The Judges War:

he Senate, Legal Culture, Political leology and Judicial Confirmation

Edited By

Patrick B. McGuigan and Jeffrey P. O'Connell

THE INSTITUTE FOR GOVERNMENT AND POLITICS OF THE
FREE CONGRESS RESEARCH AND EDUCATION FOUNDATION

The Free Congress Research and Education Foundation is a 501(c)(3) tax-exempt research organization, engaged in a variety of educational projects. Among the Foundation's many activities is the Institute for Government and Politics, which includes a Political Division, a Direct Democracy Division and the Judicial Reform Project. The Judicial Reform Project is designed to contribute to the debate on the proper role of the judiciary in a democratic society. The first phase of the Project included publication of *A Blueprint for Judicial Reform* in November 1981. A Conference on Judicial Reform was sponsored on June 14, 1982. The next phase of the project included publication of *Criminal Justice Reform: A Blueprint* (1983), sponsorship of the Conference on Criminal Justice Reform on September 27, 1983 and, in 1986, publication of *Crime and Punishment in Modern America* (scheduled for a second printing by University Press of America in August 1987).

The Project then devoted several months to an examination of the controversy surrounding the judicial nominees of President Ronald Reagan, leading to the publication of this study. The Project will next focus on tort reform, excessive litigiousness and other civil justice issues, with plans for publication of another major book in 1987–88. The Free Congress Foundation is located at 721 Second Street, N.E., Washington, D.C. 20002 (telephone: 202-546-3004).

None of the statements in this book should be construed as the policy views of the Institute for Government and Politics or its Board of Advisors, nor should the policies advocated here be taken as necessarily the policy views of the Free Congress Foundation or its Board of Directors.

The Institute for Government and Politics
Stuart Rothenberg, Director, Political Division
Patrick B. McGuigan, Director, Judicial Reform Project

Board of Advisors
Jeffrey Bell, *Citizens for America*
Richard Rahn, *Chief Economist, U.S. Chamber of Commerce*
Newt Gingrich, *Member of Congress, Georgia*
William F. Harvey, *Carl M. Gray Professor of Law, Indiana University*
Richard Woodward, *President, Woodward and McDowell*

The Free Congress Research and Education Foundation

Officers and Board

Kathleen Teague Rothschild, Chairman	Michelle Laxalt
Dr. Charles Moser, Treasurer	Marion M. Magruder, Jr.
Margaret Johnson, Secretary	John D. Beckett
Dr. Robert J. Billings	Thomas A. Roe
Senator William L. Armstrong	James Martin Hill, Jr.
Jeffrey H. Coors	Richard DeVos
Congressman Ralph M. Hall	Robert Krieble

Foundation Staff
Paul M. Weyrich, President
Patrick F. Fagan, Executive Vice President
John F. Grecco, Vice President for Finance and Administration
Eric Licht, Vice President
Martie Lawrence, Vice President for Operations
Bruce Frazer, Vice President for Marketing

Library of Congress Cataloging-in-Publication Data

The Judges War.

1. Judges—United States—Selection and appointment.
2. Political questions and judicial power—United States. I. McGuigan, Patrick B. II. O'Connell, Jeffrey P. Free Congress Research and Education Foundation. Institute for Government and Politics.

KF8776.J83 1987	347.73'14	87-19085
ISBN 0-942522-02-8 (soft)	347.30714	
ISBN 0-942522-09-5 (hardcover)		

First Printing
$9.95 soft; $17.50 hardcover

for

Orrin Hatch

CONTENTS

PREFACE

This book was conceived in the early fall of 1986, shortly after the ordeal of Daniel A. Manion ended. A qualified nominee with years of courtroom experience had suffered the most vociferous ideological assault on a federal nominee in recent memory. As the fall progressed, however, it became clear that Manion was merely a preface. The sustained political assault on judicial nominees accelerated during the confirmation struggle for Chief Justice William Rehnquist.

By the fall of 1986, many legal analysts, journalists and political "handicappers" had accepted, without critical examination, the code words which stood for generic criticisms of Ronald Reagan's judicial nominees: lack of judicial temperament, insufficient scholarly rigor, too demanding, too conservative, out of the legal mainstream, insensitivity to minorities, insensitivity to women, and so forth.

This book tells a story, but also grapples with the substance of the (largely) liberal criticisms of the Reagan judiciary. This book does not tell the entire story of the "judges war" of 1985–86, for many of the principal combatants on both sides are understandably silent about some aspects of the various engagements. As for the substantive criticisms of Reagan nominees, the authors have sought not merely to rely on persuasive force in countering the liberal criticisms, but also have gleaned highlights from the scholarly assessments thus far printed about those nominees. Finally, the contributors to this book have sought to place the dispute over judicial nominations in historical and cultural context, through an examination of the clash of contending judicial philosophies.

The cumulative evidence offered here will, I hope, foster more careful scholarly, journalistic and popular scrutiny of the assaults on Reagan's judges. I even dare to hope the book will trigger a sense of responsibility and restraint among those liberals who—while not sharing my political perspectives—share a commitment to political fair play and the rule of law. While this book may not be the definitive reply to the criticisms Reagan's judges have faced, I hope this will be the beginning of a generalized reassessment of the men and women who constitute the Reagan judiciary.

I am grateful to the scholars who provided help and support in the production of this book. It is an honor to have most of the leadership of the judicial reform movement represented in these pages. It should be noted, however, that while the contributors to this book share many legal policy views, each author's chapter represents personal views and not necessarily those of the persons or organizations with which they are affiliated. In addition, none of the specific recommendations made here should be construed as representing the policy views of the Free Congress Foundation and its Board of Directors, or the Institute for Government and Politics and its Board of Advisors.

I especially wish to declare that any typographical errors in any of these essays are entirely my responsibility. Naturally, every essay was submitted to me in perfect form, and all mistakes crept in during the editorial process. This book faced time deadlines not normally faced in production of such a study, so the chances are there are mistakes here and there—and I would not want any of these outstanding lawyers denied career advancement some years hence because of my, not their, inadequacies.

I am extremely grateful to Jeffrey P. O'Connell, who served as Visiting Fellow in Legal Studies at the Institute for Government and Politics in early 1987 and who, until his departure, helped with the editing of this study. Special gratitude goes to my staff—Kristin R. Blair, Jeffery D. Troutt and Lisa Kai—who helped in countless ways make this work easier and more pleasant. Naturally, Paul M. Weyrich and Patrick F. Fagan, President and Vice President, respectively, of the Free Congress Foundation, receive special thanks for their strong support of this timely work.

My deepest gratitude goes to my family. They tolerated hours, days and weeks of separation so that this could be completed quickly.

pbm
Washington, D.C.
June 30, 1987

INTRODUCTION

by Bruce Fein

The retirement of Associate Supreme Court Justice Lewis Powell on June 26, 1987 and President Reagan's announcement the following week of his intent to nominate United States Circuit Court Judge Robert Bork to fill the vacancy has sparked oceans of controversy.

Republican Senator Robert Packwood of Oregon has pledged to oppose Judge Bork's confirmation if he indicates hostility to the landmark *Roe v. Wade* (1973) decision creating a sweeping constitutional right to an abortion.

Democrat Chairman of the Senate Judiciary Committee Joseph Biden of Delaware and companion Committee Member Paul Simon of Illinois have voiced objections to Judge Bork. They assert that because Justice Powell was a "swing" or "moderate" vote on the Court, his replacement should hold comparable centrist views to keep High Court rulings "balanced." Biden and Simon assert that Judge Bork would imbalance the Court in a too conservative direction.

Others maintain that the idea of a perpetually balanced Supreme Court is simply a facade for opposition to conservative jurists. They note that President Franklin Roosevelt appointed nine ardent New Dealers to Supreme Court seats without encountering the complaint that a few conservative appointments were necessary to maintain a philosophical balance. Similarly, the idea of balance was no obstacle to the confirmation of Abe Fortas in 1965 to succeed Associate Justice Arthur Goldberg, and of Thurgood Marshall to succeed Associate Justice Tom Clark, although the Fortas and Marshall appointments left the Supreme Court with but one conservative Justice, John Harlan. Only three Senators voted against the Fortas confirmation, and Marshall was confirmed by a vote of 69-11, with only one Republican Senator in opposition.

The Bork nomination has also spawned heated exchanges over the role of the Senate in the confirmation process. Many insist that the Senate is an equal partner with the President in the process of appointing Supreme Court Justices, and may properly oppose candidates solely because of disagreement over judicial philosophy. Others maintain that the Senate is limited to a cameo role, serving to check only presidential nominees who are incompetent, morally wanting, or chosen because of corruption, family affiliation, or party loyalty. They note that a President frequently campaigns for office by promising the voters to change the philosophical complexion of the federal judiciary through the appointments process. Illustrative were the electoral campaigns of President Franklin Roosevelt in 1936, Richard Nixon in 1968, and Ronald Reagan in 1980 and 1984. Thus, it is argued, Presidents possess a popular mandate to appoint federal judges of their judicial philosophy, whereas Senators possess no corresponding mandate of opposition based on a nominee's philosophical approach to adjudication. Senators typically do not run for office trumpeting how they will vote on the confirmation of federal judges.

The stridency of the controversy surrounding the Bork nomination—even harsher than that evoked in the last presidential campaign—speaks volumes about the contemporary policy-making power of the United States Supreme Court and subordinate federal tribunals. Capital punishment, abortion, church-state relations, affirmative action, treatment of the handicapped, property rights, electoral apportionment, school busing and defamation are commonplace issues within the federal judicial establishment. Their resolution casts a distinctive policy hue over the actions of Congress, the Chief Executive and the states. And that is why understanding "The Judges War" is so important for the American people.

Reliance on judicial self-restraint to avoid usurpation of policy prerogatives that the Constitution assigned the elected branches of government or the States seems an inescapable fixture of contemporary American politics. The Founding Fathers expected judicial excesses to be checked by impeachment, curtailing the jurisdiction of federal courts, and constitutional amendments. But time has not honored those expectations.

The modern elected official is typically a career politician. His overriding goal is perpetuation in office. He believes that can best be achieved by avoidance of unequivocal stands on contentious policies that may divide his constituency. Thus, it is customary for an elected official to rejoice silently when federal courts reach into their policy domains under the guise of constitutional or statutory interpretation because he can censure the judges for any outcome that disturbs any portion of his constituency. Gratuitous judicial activism is an escape hatch for the vast majority of legislators who shy from controversy that might harm Gallup Poll ratings. Thus, they resist any meaningful efforts to reprimand or restrain arrogation of policymaking by the judiciary.

Executive officials managing schools, prisons, mental institutions, or other public facilities are also silent extollers of judicial activism. Sweeping constitutional or statutory decrees requiring massive upgrading or overhauling of such institutions typically means more funding by legislatures at the order of a federal judge. That type of judicial intrusion into the appropriations process was sanctioned by the Supreme Court in *Griffin v. Prince Edward County School Board* (1964).

Lawyers and scholars champion judicial activism because it endows them with greater power, prestige, and monetary rewards. In the legislative and executive branch arenas, attorneys and professors are far less potent than in the courts.

The Judges War is in essence a twofold fight: first, over the allocation of power between the judiciary and other branches of government; and, second, over the rule of law. President Reagan has endeavored to appoint judges who will leave to the elected branches of government and the states primary responsibility for crafting public policy. That is a central attribute of government by the consent of the governed. Reagan has further aspired to choose judges who will interpret the Constitution and statutes according to their text and purpose. That approach to interpretation is at variance with a dominant contemporary judicial custom of employing personalized notions of enlightened public policy as a critical component of the deliberative process.

The types of issues probed by *The Judges War* have been with the Nation ever since enactment of the 1789 Judiciary Act and President George Washington's insistence that the Supreme

3

Court appointees be adherents to the Federalist constitutional philosophy. The issues will remain after the confirmation hearings and Senate vote on Judge Bork's nomination to the Supreme Court. *The Judges War* is thus a compendium written for the ages to enhance understanding of the judicial role in the American system of government.

August 1987

ILL-ADVISED AND DISCONTENT:
UNDERSTANDING THE JUDGES WAR
by Patrick B. McGuigan[1]

Words can express our thoughts and beliefs, but they are not our thoughts and beliefs. Words all too easily shield intent and motivation. Action ultimately is the barometer for gauging an individual's intent.

This chapter is a chronology of confrontation. In the civilized combat of politics, people conceal intent by carefully chosen words and arguments. Action, however, strips away the facade words build. Temperament, sensibilities, fairness, ethics—all are words and concepts used in attempts to defeat judicial, as well as Justice Department, nominees. With two exceptions, these attacks proved unsuccessful. However, lessons were learned, and arguments were carefully honed. The gaffes of the opposition to the nominees, the gaffes which revealed intent, are largely forgotten. But even when unsuccessful, these arguments proved sufficient to spark significant challenges and, more importantly, to build the perception of "questionable nominees" among individuals with only superficial knowledge of the nominees and issues.

The critics of President Reagan's judicial nominees adopt a veneer, preferring discussions surrounding ambiguous phrases such as judicial sensibility and judicial temperament to the fundamental and relatively definable bases of judicial competence, such as performance. They prefer to dwell on the *appearance* of impropriety, while using an advocate's arsenal to argue that such impropriety actually exists. In the absence of even minimal evidence of *actual* wrongdoing, the *appearance* of impropriety becomes a sufficient cause for disqualification. The repetition of code words—temperament, sensitivity, etc.—continues in 1987, primarily because the individual, substantive arguments prove unconvincing.

Now, the ideological/political confrontation has changed. During the years of this chronology—1984-86—a single party, the Republicans, controlled both the White House and the Senate. Dramatic Democrat successes in the 1986 election once again pitted the Democrat Senate leadership against a Republican White House, mirroring the situation in virtually all of the 16 years Republicans controlled the White House prior to the Reagan Administration. The struggle over judicial selections will continue with greater vigor now that Democrats, with an opposing view of the limitations of the judiciary, control the Senate. But the battle may be waged as, if not always understood as, a struggle about judicial philosophy and/or political ideology. Although liberal advocates know they can generate enthusiasm from their usual supporters for such a confrontation, they also know most Americans will be uneasy about such political jockeying over the judiciary. Therefore, it appears the new masking "code word" in the judges war may be "balance." Reasonable sounding in itself, the "balance of the (Supreme) Court" rhetoric ignores the reality of recent American history (the Court was 8-1 liberal in the late 1960s) as well as the clear constitutional duty of Presidents to select judges who hold the limited, constitutional view on the power of judges in our unique democratic structure.

Each of the battles sketched herein—in particular, the nominations of Ed Meese, Brad Reynolds and Dan Manion—merits more detailed discussion than can possibly be offered in this limited space. The primary purpose is to offer a chronology of events, with an explicit effort to reach for underlying themes steadily perfected by opponents of the Reagan nominees. The Meese and Reynolds stories are included because, although they were not judicial nominees, subsequent confrontations demonstrate that these two nomination struggles were early vehicles for the development of the underlying opposition themes. The Manion confrontation receives the most detailed attention simply because it was the battle in which darn near every theme was evoked, at one time or another, by the Indianian's opponents.

If nothing else, this chapter should shed light on the arguments used to shield the ideological objections of those who oppose the "Reaganization"—the selection of non-activist judges who seek to restrain the judicial impulse to resolve policy is-

6

sues—of the federal judiciary. In truth, this is the story of a steady escalation of judicial politics into what one reporter called "a flat-out fight over ideology."[2]

JUSTICE DEPARTMENT: JUSTICE AT JUSTICE

Ethics and Politics: Ed Meese—the First Target. On January 23, 1984, President Reagan nominated Edwin Meese III to serve as Attorney General. Thirteen months later—the longest delay ever for any cabinet nominee—the Senate confirmed him.[3] During these long months, partisan organizations and some senators successfully frustrated the consent process of Senate, underscoring a weakness in the Senate's advise and consent procedure which is injurious to both the democratic process and smooth functioning of government.

Civil rights organizations were first to attack the nomination. Benjamin Hooks, executive director of the NAACP, viewed Meese as an "anti-civil rights devil."[4] To some, anyone associated with the Reagan Administration was *persona non grata.* Senator Edward Kennedy (D-MA) charged the Administration's civil rights policy was a "disgrace," and considered the nominee the "architect of most, if not all," of the Administration's civil rights policies. Some wished to separate the President's policies from the Justice Department, demanding that the Attorney General should somehow be independent of the Chief Executive. Joseph L. Rauh, Jr. of the Leadership Conference on Civil Rights was open about his group's motivation in the nomination. Although also questioning Meese's ethical standards, Rauh admitted his concern was ideological—that Meese "would not enforce vigorously and objectively our nation's civil rights laws," as Rauh defined proper enforcement.[5]

The most significant and effective attacks questioned Meese's ethical standards. In one instance, Meese's California home—burdened by a delinquent mortgage—sold, but only with the assistance of a real estate developer who thereafter secured a post as assistant secretary at the Department of Interior. Although the home was actually purchased by a third party, the developer, Thomas Barrack, loaned $70,000 of the $307,500 sale price to the purchaser and, subsequently, forgave the loan. Barrack maintained, however, that he did not know Meese and assisted him only at the request of White House Personnel Director Pendleton James. Meese also testified he knew nothing of the loan by Barrack.[6]

Meese's tax advisor, James R. McKean, arranged $60,000 in loans for Meese. McKean, after discussions with White House advisor Michael R. Deaver, was appointed chairman of the Postal Service Board of Governors. Meese denied recommending McKean for the position. An additional flap ensued when it was discovered that Meese mistakenly omitted from a disclosure statement, filed under the Ethics in Government Act, an $18,000 loan to Meese's wife from Edwin Thomas, a former deputy to Meese. However, Meese never hid this—or any other—financial dealings, which previously had been disclosed in one document or another.

Other complaints included Meese keeping a gift of cufflinks (worth $375) presented by the South Korean Government in 1983, and the circumstances under which Meese became a general in the army reserve. To stop the complaints, Meese eventually returned the gift to South Korean on March 28, 1984.[7]

In addition, Democrat Senator Carl Levin (D-MI) made political hay by resurrecting the old issue of Jimmy Carter's 1980 campaign strategy papers and Meese's supposed personal knowledge of the papers.[8]

To resolve the charges, Meese requested that an independent counsel be appointed. Attorney General William French Smith petitioned a three judge panel to select an independent counsel. The panel appointed Jacob Stein, a Washington trial attorney, in April 1984 to carry out that mandate. Stein, along with five assistants, investigated 11 separate allegations, during a five month investigation. An exhaustive 385 page report, released in September 1984, documents the investigation and its conclusion—no basis for prosecution of Meese was found.

The independent counsel's report did not stop some critics, particularly Senator Metzenbaum. They did not exhaust all inquiries into the nominee's ethical conduct. An irony of the criticism is how prominent Metzembaum was. Perhaps you have to have climbed the mountain to be such an expert on the subject. Metzenbaum admitted receiving a $250,000 finder's fee for assisting in the sale of Washington's Hay Adams Hotel. According to Metzenbaum, his work for the fee consisted largely of two phone calls. Although defending the legitimacy of the fee, he chose to repay the fee with interest.[9] In another situation, the senator came to the aid of a relative. Metzenbaum called the Immigration and Naturalization Service in 1983 to use his influence in preventing a nephew from being fired.[10] Federal regulations prohibit hiring officials from considering recommendations for job applicants from members of Congress "except as to the character or residence of the applicant."

Further Judiciary Committee hearings were not scheduled during the session, requiring the President to resubmit Meese's nomination in January 1985. New hearings were held on January 29 and 30, 1985.

The Judiciary Committee approved Meese on February 5 by a 12-6 vote, with two Democrats—Dennis DeConcini (D-AZ) and Howell Heflin (D-AL)—breaking ranks to vote for the nominee. The Senate finally confirmed Meese 63-31 in a Saturday session, February 23, with Democrats casting all 31 negative votes.[11]

Brad Reynolds' Trial by Fire. In 1985, President Reagan nominated William Bradford Reynolds to be Associate Attorney General, the number three office in the Justice Department, intending to elevate him from his position as head of the Justice Department's Civil Rights Division. Things did not work out, however. As Senator Orrin Hatch (R-UT) put it:

> What it really came down to was that it didn't make any difference how good a man Brad Reynolds is. One of the leading Democrats told me personally, "It is a shame that we have to be against him, because he is one of the finest lawyers in government. We know he is a man of integrity and we know he is a good man. But we have to defeat him."[12]

Reynolds' dilemma was that he carried out the policy of the Reagan Administration, failing to subscribe to all the advances demanded by the Civil Rights Establishment. The Administration and, therefore, Reynolds were in a no-win situation. There was little either could do to win the plaudits of the Civil Rights Establishment. Reynolds was targeted. The attacks were vociferous. Kennedy complained Reynolds had done "enough damage to civil rights," while Metzenbaum declared the nominee was on the side of "bigots." Many members of the Senate Judiciary Committee found it politically expedient to accept the accusations of the Administration's opponents rather than vote for a qualified, experienced Justice official. Reynolds' personal qualifications simply could not overcome the wall imposed by those who made him a test case for conformity to prevailing liberal civil rights proposals.

This raises a fundamental question: to what extent does a president—any president—have a right to appoint qualified individuals, willing to support the policies of his or her Administration, to key policy posts? If a president is denied qualified individuals who possess a common philosophy and goals, the electoral mandate is undermined.

The Committee Struggle. The initial signs of success against Reynolds' nomination became apparent when a majority of the Judiciary Committee members were able to delay hearings from May until early June. Hearings were held June 4 and 5. After the initial hearings, Senator Charles McC. Mathias, Jr. (R-MD) requested an additional day of hearings eventually scheduled for June 18. The two seat Republican edge in the Judiciary proved tenuous, as it frequently was in the Ninety-ninth Congress, because of the positions of Mathias and Senator Arlen Specter (R-PA). After the third day of hearings, the Democratic leadership wanted an immediate vote on Reynolds, but relented at the request of Heflin.

Three days prior to the Judiciary Committee's vote on Reynolds, several leading judicial reform activists met with Specter to stress the significance of Reynolds' confirmation. Participants in the confidential meeting included key leaders from both the judicial reform and pro-family movements. Specter was bluntly informed only a "yes" vote on the Reynolds nomination would be "acceptable." Specter responded that his mind was still open. One participant described the meeting as "successful," despite Specter's ultimate vote against Reynolds. Shortly before the Committee vote Specter called several of those who attended the earlier meeting personally, informing them that he would vote against Reynolds "on the merits" but would support a motion to send the nomination to the full Senate without a recommendation.

The Committee rejected Reynolds on June 27 by an 8 to 10 vote to report the nomination favorably. The committee then considered a motion to send the nomination to the floor without any recommdation. Specter, as he promised, voted against Reynolds in the initial tally, but did vote to send the nomination to the full Senate for its consideration. The final tally was a 9-9 tie, insufficient to secure movement to the Senate floor. A third vote, also a 9-9 tie, failed to send the nomination to the floor with an unfavorable recommendation. The last vote, proposed by Senator Paul Laxalt (R-NV), was a surprise and caught Joseph Biden (D-DE), the ranking Democrat, off guard. Biden wanted time to consider the motion. He was rebuffed, and the roll call was taken as he and five other Democrats walked out of the Committee room. The initial tally was 9 to 3 in favor of the unfavorable recommendation. Biden managed, however, to postpone the final vote until he could talk to Senator Robert Byrd (D-WV), the Senate Minority Leader. After conferring, the Democrats, who first refused to vote, cast their ballots against the motion, creating the deadlock and killing the nomination.

In a last ditch effort to secure Reynolds' confirmation, Senate Majority Leader Robert Dole (R-KS) sought the support of 51 Senators for a discharge petition to force the nomination out of Committee in mid-July. The strategy among the Department of Justice leadership apparently was to wait until early August, after the Senate recessed, and simply name Reynolds to the post as a "recess" appointment, allowing him to serve through 1986. Vigorous opposition to both the petition and the recess appointment surfaced in mid-July after press reports, leading to withdrawal of both possibilities.

The Reynolds nomination provided another opportunity for the entrenched Civil Rights Establishment to demonstrate its continuing power in Washington. Testifying against Reynolds were groups such as the National Urban League, the National Organization for Women (NOW), the Leadership Conference on Civil Rights, the Lawyers Committee for Civil Rights Under Law, the National Women's Political Caucus and the NAACP, among others. John Jacob of the National Urban League accused Reynolds of turning the Civil Rights Division into "an obstacle to the elimination of racial barriers in our society." Benjamin Hooks of the NAACP claimed Reynolds had "launched an all-out attack on civil rights." NOW president Judy Goldsmith described Reynolds as the "Scrooge of the Justice Department."[13]

A broad range of witnesses appeared before the Committee to support Reynolds' confirmation. Paul Kamenar of the Washington Legal Foundation, Robert Kliesmet, president of the International Union of Police Associations (AFL-CIO), and David Zwiebel of Agudath Israel of America were among those who supported Reynolds. Linda Childs, East Coast president of the Professional Bail-Agents of the United States (PBUS), Roy Innis of the Congress on Racial Equality (CORE), Charles Ord of the Association of American Physicians and Surgeons (AAPS), and Richard Fox of the National Jewish Coalition submitted statements endorsing Reynolds for Associate Attorney General. Kamenar testified that Reynolds had "made it clear that our constitution is color-blind and that racially divisive affirmative action quotas violate the fundamental principles of equal opportunity." Childs stated that PBUS was supporting the nominee because of his "steadfastness and forthrightness in upholding the Constitution's guarantees for equal protection for All, *not* special treatment for anyone." AAPS' Ord applauded Reynolds for waging a "vigorous war against discrimination without resorting to the pro-quotas/anti-business tactics which have done so much to cripple the economy and disrupt our society."

Particulary irksome to grass roots supporters of Reynolds was the cavalier approach of Committee Republicans toward pro-Reynolds witnesses. All the Democrats and most Republicans attended when anti-Reynolds witnesses testified, but frequently only Senator Howard Metzenbaum (D-OH) was present to listen to and question the pro-Reynolds witnesses. Metzenbaum limited each pro-Reynolds witness to four minutes—at one point vigorously interrupting witness Bob Kliesmet—only a fraction of the time allotted to anti-Reynolds witnesses.

The *Wall Street Journal* described what happened to Reynolds as part of a successful and continuing liberal attempt to "frustrate the policies implicit in the (1984) election," which took the form of "a personal assault on the president's nominees." the emerging strategy of Reagan Administration opponents was to engage in a steady assault on the character of the nominee in question, building the perception of serious personal defects. In the wake of the nominee's defeat, however, critics shifted gears, characterizing the results as a rejection of the Administration's policies. This is precisely what transpired with Reynolds.

KOZINSKI: FIRST THEY ACTED, THEN THEY PRAYED

Alex Kozinski found that being an experienced, intelligent attorney—and a judge—with superior academic credentials was insufficient to ensure quick confirmation to the Ninth Circuit Court of Appeals. After months of struggle, Kozinski won confirmation on a 54-43 roll call vote. Looking back, one is reminded of the scene from the ABC miniseries, *Amerika* in which a mother, living in a United States under Soviet domination for a decade, is distraught to find that her talented, inventive daughter could not win approval for state sponsored ballet instruction. A committee woman advised the mother that *cooperation* is more important than *talent*. Kozinski's "lack of cooperation" with the Senate Democrats flowed naturally from his beliefs as a conservative supporter of Reagan. His is perhaps the clearest case of how the system, or at least those who possess the power to interfere with it, can impede a nomination for baldly political reasons.

At the time of the nomination, Kozinski was Chief Judge of the Claims Court.[14] He graduated first in his class at UCLA Law School, received his baccalaureate degree *cum laude* from UCLA and is a Phi Beta Kappa member. His superior academic achievements produced a coveted law clerkship with Chief Justice Warren Burger. (The acquisition of such a clerkship invariably assures the law clerk of a legal future marked by distinction and, if he chooses, wealth. But Kozinski chose public service.)

When President Reagan submitted the nomination to the Senate, it sailed through the Judiciary Committee without a single negative vote. However, a Democrat not on the Committee, Carl Levin, objected to the nominee based on complaints received through the Government Accountability Project ("GAP"), a leftist organization.[15] The complaints were in the form of affidavits from former employees of Kozinski during his fourteen month stint as special counsel with the Merit Systems Protection Board, the agency charged with protecting the rights of federal employees in disagreements with their superiors.

13

In an unusual move Levin, with the assistance of Senator Howard Metzenbaum (D-OH), wrestled a second confirmation hearing on November 1, 1985, six weeks after the original Committee approval. During the new hearings, Tom Devine of GAP, incredibly, argued that Kozinski was hostile to whistleblowers and that he was the "most effective opponent of the First Amendment in the federal system in the last five years."[16]

The primary objection, emerging as a familiar refrain against Reagan nominees, was a lack of "judicial temperament and sensitivity." Levin claimed the nominee was unfit because he did not have the "judicial temperament, the fairness, the sensitivity and the compassion" that judges should have. The specific charges were that:

• He summarily fined, without notice, two attorneys for bringing an unmeritorius complaint for judicial misconduct. Some Senators complained that the 25 cases that the nominee presented as precedent were inapplicable to the judge's decision.

• He concealed poor relationships with his staff when he indicated in his first hearing that his relationships with employees were excellent.

• He misrepresented the results of a settlement with a former employee that he fired by not revealing that the settlement gave her back wages and attorney's fees.

Kozinski was also accused of attempting to discredit GAP by supplying information for an editorial by radio broadcaster Avi Nelson. The editorial indicated that GAP was sponsored by the Institute for Policy Studies ("IPS"), a "revolutionary group" hostile to the U.S., with ties to terrorist groups such as the PLO. Although no one denied GAP's relationship with IPS, GAP had broken from the Institute for Policy Studies the prior year. Kozinski's part in this was seen by Levin as part of a "pattern" of intemperate conduct.

Some arguments bordered on the trivial. Kennedy, arguing the nominee lacked compassion and basic decency in dealings with his subordinates, noted that he edited staff work in "technicolor," that is, he used different colors of ink.[17] Rough stuff, indeed! Multi-colored pens are less than a smoking gun.[18]

What this all suggests is that opponents were grappling hard for issues to cripple the nomination. The charges, however, did not deal with judicial capability. Indeed, these were no complaints of his actions as a judge in a trial or administrative capacity. Biden was forced to admit that Kozinski is "exceedingly intelligent and competent."[19] The sum of the complaints was that his people handling skills were questionable. Senator Pete Wilson (R-CA) defused the criticism when he suggested to his peers that he who was without sin should cast the first stone:

> If there is a Senator on this floor who has never been unkind, short of patience, overly painstaking with an employee, let him hold up his hand. If there are any in that category, and we are to limit the vote on those, then we will not have a vote today.[20]

What some view as abusive, others consider tough, demanding and decisive. The qualities of leadership do, on occasion, offend. Toughness is a necessary prescription in difficult situations. Indeed, the basic characteristics criticized by Democrat opponents were important in his role with the new Claims Court. Kozinski did not simply become a judge of a Court. He was Chief Judge of a new Court whose birth rights included a congested docket, significant administrative obligations and a staff one judge short. Judge John Weise worked with Kozinski and his analysis was plainly different from that of the critics:

> Confronting the new court were many problems: an inherited backlog of over 1,700 cases; the uncertain burden of coping with an expanded Tucker Act jurisdiction; a significant reduction in overall staffing; and, indeed, even the inefficiencies of a physical plant in drastic need of improvement.
>
> By personal example Chief Judge Kozinski showed that the court could manage its docket with efficiency and fairness; he performed the administrative duties of his office while concurrently maintaining a full trial docket and achieving one of the highest case disposition rates. More could indeed be done with less.[21]

Thurmond and his staff remained confident of an easy victory for Kozinski until late in the contest. The day before the vote, rumors circulated on Capitol Hill that the Democrat leadership might make the confirmation vote a "test vote" of party loyalty. Judicial reformers organized a last minute surge for Kozinski. On the morning of the vote, activists in the Library Court Coalition (the leading conservative social justice/moral issues coalition) and the 721 Group (the leading anti-crime/pro-judicial reform coalition) identified 30 key Senators whose votes were uncertain. In particular, supporters of Kozinski focused on about 10 key Senators—four Republicans and six Democrats. Of some 60 organizations contacted, 30 agreed to do what they could to support the confirmation.

One organization—an evangelical Christian group—went the extra mile for the nominee, himself a Jew. On behalf of the organization's thousands of supporters, the group contacted all 30 Senators on the "target list" between mid-morning and early afternoon on the day of the vote. With the roll call slated to begin shortly after 2 p.m., the organization's employees gathered and prayed for Kozinski himself, his family and his confirmation. As one organizer of the last minute surge of pro-Kozinski activity put it, "First they acted, then they prayed." The effectiveness of the last minute activity cannot be discounted. All four targeted Republicans backed Kozinski, as did four of the six key Democrats.[22]

The rancor of the Kozinski debate foreshadowed developments in future nominations. Judiciary Committee Democrats were embarrassed because one of their colleagues raised issues that they "should" have raised themselves. Some criticized the Democrats for not effectively opposing the Reagan nominees. The Democrats were firm that it would not happen again. Judiciary Democrats began to slow down the nomination process to give further time for investigation, with the excuse that the current nominees were "younger, less experienced and more ideological than in Reagan's first term." According to the Washington Post's Howard Kurtz, "the attempted slowdown is the latest [Democratic] tactical move in one of the most important. . .ideological battles" in Congress.[23] The Kozinski nomination above all was an exercise in refining the tactics of opposition without the overt appearance of ideological confrontation. As Kurtz wrote:

> Since (the Democrats) are loath to oppose a nominee solely on ideological grounds, the Democrats have trained their fire on other issues—credibility, temperament, discrepancies in testimony—to wound the most conservative nominees for judgeships and Justice Department vacancies. At one recent Committee hearing, a ranking Democrat (Biden), told Charles J. Cooper, nominated as the Justice Department's chief legal advisor, that he was looking for a reason to vote against him because he didn't like Cooper's civil rights policies.[24]

The slowdown, however, had an additional objective—simply to delay further judicial confirmations. The Democrat leadership's eye was to the 1986 elections with the opportunity to post further Democrat gains in the Senate, enabling them to pick up crucial votes to prevent further conservative nominations.

FITZWATER: OF STREET MONEY AND JUDICIAL POLITICS

Sidney Fitzwater was nominated to be a judge for the District Court for the Northern District of Texas. At first appearance, his confirmation seemed assured. If there *is* some "objective" criterion to determine a nominee's judicial capabilities, actual performance on the bench should be the basic barometer. Already a Texas district court judge, Fitzwater's Dallas Bar Association ratings, based on attorneys' responses, produced superior results: 97 percent of responding attorneys indicated Fitzwater was an outstanding judge; 98 percent indicated he is hard working; 97 percent said he is impartial; 95 percent believe he applied the law correctly; and 97 percent felt he had proper judicial temperament and demeanor. His performance was considered so superior that he was rated higher than any federal, district or county judge in his location.[25] Even with such impressive statistics, the ABA Standing Committee on the Judiciary only found Fitzwater qualified, with a minority considering him unqualified. Metzenbaum myopically ignored the state ratings of the nominee, preferring to dwell on the ABA rating.[26] In addition to the superior ratings, Fitzwater had one other distinctive characteristic. He was young. Approval would make him, at 32, the youngest federal judge, with the likelihood of a long and productive career.

The main charge, indeed, the only charge, against Fitzwater was that he posted three signs in the 1982 election in one predominantly black precinct in southern Dallas County warning against voter fraud. The controversial signs, posted by Fitzwater at the request of a senior judge on the Dallas Court of Appeals and with the understanding that the signs were approved by the Texas Secretary of State, read:

17

YOU CAN BE IMPRISONED —
1. If you offer, accept or agree to accept money, or anything else of value to vote or not to vote.
2. If you influence or try to influence a voter how to vote.
3. If you vote without being registered.
4. If you let a person vote more than once.
5. If you vote with someone else's registration.
6. Violate Texas Election Code or Texas Penal Code.
DON'T RISK IT
OBEY THE LAW[27]

According to Kennedy, the three posters amounted to personal participation in a "partisan scheme to disenfranchise minority voters. . . "[28] Senator Gary Hart (D-CO) felt that because Fitzwater was a judge at the time that he "compromised the public perception that judges and courts are a forum for the fair, unbiased, and impartial adjudication of disputes."[29] Metzenbaum was able to see this as an issue of "judicial temperament" and "sensitivity," questioning "what kind of sensitivity [Fitzwater] would bring to issues that would affect minorities and others as well, the poor, when they appear before you in [the] courtroom."[30]

However, the reasoning behind the signs is not as black and white as Kennedy, Hart and Metzenbaum suggested. The 1980 elections in Dallas County were tainted by massive voter fraud, with the bulk of the fraud concentrated in south Dallas County. A grand jury indicted eleven individuals; six were eventually found guilty.[31] As a result for the 1982 voting the Dallas Sheriff's Department, in consultation with members of the judiciary, established a Ballot Security Program, under which the signs were posted. Signs appeared primarily in black precincts, but were also posted in predominantly white north Dallas. A suit was brought in federal court, naming Fitzwater (later dropped from the suit) as one of the defendants. The suit itself was eventually dismissed for plaintiffs' lack of standing to contest the suit and, additionally, for lack of jurisdiction in the court to hear the case.

In response to the charges, concern set in when Democrat Texas Senator Lloyd Bentson withdrew his support for Fitzwater. Senator Phil Gramm (R-TX)—the nominee's strongest defender—commented on the charges that "I never understood why people get so upset if you put up a sign that says do not violate the law."[32]

Fitzwater clarified during the nomination hearings that his actions in posting the signs were based on an incomplete understanding of what had transpired. Specifically, he had been informed that the signs, as part of the Ballot Security Program, were to be posted throughout Dallas. The circumstances under which the nominee accepted the signs clarify the reasons for his actions. Justice Pat Guillot requested that he participate, explaining that the reason that judges were asked to assist was because there were not sufficient volunteers or sheriff's deputies to post the signs in all precincts. Guillot's cover letter, accompanying the signs, stated that the Secretary of State had approved the signs.[33] If all the facts had been presented to him, the nominee indicated that he would not have posted the signs.

Theodore Steinke, Jr., Assistant District Attorney and Chief of the Public Integrity Section of the Dallas County Specialized Crime Division, indicated that their investigation showed that there was no evidence the signs were intended to "intimidate or disenfranchise voters."[34]

Even liberal Senator Paul Simon (D-IL) disagreed with the accusations against the nominee. Admitting he attended the hearings "expecting to vote against" Fitzwater, Simon explained that the real question, as he perceived it, was whether Fitzwater's actions reflected a racist intent. Simon found no such intent.[35] Looking at the Fitzwater's considerable qualifications, Simon said he saw no choice but to vote in favor of the nomination. He stated: "My conclusion...is that it would be a mistake on the basis of one mistake...to deny him a federal judgeship."[36]

The entire voter issue quickly degenerated into a political squabble. Support for the charges against Fitzwater came from Democrat Texas Attorney General Jim Mattox. In reviewing the warnings in the signs, Mattox wrote to Congress that he considered the signs overly broad or out of context. Mattox, however, was scarcely a neutral party. Senator Phil Gramm, Fitzwater's stalwart supporter, recalled that two Mattox aides were indicted in the earlier 1980 scandal. Disproving the accusations of voter fraud in the 1980 elections and, at the least, smearing Texas Republicans was in the best interests of Mattox.

Senator Hart, opposing the nomination, observed:

> Less than a month ago we celebrated a democratic revolution in the Philippines. We gloried in televised images of average citizens protecting ballot boxes with their very lives. We understood the yearning of the Filipino people for the fair and unfettered exercise of the right to vote.[37]

But Hart's vivid picture left out what triggered the heroics he described, namely protection from voter fraud. No one suggested Fitzwater stuffed ballot boxes. On the contrary, he preserved precisely the same ideals in north Texas as did those average citizens in Manila—protection against fraud. Voter fraud is not more or less heinous depending upon who performs the act. If street money is wrong in Manila, it is also wrong in north Texas.

Ideological opponents attempted, based on a single event, to derail a judge with an unblemished judicial record, a man literally among the best on the bench, as perceived by lawyers who practiced before him. From one incident, suggestions of racism abounded.

The Judiciary Committee vote recommending Fitzwater was 10-5. Opponents attempted to derail the nomination with a filibuster, but on March 18 cloture was invoked 64-33. Later that afternoon, Fitzwater was approved 52-42.

SESSIONS: UNPOPULAR CASES AND POT SMOKERS

Jefferson B. Sessions III was the U.S. Attorney for Mobile, Alabama when nominated to the federal district court in Alabama. Civil rights groups, reported the Washington *Post*, targeted Sessions from the beginning for his prosecution of three civil rights activists—including a former aide to Martin Luther King—for the alleged distribution of "street money" (vote buying) in Alabama elections.[38]

With the civil rights attacks and allegations of racism, critics jumped on a remark Sessions made to a black assistant which, on paper, appeared to support the Ku Klux Klan. Immediately after learning of the apprehension of suspects for the beating of a black man, Sessions said: "Those bastards! I used to think they were o.k., but they're pot smokers." The comment came from the Klansmen's contention—told to arresting officers and described to Sessions over the phone—that they were "high" on marijuana during the crime. Sessions defended the remark by indicating it was "silly" and "ludicrous," and said in quite evident jest, believing that no one could have taken it seriously. Even the New York *Times* refused to criticize Sessions for the street money litigation, which it characterized as the trying of an unpopular case. Subjecting prosecutors to such criticism could stifle the need for justice to be applied regardless of the politicial climate. Nor would the *Times* accept criticism for the KKK comment, which it understood, by its context, not to be taken literally.

Senator Jeremiah Denton (R-AL) led an aggressive and at times indignant fight for Sessions, charging that some actions by Session opponents were "cheap gutter politics," with ulterior motives—an attempt to injure Denton by suggesting that Sessions was involved in actions which had an impact on the election of Denton. (Some observers later told this writer Denton's tough and argumentative defense irritated other Senators beyond the level of normal disagreements in the collegial upper chamber.)

The Judiciary Committee rejected Sessions 10-8, with Republicans Specter and Mathias voting with the solid bloc of Democrats against the nominee. On a vote to send the nomination to the floor of the Senate without a recommendation, Specter shifted his vote, producing a 9-9 tally, insufficient to carry the motion. The Administration briefly considered a discharge petition to get the nomination to the floor, but dropped the idea as unworkable. Sessions became the first Republican judicial nominee to be defeated since Clement F. Haynsworth, Jr. and Harrold Carswell during the Nixon Administration.[39] The Democrats had finally drawn judicial blood.

MANION: A FLAT-OUT FIGHT OVER IDEOLOGY

The Democrats have refrained from challenging any nominee explicitly on grounds of being too conservative, focusing instead on questions of temperament and personal conduct. But the Manion nomination is a flat-out fight over ideology.

— Washington *Post*[40]

Daniel Manion was prejudged. When his nomination came before the Judiciary Committee, he was presumed guilty until proven innocent. His "crime" was the assimilation of conservative precepts. The presumption of Manion's "guilt" arose through guilt by association—his natural relationship with Clarence Manion, his well known, conservative father. Unlike other conservative nominees such as Kozinski and Fitzwater, he possessed more than a conservative background. His was a well-known name—one long associated with conservative views.

In one well-reported remark, Senator Joseph Biden (D-DE) made the ideological struggle clear in Judiciary Committee hearings, indicating: "I think you are a decent and honorable man, but I do not think I can vote for you becaue of your political views." Should a nominee's politics be an issue? Under other circumstances—the nomination of a liberal, controversial Congressman, Rep. Abner Mikva (D-IL), to the D.C. Court of Appeals—Biden offered a different understanding of the relevance of the nominee's philosophy:

> Although a nominee's personal views on matters likely to come before him are relevant, they are not nearly as important as the more elusive qualities of demeanor and personal temperament.
> Specifically, I do not believe that elected officials should be disqualified for service on the Federal bench simply because during the course of their political careers they have advocated positions with which some disagree.[41]

Indeed. Biden apparently prefers a higher standard for private citizens.

Manion's qualifications included 13 years as an attorney. He was a state senator for four years before refusing to run for re-election because of a battle (since won) with multiple sclerosis, and served as a Deputy Attorney General for Indiana. His father's national reputation gained the nominee his notoriety. The elder Manion, dean of Notre Dame Law School for eleven years, was a conservative Democrat all his life. Active in Franklin Roosevelt's Administration, he had been appointed by Eisenhower to serve on a federal commission. During this time, Manion supported the Bricker Amendment, which would have limited the authority of international treaties, clearly delineating the supremacy of the United States Constitution. Early in the Eisenhower Administration, someone—Sherman Adams, Daniel Manion believes—propositioned the elder Manion. The next appointment to the Supreme Court would go to a Catholic Democrat, and the heavy implication was that Manion would get the nod. As Daniel Manion describes it:

> My father had been the leader of Democrats for Eisenhower. There can be no doubt that the offer was a serious one. But Dad replied: "I believe in the Bricker Amendment. I am not going to abandon my principles in order to get some sort of a patronage appointment."[42]

The next Court appointment did go to a Catholic Democrat. His name was William Brennan.

The problem Dan Manion's enemies confronted was that a substantial investigation into Manion's legal abilities clarified that those who knew him and his work overwhelmingly considered him a man of integrity and fairness. Even the Chicago Council of Lawyers, a liberal association that criticized the nomination, could only remark:

> Mr. Manion has a high reputation for integrity, conscientiousness, and fairness. The reports... also indicate that Mr. Manion has excellent interpersonal skills, and that lawyers who work both with and against him like and respect him. Many of the lawyers to whom we talked also thought that despite his reputation for political conservatism, Mr. Manion would struggle to be fair in ruling on cases which present issues on which he has strong political views.
> The majority of lawyers to whom we talked regarding Mr. Manion's legal experience thought that he was a competent lawyer... All vouched for his forthrightness and his adherence to high ethical standards.[43]

Richard M. Biven, Chief Justice of the Indiana Supreme Court, praised the nominee's "outstanding career as a attorney", his "high academic credentials," and "impeccable personal integrity."

A noted liberal, Father Theodore Hesburgh, until recently President of Notre Dame University and former member of People for the American Way, wrote that Manion is a "reflection of the strong morals and high values" that have been a part of his family, and continued:

I believe he will bring dedication, integrity, and a keen knowledge of the law to that position. His life has been one of service and commitment to justice. I believe that he will exhibit these same qualities sitting on the federal bench, and that his appointment will be a strong one.[44]

Manion's supporters were not merely conservative Republicans. Former Indiana Senator Vance Hartke, a liberal Democrat, supported the nominee. Democrats within Indiana, including John J. Sullivan, partner of a prominent Indianapolis law firm and former Democratic Indianapolis mayoral candiate, while admitting to a different political philosophy, urged confirmation of the nominee.[45]

Non-Republican liberals outside Indiana agreed. Eugene I. Goldman, a partner of a nationally known Washington law firm, a Democrat, and a director of the Executive Committee of the Washington Council of Lawyers, wrote that Manion was an excellent lawyer and would be a "distinguished member of the Seventh Circuit." Goldman disagreed with the Chicago Council's negative assessment of Manion, considering it a speculative conclusion.[46]

The strident attack by many upon Manion provoked Senator Daniel Quayle (R-IN) to reply:

I would say I was perplexed by all this criticism of the personal and professional qualifications of Dan Manion if I were not so outraged by the inaccuracy and misleading information which characterizes it. What I find most disturbing is that the criticism comes from people who have never met Dan Manion. I believe any fair examination of a man and his record should assign greater weight to the first hand knowledge of his acquaintances and colleagues than the exaggerated charges of lobbyists looking for a convenient focus of all their efforts to overturn the clear results of the 1980 and 1984 elections.

Manion's opponents, faced with a dearth of negative opinion from Manion's peers, produced a novel strategy, blending varied arguments that he was ill-equipped for the appellate bench. Four primary arguments were raised.

The first argument was that Manion had produced no scholarly writing. This was a make-shift argument because it did not reflect the reality of most competent lawyers who work long hours pursuing their clients' interests. A successful attorney's obligations leave the practitioner little time for writing. Scholars who possess the luxury of time to write legal articles frequently lack the fundamental working knowledge of the day to day problems of practice. David T. Ready, former U.S. Attorney for the Northern District of Indiana under President Carter, noted:

> The most recent appointments to our Seventh Circuit have emanated from the area of academia. I have no problems with the qualifications of many of those persons who were so appointed. However, I believe that our Courts of Appeals are best served when they are comprised of former trial judges, academics, and practicing lawyers. It is my opinion that Mr. Manion is an excellent representative of the latter group and will well serve on the Court of Appeals.[47]

Because Manion did not have any publications, critics attacked his legal briefs. The second argument was that Manion's legal briefs did not reflect a structured legal mind because the briefs were filled with misspellings and grammatical errors. If five best representative briefs of his own choosing contained numerous errors, what problems, the argument continued, would be discovered in lesser briefs? However, the circumstances behind the choice of the briefs were thus: Laurie Wesley, chief counsel to Simon, called Manion on Thursday, April 17, 1986 indicating that five of his best briefs were urgently needed for the April 30 Committee hearing. Manion, however, was in federal court all day Friday and Saturday. Subsequently, he went to his office and hurriedly took five briefs from *recent* cases, ones he admitted were not his best and which he knew contained errors. The briefs were chosen because they covered a variety of subjects: civil rights, land condemnation, personal injury, taxation, and securities and corporations.[48] These briefs were sent by Simon and other Senators to a number of law professors and interest groups for intense scrutiny. They were criticized for misspellings, grammatical errors and poor legal analysis. Astoundingly, this issue took on front page significance, submerging the significant criteria, when People for the American Way began circulating copies of the briefs to reporters and editorial writers across the nation.[49] The *Legal Times*, however, also submitted Manion's drafts to numerous appellate lawyers in Washington. The conclusion of these lawyers was that the "briefs are entirely typical of briefs prepared in cases at the state court level and of briefs submitted by small firms."[50]

Fate has a way of demonstrating the triviality of some arguments. Senators Kennedy, Biden, Metzenbaum, Simon and Patrick Leahy (D-VT) sent a "Dear Colleague" letter in which they criticized the nominatiion.[51] Whatever measures all *five* senators took to ensure the quality of their product, the letter, nevertheless, contained numerous misspellings, syntactical and grammatical errors—so much so that Senator Hatch introduced the letter into the *Congressional Record*. Similarly, professors Laurence Tribe and Philip Kurland criticized Manion's briefs in a report; the meticulous, careful professors managed, however, their own misspellings, including the word, "ingelligently," and grammatical errors. Senators and professors would apparently hold Manion to a higher standard than they set for themselves.

The arguments misapprehend the nature of a lawyer's activities in a small, hard-working firm. Discovery, balancing heavy loads, and the special nature of trial practice frequently place full information at the hands of the lawyer with only a minimum of time to analyze the facts and research the law. Deadlines in the judicial system are not geared to the convenience of lawyers (even potential judicial nominees) but to the needs of an effective judicial machinery. (Understandably, Congress may not apprehend the significance of such deadlines—consider its inability to produce budgets on time.) With the pressure generated from these demands, the practitioner must ensure that substance prevails over style. Moreover, the impeccable, but costly, briefs that come from large firms are very difficult to justify in a small firm. There is a characteristic difference between a small law firm—meeting the needs of individuals and small and medium size companies—and large law firms catering to large businesses. The smaller the firm size, the fewer the attorneys, paralegals and other staff to assist in the preparation and review of documents. The small firm normally does not budget to invest in the most modern and expensive computer equipment, which today can cost over $500,000. The size and dollars available to the "megafirms" permit prettier briefs, but that is little indication of the quality of the representation of the client or the attorney's knowledge of the law, let alone the dedication and inherent legal capabilities of the attorney. The attorney in a small firm must constantly strive to balance substantive performance against grammatical detail. As Manion himself put it, in a small firm you do not get less quality, just less "workover."[52] The savings to the small firm's clients frequently are what makes an attorney affordable. As Manion himself indicated:

> Justice is not only for big corporations and big law firms. It is also for the little guy. It is for the people who have day-to-day problems. When they come up on appeal, I think my sensitivity to justice for such people will be, frankly what a Court of Appeals judge should have.[53]

The fundamental rule for the attorney is that he must successfully represent his client, while keeping well within the bounds of ethics. Manion and other judicial nominees from small law firms can reasonably be judged on that criterion. Look at the *results* produced as a result of the five "notorious" briefs: Manion won four of the cases.

A third argument was that Manion's daily practice did not sufficiently encompass complex litigation or constitutional law to permit the requisite knowledge necessary for a federal appellate judge. Contitutional law practice may be desirable but it is hardly necessary. Few attorneys possess that experience, outside of criminal attorneys and law professors. Moreover, this is not the Supreme Court, where constitutional issues are almost exclusively considered. The appellate judge determines all types of appeals brought from the federal and, to a lesser extent, state courts. The cases include questions of state law (under diversity of citizenship jurisdiction and ancillary jurisdiction) and federal (but non-constitutional) law. The floor speeches of some Senators show a surprising innocence in an inability to distinguish issues of federal law (federal legislation) from constitutional law.

For complex litigation, there would be a better basis for the argument if the nomination was for a district court position, where trying such cases on a daily basis would require that knowledge. At the appellate level, the necessary requirement is precisely a *broad* knowledge of law. As any litigator would indicate, the value of the litigator (and judge) is not found simply in an encyclopedic knowledge of the law, although that is certainly no detriment. Because of the wide variety of factual situations and legal issues that litigators deal with, the key stock in trade in his ability to analyze legal issues and apply the law to those issues.

The fourth argument was that Manion possessed little federal court experience, most of his litigation occuring in the Indiana state judicial system. Little time need be spent on this. Knowledge of federal practice is important, but is is not the realistic requirement on which to base the qualifications of a nominee. Legal capability is the proof of the pudding.[54]

Beyond arguments over legal abilities, critics challenged Manion's comprehension and adherence to the Constitution. In 1980, Manion, as an Indiana state senator, co-sponsored a bill— which passed overwhelmingly—along with a majority of Republican and Democrat senators, which authorized the voluntary display of the Ten Commandments in public classrooms, provided funding came from non-public funds. An 81 word inscription describing the secular purpose of the Ten Commandments would have been appended to the display. The bill followed in the wake of a Supreme Court decision, *Stone v. Graham*, which by a narrow 5-4 margin struck down a Kentucky statute providing for mandatory display of the Ten Commandments.[55] In a Dear Colleague letter, Kennedy, Leahy, Simon, Metzenbaum and Biden protested that Manion's actions demonstrated a lack of understanding of the Supreme Court decisions as the supreme law of the land, that he instead "substituted his own personal notion of what the law should be for the established rule as enunciated by the Supreme Court."[56] This concept that the Supreme Court's opinion on an issue of law is somehow of equal weight with the Constitution itself mistakes the nature of the Court's process. The Supreme Court *interprets* the Constitution; it is not *the* Constitution. If the Court's decisions held such significiance, even the Court would be restrained from overruling its prior decisions. One simple example is that *Brown v. Board of Education*, (1954)[57] the school desegregation case, could not have overruled *Plessy v. Ferguson*, (1896)[58] which established the "Separate but Equal" principle. Because the Supreme Court only interprets the Constitution, and is not equal to it, it can question its own decisions. But coequal branches also have that ability. It is a troubling suggestion that after the Supreme Court speaks, the other branches stop thinking, even with issues involving different facts, such as the Indiana bill contemplated. Indeed, it suggests that a 5-4 Supreme Court decision is etched in granite, even though the dissents displayed considerable disagreement with the fundamental proposition of *Stone*. Importantly, however, this concept of total deference fails to recognize the proper role of the different government branches in the American constitutional scheme. Andrew Jackson showed no hesitancy in his 1832 veto of a bill to extend the charter of the Bank of the United States. Jackson's veto message declared that the Bank was unconstitutional, notwithstanding a Supreme Court ruling to the opposite effect. Jackson's veto message stated "Each public office who takes an oath to support the Constitution swears that he will support it as he understands it, and not as it is understood by others." Under the constitutional interpretation suggested by this Dear Colleague letter, Abraham Lincoln would also have been criticized for intending to resort to his "personal notion" on slavery in disregard of the Supreme Court's *Dred Scott* decision. During the Lincoln-Douglas debates, he noted: "If I were in Congress, and a vote should come up on a question whether slavery should be prohibited in a new territory, in spite of that *Dred Scott* decision, I would vote that it should."[59]

Finally, much was made of the fact that the American Bar Association Standing Committee on the Federal Judiciary gave Manion a rating of qualified, with a minority giving him an unqualified rating. Some misrepresented the significance of this in their advocacy. Senator Paul Sarbanes (D-MD), for example, characterized him as "barely qualified."[60] A few, including a letter from 40 law school deans and certain editorials disapproving of the nomination, translated this into the ABA considering him "barely qualified." Behind the rehetoric is the reality that most nominees receive a "qualified" rating. Under Presidents Johnson, Nixon, Ford and Carter, 555 federal district court judges were appointed, and 50.8 percent, or 282 of them, received a qualified rating.[61] The law school deans could have, one would like to think, more intellectual honesty. To be fair, most of the deans signed a letter drafted by a few whose intentions can be questioned. Indeed, there is some question that the law school deans possessed adequate information to form their conclusions. The deans of Duke and Loyola Law School admitted surprise at the level of support for Manion among his Indiana colleagues. Loyola's Dean Arthur Frakt said: "I'm feeling a little sheepish. If it turns out he is someone of subtantial ability, I would feel it was unfortunate he got caught up in this." Paul Carrington, Dean at Duke Law School, was reminded of the "false views" on appellate court Judge Clement F. Haynsworth, Jr. when the Senate rejected his Supreme Court nomination in 1969.[62] The real tragedy, however, arises from editorials that preferred to use the misleading language, for they were engaged in influencing citizens who were unaware of the ABA rating system and the history of judges who traditionally receive the same "qualified" rating. Other presidents made six district court nominations—three from Carter and three from Johnson—that received *unqualified* ratings from the ABA, yet each was confirmed by the Senate.

The argument that a "qualified" rating effectively disqualifies a nominee substantially misstates the facts. Indeed, a qualified rating puts one in good company indeed. When Associate Justice Antonin Scalia was appointed to the Court of Appeals for the District of Columbia, he received only a qualified rating despite a distinguished academic background. Similarly, as Senator Hatch noted on the Senate floor, Judges Richard Posner and Frank H. Easterbrook, both appellate judges, received only a qualified rating when nominated to their posts.[63] Each had been a professor of law at a distinguished law school. Posner and Easterbrook also had a minority of the Standing Committee members voting them unqualified. In light of the intelligence and legal background possessed by both, those members of the ABA Standing Committee who voted these men unqualified had questionable grounds to reject them, except that both men were considered conservative.

Despite denials of any ideological considerations, it is clear that political philosophy was the litmus test some Senators and others applied to Dan Manion. Some gathering information on Manion were less interested in an honest appraisal than in what would support their preconceived view. David Ready, for example, reported what happened when a People for the American Way representative called him:

> I must say that I was disappointed in the nature of their inquiry and the questions they asked of me. . . . However, I must say that the overall tone of their inquiry was not one in which they were seeking my opinion on Mr. Manion's qualifications, but rather looking for something negative concerning Mr. Manion. When it became apparent that I was not going to accommodate them, simply because I do not know anything negative about Mr. Manion, their interest in talking to me waned sharply and the conversation terminated abruptly.[64]

On July 10, PAW began airing television and radio spots against Manion. One PAW newspaper ad proclaimed: "Our highest courts deserve first-rate judges, not second rate extremists."[65] The organization spent over $300,000, some observers believed, to oppose the confirmation. PAW also found a form of political encouragement for the four Republican senators who voted against Manion. As a reward for the senators' actions, PAW paid for "thank you" messages broadcast in their home states.

A number of Senate opponents defended ideology as a legitimate consideration. Simon considered it appropriate, saying he feared large swings in the law if there were "ideologues" on the bench. Although Simon was careful to say that this was a fear of both liberal and conservative ideologues, this was not a discussion of liberal men, and it is questionable whether he would oppose someone who possessed the liberal credentials that he suggested would be inappropriate. More importantly, one must wonder if the definition of liberal extremist would differ significantly when viewed by a liberal senator.

Earlier, a Washington *Post* editorial rejected decisions against confirmation made on the basis of ideology.

> The president has the right to choose judges with whom he is philosophically compatible, and they should not be denied confirmation for this reason.[66]

For those who deny decisions were made on the basis of Manion's political views, is there any doubt that the nomination would have encountered little resistance if the nominee subscribed to a less conservative position? An editorial in the Chicago *Tribune* concluded:

> You cannot help but conclude that the real reason Mr. Manion's nomination is in trouble is that half the members of the Senate Judiciary Committee think he is too conservative for their tastes, even though his views are well within the mainstream of American legal discourse. They seem to be opposing his name and his ideas. And if that is the reason, then Mr. Manion is being ill-treated.[67]

If his father was not Clarence Manion, how many people would have rallied to attack him? Would PAW or the Chicago Council of Lawyers have been so vigorously involved? The central issue in the Manion nomination was ideology, with convenient non-ideological arguments providing a thin facade. In sum, the objection was to a person whose father was a famous conservative.

The Senate Battleground. The Judiciary Committee vote for a favorable recommendation was a 9-9 tie, insufficient to carry the recommendation. The Committee, subsequently, voted 11-6 to send the nomination to the floor without recommendation, permitting the entire Senate to evaluate the nomination.

On the floor everyone knew the vote would be close. Dramatically, filibuster plans were dropped by the Democrats minutes before a cloture vote. According to a Democrat head count the vote "on the merits" appeared to be 46 votes for and 48 votes against the nomination. The initial proposal by the Democrats for an immediate vote on the merits was rejected by Robert Dole because two Republican senators, Paula Hawkins (R-FL) and Robert Packwood (R-OR) were absent. Two Democrats agreed voluntarily to abstain to balance the absent Republicans. [Packwood later said he was surprised that his name was thrown into the fray to secure one of the two Democrat pairs, publicly saying Dole had no authority to pair him; he eventually repudiated Dole's action by voting for reconsideration of the nomination (an anti-Manion vote) on a later day.] Slade Gorton (R-WA) shocked the Democrat leadership when he voted for Manion after being informed that the President would nominate a liberal Democrat associate for a judgeship. Quayle, working the floor in favor of the nomination, convinced Nancy Kassebaum (R-KS), who opposed Manion, to withdraw her anti-Manion vote and "pair" with Barry Goldwater (R-AZ), who, she was informed, could not be located and was likely to vote in favor of Manion. (Later some said that Goldwater had intended either not to appear or to vote present.) Early in the balloting, Biden realized that he had given away one too many votes in his pairing stratagem. In front of a national television audience on C-SPAN (broadcasts of Senate proceedings had begun only a few days before), Biden declared that he wanted to withdraw his paired vote. Such a withdrawal would have been a nearly unprecedented violation of senatorial courtesy. Apparently sensing this, Biden quickly said "Forget I said that." (When the *Congressional Record* appeared the next day, these comments had been stricken from the official record of the proceedings.)

As the roll call was ending, the vote appeared to be a 47-47 deadlock. When it became evident that a tie-breaking vote by Vice President George Bush would push Manion over the top, Byrd switched his vote from no to yes, bringing the tally to 48-46 in favor of the nomination. Byrd then moved immediately to reconsider the vote (which he could not have done if he had voted against the nomination).

Biden threatened to tie the Senate up in procedural knots unless the reconsideration vote was postponed until after the Independence Day recess, which ran until July 14. The Republicans agreed to the delay.

On July 23, 1986 the motion to reconsider came to a 49-49 tie which Vice President Bush, presiding over the Senate, broke by voting against the motion. (His vote was not strictly necessary because a tie was insufficient to carry such a procedural motion.) The vote changes in the motion to reconsider showed Manion retaining all 47 "solid" votes originally cast in favor of his nomination (Byrd, of course, voted to reconsider) while picking up Hawkins, who had been out with an injury, and Daniel Evans (R-WA). Evans thought the matter should be put to rest, although some analysts believed that he was covering for his embattled colleague Slate Gorton, who had come under fire for his last minute switch to Manion in the earlier vote.

Manion was finally confirmed.[68] He was sworn in on the day before Thanksgiving.

The Aftermath. Needless to say, many Democrats and activists were sorely disappointed with the maneuvering that produced the vote on the merits. Biden took much of the blame—not only for his mishandling of the floor fight, but also for his attitude and actions throughout the Manion nomination.

Months after Manion's swearing-in, the letters to the editor section of *The Nation*, featured this post-assessment:

> One usually temperate legal expert said angrily: "Off the record, Biden's a [scatological reference]. He takes credit for what others do. On the Manion nomination, he came in later than anyone else, and then insulted everyone else. Of course, he wanted to work with People for (the American Way); it has 300,000 well-heeled members. But he has specialized in spitting in the face of the civil rights community in order to position himself in the center and distance himself when it's convenient."
>
> . . . Biden boasted to guests at a dinner in his honor in Los Angeles that he had "put together" letters from law school deans and law professors around the country in opposition to the Manion nomination. In fact, those projects were largely developed and directed by People for the American Way and other extraparliamentary civil liberties activists. Biden's hosts couldn't believe their ears; one later said he thought the Senator was "certifiable" for claiming credit where none was due.
>
> Biden did not assume leadership until he became convinced by advocacy organizations that it was winnable, another leading civil libertarian said. (I'm sorry for the blind quotations, but nobody wants to get on Biden's black list.)
>
> On the Senate floor, Biden allowed himself to get mouse-trapped by the Republican leadership.[69]

CONCLUSION

As doubts about the accuracy of the various "code word" attacks on Reagan judges increased in 1987, the resurgent Democrats resorted to an outright slowdown, which this writer has described as a "stall" similar to the old four corners offense in college basketball: If you have a small lead, send a man to each corner of the court and just pass the ball around to eat up time on the scoreboard.

The analogy is not all that mixed: Under Senator Edward Kennedy's chairmanship in the late 1970s, the average time to elapse between a judicial nomination and a hearing of that nominee was 6^1/$_2$ weeks. Under Republican Strom Thurmond, the average time between nomination and hearing in 1985–86 was 3 weeks. But under Democrat Joe Biden of Delaware in the 100th Congress, the average time stretched to 9 weeks, with seven nominations actually held 12 weeks or more and three held for 20 weeks. One respected nominee, Professor Bernard Siegan of

San Diego University, was nominated in early February and had his first, tenuous hearing (with no firm commitment it would not be delayed or cancelled outright) slated for the late summer of 1987.

Surely no one, least of all the Democrats, could object if an interested observer suggested that perhaps Senator Kennedy's relatively more expeditious rate for confirmation hearings—which just happens to lie exactly between the two extremes—could become the standard. Fair play for Reagan judicial nominees may require the senatorial equivalent of the 30 second shot clock introduced in basketball when the four corners offense became an abuse of the rules.[70]

As for the "judges war" of 1985–86, an excuse—any excuse—was turned into an issue of judicial temperament, fairness and sensitivity. Opponents criticized Kozinski's interpersonal skills while overlooking his accomplishments as Chief Judge of the Claims Court. Fitzwater's "minority disenfranchisement" produced the illusion of racism. Neither the circumstances of his actions—he understood himself to be part of a broader anti-fraud project—nor his accomplished, and documented, record as a state court judge overcame this perceived stigma in the eyes of dissenters. Sessions' decision to obey his oath of office and accept an unpopular case—attempting to preserve the integrity of the ballot box—ironically brought the Civil Rights Establishment against him. Manion's personal and legal qualifications were ignored in the rush to stop the advancement of an unabashed conservative. Later, Rehnquist's record on judicial restraint and his posture against result-orientation in constitutional adjudication made him a choice target for those using the judiciary to establish their social agends.

The travesty of postured philosophical neutrality in judging the nominees does not hold up to scrutiny. *The overriding concern of many senators and interest groups opposing Reagan's judges is whether or not a particular judge will carry out their social agenda.* If ideology is the factor, then say so. If a Senator believes that his constitutional mandate requires that ideology be a criterion, then put it on the record for reasoned discourse. Hiding behind vague terms to justify voting against a nominee serves no legitimate purpose and cheapens the confirmation process.

David Brooks of the *Wall Street Journal* discussed the new and unpleasant realities of judicial politics in the *National Review*. A Reagan Administration official who did not want to be identified told Brooks:

> It's a myth that we lose a lot of government recruits because they don't want to take the kinds of pay cuts that are involved. They don't want to have their backgrounds laundered the way the Judiciary Committee has in the past few years.

Everyone needs to understand something: Republicans and conservatives are not dumb. They are watching very carefully what is happening to their friends. In politics, what goes around, comes around—all too often. Republicans told Brooks, "during future liberal presidencies they intend to fight just as dirty as the Democrats are doing now."[71]

Is this really what Americans want for present, and future, judicial nominees?

It is time to stop hiding motivation with words. "Objectivity" in politics may not be an obtainable goal. But fairness and honesty are both, surely, still possible.

The confirmation process that has emerged over the last few years is disturbing not merely in the short run. Easily established is a pattern where the dominant criterion for all things becomes ideology. With understandable reciprocity from conservatives facing a future liberal Administration, America is courting a permanent state of judicial warfare. The "judges war" of 1985-86 was not about qualifications, temperament, sensitivity or typographical errors. It was, rather, an unedifying series of engagements in the essential legal confrontation of this era: the national debate over the proper roles of judges in a democratic society.

REFERENCES

Ill-Advised and Discontent: Understanding the Judges War, by Patrick B. McGuigan

1. I would like to express my appreciation for the work and research performed by this book's co-editor, Jeffery P. O'Connell, Visiting Fellow in Legal Studies at the Free Congress Foundation's Institute for Government and Politics in 1987. I would also like to acknowledge the assistance and research of Jeffery D. Troutt, Research Director for the Judicial Reform Project, and Jon Pascale, the project's former Assistant Director, in the preparation of stories in *Judicial Notice*, where some of this material first appeared.

2. Howard Kurtz, Washington *Post*, May 7, 1986.
3. "Meese is confirmed by Senate in an Unusual Saturday Session," *Congressional Quarterly*, March 2, 1986, p. 385.
4. "Probe of finances Stalls Meese Nominations," 1984 *Congressional Quarterly Almanac*, p. 248.
5. "Panel Set to Vote on Meese After Querying Ethical Fitness," *Cong. Quar.* February 2, 1985, pp. 200, 203.
6. "Probe of Finances Stalls Meese Nomination," *supra* n. 4, p. 249.
7. *Id.*, p. 252.
8. *Id.*, p. 250.
9. "Senator's Pay for Night's Work: $250,000," *U.S. News and World Report*, June 4, 1984, p. 14; William Rusher, "Finder's Fee Stain Tough to Cleanse," Washington *Times*, August 17, 1984.
10. Pete Early, "Metzenbaum called Agency about Nephew," Washington *Post*, March 31, 1984.
11. 131 *Cong. Rec.* S1993 (daily ed. February 23, 1985).
12. Patrick B. McGuigan, "Senator Hatch Comes Down Hard Against Judicial Legislation," *Conservative Digest*, May 1986, pp. 99, 106.
13. Jon B. Pascale, "Reversing the 1984 election, Continued: Senate Judiciary Committee Rejects Reynolds," *Judicial Notice*, July/August 1985, pp. 1-2.
14. The Claims Court was created by the Federal Courts Improvement Act of 1982.
15. It was until recently an affiliate of the Institute for Policy Studies, which the *Wall Street Journal* called "left wing" and *Human Events* referred to as "one of the most unabashedly radical-Socialist advocacy centers in America." Foundation for Public Affairs, *Public Interest Profiles* (1986), pp. L27-29.
16. Howard Kurtz, Washington *Post*, November 1, 1985, p. A4.
17. 131 *Cong. Rec.* S15038 (daily ed. November 7, 1985).
18. It is impossible to resist, at this point, a personal digression. The finest teacher I had in my four years in graduate school was Odie B. Faulk, a prolific writer and an excellent historian of the American West. The man was absolutely merciless in his critiques of the papers submitted in his graduate seminar, "The Writing of History." Indeed, he used multi-colored pens and scathing editorial commentary in the margins of the essays he received from myself and a half-dozen colleagues. Enduring this course—and several others I eventually took from him — was among the least pleasant experiences of my college years. But when it was all over, I had emerged as, at the least, a prolific and efficient writer. Nearly a decade has passed, but what remains with me from those years is a variety of maxims of good writing — Maxims which I am passing on to the dozens of interns, reporters and staff writers who have worked with me in my professional life. Those rules of good writing were not always imparted to me and my colleagues with a light touch, but they were conveyed with a sincere concern about our futures as scholars and historians representative of the quality of education at our school. Today, I am grateful for every merciless moment of those seminars. Some of those on the receiving end of Judge Kozinski's "Technicolor" editing might have benefitted from such moments in their own college experiences.
19. 131 *Cong. Rec.* S15038 (daily ed. November 7, 1985).
20. 131 *Cong. Rec.* S15037 (daily ed. November 7, 1985).
21. *Id.*
22. "Kozinski Battle Signals Liberal Assault on Reagan Judges," *Judicial Notice*, November/December 1985.
23. Washington *Post*, November 12, 1985.
24. Howard Kurtz, Washington *Post*, November 12, 1985.
25. 132 *Cong. Rec.* S2916 (daily ed. March 18, 1985).
26. 132 *Cong. Rec.* S2387 (daily ed. March 10, 1986).
27. 132 *Cong. Rec.* (daily ed. March 11, 1986).
28. 132 *Cong. Rec.* S.2390 (daily ed. February 18, 1986).

29. 132 *Cong. Rec.* S2921 (daily ed. March 18, 1986).
30. Confirmation Hearings on Federal Appointments: Senate Hearing 99-141, Part 3, pp. 34, 36.
31. 132 *Cong. Rec.* S2915 (daily ed. March 18, 1986) (statement of Sen. Gramm).
32. Jon S. Pascale, "New Fronts Opened in the Judges War," *Judicial Notice*, March/April 1986, pp,1-2.
33. Confirmation Hearings, *supra* n. 30.
34. Letter of Theodore P. Steinke, Jr., Dallas County Assistant District Attorney, Chief, Public Integrity Section, Specialized Crime Division, dated January 29, 1986 to Sen. Strom Thurmond, reprinted in Confirmation Hearings, *supra,* n. 33, p. 23.
35. 132 *Cong. Rec.* S2916 (daily ed. March 18, 1986).
36. *Id.*
37. *Id.*
38. Washington *Post,* May 7, 1986, p. A8.
39. This chapter covers only individuals that were nominated by the Reagan Administration and went through the rigors of Senate consideration. Others could properly be considered if the chapter were broadened. Some nominations were preempted by other circumstances. Perhaps the best known situation involves University of Texas constitutional law professor Lino A. Graglia. With the intention of nominating Graglia to the Fifth Circuit Court of Appeals in New Orleans, the Justice Department submitted his name to the ABA Standing Committee on the Federal Judiciary. He was rejected with an unqualified rating. Interest groups, including the People for the American Way (PAW), lobbied extensively against Graglia, claiming insensitivity to minorities and disrespect for the rule of law. *See* David Sellers, "Justice Seeks Second Opinion on Nominee Rejected by ABA," Washington *Times,* May 14, 1986, p. 3A. PAW, which invested heavily in selected attempts to defeat Reagan nominations, published a 50 page booklet attacking Graglia and charging him with racism. After the ABA rejection, the Justice Department requested Griffin Bell, former Attorney General under Jimmy Carter to assess Graglia's qualifications. Unhappily for his many admirers in conservative judicial reform circles, Graglia was no more popular with Bell than with the ABA. The decision to consult Bell, an unusual second step for candidates deemed unqualified by the ABA committee, was significant in light of the suit pending against the ABA. The Washington Legal Foundation, in a suit filed in December 1985, asked the court to force the ABA to open its meetings to the public. Even Mr. Bell, while acknowledging that the ABA was useful, admitted that the Carter Administration did have some problems with them. *Washington Legal Foundation v. ABA Committee on Federal Judiciary,* C.A. No. 85-3918 (D.D.C. filed December 11, 1985). The Washington Legal Foundation alleged that the confidentiality of the ABA Judiciary Committee violates the Federal Advisory Committee Act of 1972. *See* Popeo and Smith, "The Questionable Role of the ABA . . . ," in this book.
40. Howard Kurtz, Washington *Post,* May 7, 1986.
41. 125 *Cong. Rec.* S26029. (daily ed. Sept. 25, 1979).
42. Patrick B. McGuigan, "Manion and Reagan win a Big One for Middle Americans," *Conservative Digest,* October 1986, pp. 5, 11.
43. Letter of the Chicago Council of Lawyers to Senator Paul Simon dated April 9, 1986, reprinted in 132 *Cong. Rec.,* S8476 (daily ed. June 26, 1986).
44. 132 *Cong. Rec.* S8478 (daily ed. June 25, 1986).
45. Letter of John J. Sullivan to Sen. Robert Byrd dated May 9, 1986, reprinted in 132 *Cong. Rec.* S8479-80 (daily ed. June 25, 1986).
46. Letter of Eugene I. Goldman to Sen. Strom Thurmond dated April 23, 1986, reprinted in 132 *Cong. Rec.* S8479 (daily ed. June 25, 1986).
47. Letter of David T. Ready to Sen. Strom Thurmond dated April 28, 1986, reprinted in 132 *Cong. Rec.* S8479 (daily ed. June 25, 1986).
48. McGuigan, *supra* n. 42, p. 10.
49. See Jill Abramson, "Manion: Look for Experience, Not Speling (sic)," *Legal Times,* June 23, 1986, p. 1.

50. *Id.*, p. 4.

51. Dear Colleague letter of Senators Kennedy, Metzenbaum, Biden, Leahy and Simon dated May 5, 1986, p. 3, printed in 132 *Cong. Rec.* S8482-3 (daily ed. June 25, 1986.

52. Patrick B. McGuigan, "Manion and Reagan Win a Big One for Middle Americans," *supra*, n. 42, p. 9.

53. *Id.*, p. 10.

54. The lack of legal experience did not stop President John F. Kennedy from appointing his brother as Attorney General.

55. 449 U.S. 39 (1980).

56. Dear Colleague letter, *supra* n. 51.

57. 347 U.S. 483 (1954).

58. 163 U.S. 537 (1896).

59. Lincoln-Douglas Debates, Chicago, July 10, 1858, quoted in Charles E. Rice, "What the Manion Fight is All About," Washington *Times*, June 18, 1986, p. 30.

60. 132 *Cong. Rec.* S8543 (daily ed. June 26, 1986). For elaboration on ABA ratings, see Popeo and Smith herein.

61. 132 *Cong. Rec.* S8476 (daily record June 25, 1986).

62. Paul Houston, "Political Foes Also Support Manion Court Nomination," Los Angeles *Times*, July 13, 1986, p. 1.

63. 132 *Cong. Rec.* S8480 (daily ed. June 25, 1986).

64. 132 *Cong. Rec.* S8479 (daily ed. June 25, 1986).

65. Stephen Wermiel, "Conservative's Nomination to U.S. Appeals Court Spurs Debate over Quality of Reagan-Era Judges," *Wall Street Journal*, June 6, 1986, p. 44.

66. Washington *Post*, November 14, 1985.

67. See, for example, editorial, "The Fight over Reagan's Judges," Chicago *Tribune*, June 13, 1986.

68. The Manion confirmation struggle was one of the most intense political confrontations of the last six years, and it produced countless stories and vignettes impossible to describe in this limited space. Among the stories that could be told at some length, however, was the aggressiveness of Republican Leader Robert Dole in securing the final result. Another tale would be of the first Manion confirmation victory party, held at the offices of Coalitions for America only a few hours after the vote. Yet another story would be that of a young employee working with a conservative organization who, angered by the scurrilous assaults on Manion's integrity and qualifications, called a well-known Washington, D.C. radio station for days, complaining of the unfairness of the Anti-Manion advertisements running on that station. This unsung heroine's efforts led the station manager to offer equal time to Manion's supporters, which led to this writer's introduction to the world of big time radio political advertising. In short, there were enough stories in this one battle to fill a book — one I hope will someday be written.

69. Letters, *The Nation*, May 9, 1987. p. 596.

70. *See* George Archibald, "Hill politics blamed for slow action on judges," Washington *Times*, July 6, 1987, p. A1.

71. David Brooks, "The Young Pol's Guide to the Brave New World," *National Review*, April 10, 1987.

2

REHNQUISITION: RITE OF PASSAGE FOR A CHIEF JUSTICE

by Jeffrey P. O'Connell & Patrick B. McGuigan

The struggle over the nomination of William Hubbs Rehnquist as Chief Justice of the United States is the classic case in point of the ugly side of increasingly confrontational tactics utilized by some who are more concerned with their social agenda than with equal justice under law. In the words of Senator Orrin Hatch, the nomination process was transformed into a "Rehnquisition."[1] Rehnquist's opponents "left no stone unturned" attempting to find incriminating evidence. They inspected 20 year old records of the Justice Department's Office of Legal Counsel, memoranda 34 years old from his days as Associate Justice Jackson's law clerk, FBI reports "20 years and 20 minutes old," and over 50 witnesses.[2]

A perspective on Justice Rehnquist is helpful. He graduated first in his class at Stanford Law School (the only classmate ahead of the young Sandra Day O'Connor). At 61 years old, he had served as an Associate Justice on the Supreme Court for 15 years since his confirmation to that post in 1971 by a Senate (and Judiciary Committee) controlled by Democrats. The American Bar Association Standing Committee on the Federal Judiciary rated him "well qualified" for the Chief Justice slot, the highest rating given to Supreme Court nominees. In the process of the evaluation, the ABA interviewed all current Associate Justices of the Court, over 180 federal and state judges, 65 practicing attorneys, and over 50 law school deans and professors. Justice Rehnquist received accolades as a justice and scholar. Even Justice William Brennan, his jurisprudential counterpart on the High Court, applauded the choice. The ABA Committee also examined over 200 of the nominee's opinions. Those supporting the confirmation included Griffin Bell (Attorney General under President Jimmy Carter), Erwin N. Griswold (Solicitor General under Presidents Jimmy Carter and Johnson), William French Smith (former Reagan Attorney General), Gerhard Casper (dean of the University of Chicago Law School), and Rex Lee (former Solicitor General under Reagan).[3]

What Rehnquist possessed that irritated many activists was a firm belief in judicial restraint, or interpretivism (considered in more detail in chapter 13), which recognizes that Justices, like Congress and the President, are subject to limitations in the performance of their constitutional responsibilities. In most situations, the democratic process, not the judiciary, must determine policy decisions.

EXTREMISM IN THE PURSUIT OF INTERPRETATION?

Opposition to Rehnquist and his traditional view of judicial restraint was expected, particularly from the more liberal senators, as well as from activist organizations that seek policy mandates from the judiciary. Rehnquist's understanding of judicial restraint—which accepts the premise that some solutions to the nation's problems are properly left to Congress, state legislatures and the democratic process—makes him anathema to such groups. The attacks, however, were surprisingly harsh by any measure. Senator Alan Cranston (D-CA) attacked Rehnquist as an "unrelenting supporter of segregation" who does not support equal justice under law.[4] Cranston also inveighed that Rehnquist was an "extreme ideologue, whose judicial philosophy is far beyond the mainstream" and "whose very zeal prevents detached judicial consideration and affects his ethical judgment."[5]

During the floor debates, Senator Edward Kennedy (D-MA) declared:

On the merits, Justice Rehnquist is not mainstream but too extreme—he is too extreme on race, too extreme on women's rights, too extreme on freedom of speech, too extreme on separation of church and state, too extreme to be Chief Justice.[6]

Kennedy concluded that Rehnquist "is outside the mainstream of American constitutional law and American Values."[7] The debate's polemic hyperbole continued as Senator John Kerry (D-MA) contributed:

I believe that Justice Rehnquist's views are so far outside the mainstream of legal thought that he is irredeemably handicapped in his ability to effectively fulfill the essential role of a Chief Justice as a builder of consensus on the Court.[8]

Besides, Kerry added, Reh́nquist wanted women to be second class citizens.[9]

Professor Gary Born, once Rehnquist's law clerk, questions those who call, as Kennedy, Cranston and Kerry did, the nominee outside the mainstream of constitutional law and American values.

Opposition to Rehnquist's appointment boils down to a single complaint: Rehnquist's critics wish that he would more frequently invoke the U.S. Constitution to overturn state and federal laws that they disagree with. Rehnquist's refusal to interfere with the democratic process in this way reflects his commitment to the most basic principles of the American Constitution—not his rejection of them. Rehnquist believes judges are bound by the Constitution to respect the policy choices made by the democratically-elected representatives of the people, ... the Justice responds with caution when litigants ask unelected, life-tenured judges to overturn democratically-enacted laws.[10]

Some Senators characterized Rehnquist as a major dissenter. According to Cranston, Rehnquist "dissented alone more than anyone else."[11] This charge is not only inaccurate as applied to Rehnquist, but dissent as a criterion of qualification is of dubious validity. Lone dissents are a questionable criterion for determining the legitimacy of the views of a justice. Associate Justices John M. Harlan (1877-1912) and Oliver Wendell Holmes (1902-1932) were known for their eloquent dissents, some of which eventually became the dominant philosophy of the Court. In any event, the facts disprove the charge. Justice John Paul Stevens, in the first ten years their terms overlapped (Stevens was appointed to the Supreme Court in 1975 by President Gerald Ford), surpassed Rehnquist 50-41 in lone dissents. Stevens also was the greatest dissenting author—with 145—from 1980-84. During the same four year period, Brennan wrote 106 dissents, while Rehnquist wrote only 75. Looking from a slightly different perspective—votes (rather than opinions) against the majority—during 1980-84, Rehnquist cast 182 losing votes, compared with Brennan's 345 such votes. If the criterion for "being mainstream" is conformity with the majority, Rehnquist does well. Indeed, no one authored more majority opinions over the four terms prior to his nomination.[12]

Fundamentally, the issue is not whether a justice dissents. The issue is whether he properly applies the Constitution. The clear concern voiced by groups such as the American Civil Liberties Union was whether Rehnquist acted in conformity with a liberal social policy agenda. That agenda required that the courts act where Congress or state legislatures failed to enact the agenda of such groups. The ideological extremism, if found, would be in those who demanded that there be purity of belief in policy. This result-orientation leaves no room for the expression of the restraint necessary in judges, for the resulting judicial process finds no correcting impulse for errant actions of the judiciary other than the self-correcting behavior of individual judges.

Kerry's tactic on the Senate floor was to numb everyone with statistics. He asserted that in 80 of 83 cases where members of the Court disagreed on interpretations of modern civil rights statutes, Rehnquist took the position least favorable to minorities, women, elderly or disabled. In 23 cases challenging statutes on the basis of sex discrimination, Rehnquist voted for constitutionality in 20, and partial constitutionality in two others. Rehnquist also voted against individuals challenging government action in 120 of 124 cases. In cruel and unusual punishment cases, he cast his ballot in favor of the constitutionality of all 30 cases to come before the Court.[13]

Kerry and other critics equated votes against constitutional claims as evidence of insensitivity to the rights of women and minorities and a disregard for equal justice under law. Such conclusions are specious, providing a notorious, selective approach to evaluating Rehnquist's qualifications. Such statistics do not explain constitutional claims before the Supreme Court, let alone the heart and soul of a judge. The nature of the claim and the constitutional justification of claimants must be independently evaluated. Most claims before the Supreme Court are attempts to expand the current boundaries of constitutional law. A decision of a justice that he cannot expand constitutional law does not make that justice insensitive to individuals' rights. Expansion of those constitutional boundaries ought to occur only after the most rigorous examination, and only when the facts of the case, the language of the Constitution or the clear intention of the framers allow no other result. The wrong approach, clearly, is a result-oriented approach, which looks not to the law and its limitations but to "good" results for the individual litigant. A vote for a statute's constitutionality, rather than evidence of hostility to women or minorities, can reflect an understanding of the limitations under which the judiciary must work if it is to fulfill its role in a democratic government. Many issues are for the Congress or the state legislatures to resolve and cannot be the province of the judiciary. The judicial restraint philosophy, which Rehnquist holds, simply recognizes that the Constitution defers most policy decisions to the democratic process.

Senator Christopher Dodd (D-CT), however, concluded that Rehnquist's civil rights decisions mirror "an icy cold indifference to the equal protection guarantee embodied in our Constitution."[14] Because of the limitations of the judiciary in "legislating" by judicial fiat, Dodd's criticism is better redirected to himself and the other members of Congress or the state legislatures— those who bear the fundamental responsibility for enacting the legislation necessary to deal with policy issues. *Their* failure to enact the legislation they believe "essential" does not justify the judiciary resolving cases by constitutional manipulation.

Senator Barry Goldwater (R-AZ), in his inimitable way, went to the heart of the matter on the attack on the nominee's "insensitivity" to the rights of minorities and women:

> He has not decided cases on the way they would have wished and it is supposedly "insensitive" for anyone to disagree with [the opponents'] liberal agenda. A person becomes a racist or sexist because his reasoned judgments guide him to a different outcome from the tenets of liberal philosophy.[15]

JUSTICE

Some simply did not like Rehnquist's brand of justice, which is to say Rehnquist's judicial restraint philosophy was unacceptable to them. Senator Donald Riegle, Jr. (D-MI) felt that Rehnquist's pattern of decisions over the years made it difficult to obtain equal justice. Senator Lowell Weicker (R-CT) wanted justice achieved, even at the cost of transforming the fabric of the Constitution with novel and evolving meanings—the Supreme Court as the continuing constitutional convention.[16] Senator William Roth, Jr. (R-DE), speaking immediately after Weicker on the Senate floor, served as the perfect counter point to Riegle, recognizing the necessary judicial restraint of the Supreme Court Justice:

> I believe it is important to keep in mind that our duty is not to select and advance those individuals who will carry out our political ideologies to the hallowed chambers of the Supreme Court, but to approve those who are dedicated and faithful to the Constitutional plan.
>
> Within this framework, the substantive value judgments concerning the Government of America—or the making of laws—were assigned to those officials politically accountable to the people. . . .
>
> . . . Therefore, there is no place in the constitutional plan for the courts to impose their notions of what is right or just or popular.[17]

Underscoring the extremist theme, some argued Rehnquist could not be the consensus builder that a Chief Justice should be. Kerry argued that Rehnquist did not have the "record of a man who will build consensus and lead the Court."[18] Kerry, however, called not for consensus, but for the capitulation of principle to expediency—surrendering one's view and vote to achieve a more ambiguous objective. What "justice" is served to the litigants when one of them is sacrificed for a "consensus?" Senator Max Baucus (D-MT) perceived Rehnquist as more likely to divide the Court than unite the nation.[19] Baucus's dislike of the nominee's constitutional philosophy transformed intellectual disagreement into divisiveness—something the other Justices could not find. His Court peers, according to the ABA Judiciary Committee interviews, favored the nomination. Even Justice Brennan, his jurisprudential antithesis on the bench, thought Rehnquist would make a "splendid Chief Justice."[20] Certainly after 15 years on the court, any divisive quality in the nominee's personality or jurisprudence would have manifested itself to the other justices.

Although virtually every Senator opposing Rehnquist's elevation carefully recited that ideology was not the rationale for his negative vote, there is no way to square their arguments with the facts—unless the political viewpoint of the Senator is considered. The makeshift arguments hid the actual rationale—opposition to judicial restraint, as evidenced by the Justice's 15 years of decisions.

Professor Born, from his personal perspective of working with the Justice at the court, disagreed with arguments that Rehnquist could not be an effective consensus builder:

> Rehnquist ... devotes special attention to building consensus for opinions of the court and encouraging collegiality among the members. He frequently visits the chambers of other justices, either to discuss cases or simply to chat. Likewise, he maintains warm personal relations with other members of the court, and he is keenly aware of the personal interests and sensitivities of his fellow justices. These personal qualities will go far toward preventing the internal divisiveness that sometimes has beset the court.[21]

Professor A. E. "Dick" Howard of the University of Virginia also noted the genuine warmth and leadership abilities of the nominee.[22]

Biden was particularly troubled because Rehnquist refused to concede that he would have changed his mind on any one of his 8-1 dissents in the hopes of building a consensus.[23] This perspective of Biden, also a lawyer, is troubling. Apparently, Biden has more regard for a common result than a principled decision based on an understanding of the law. No Justice, let alone the Chief Justice, should follow such a formula of capitulation. Biden, who at one point admitted that he would not be qualified to sit on the Supreme Court, would have difficulty with another Chief Justice—John Marshall. Marshall's famous admonition in *Marbury v. Madison* is that we are blessed with a government of laws, not of men.[24] Biden's conception of law reduces judges to negotiators who decide cases based on policy discussions with other jurists, ignoring the need soundly to premise the decision *on the law*, as understood by the judge. Biden's advocacy suggests a system that depends less on the merits of the individual cases than on pragmatic considerations of judicial negotiations. The Supreme Court is not a jury struggling to reach a unanimous verdict but a panel obligated under the members' constitutional oath of office to recognize and apply the Constitution as the supreme law of the land.

RESTRICTIVE COVENANTS

Two houses that Rehnquist owned contained restrictive covenants against blacks and Jews. His Phoenix house, purchased in 1961 (and subsequently sold), contained a covenant against non-whites. This covenant had existed since the real estate was initially developed in 1928—an unfortunate era when such covenants were common. A Vermont home, purchased in 1974, prohibited its ownership by anyone of the "Hebrew race." Both of the covenants are unenforceable and have been since 1948 when the Supreme Court decided *Shelley v. Kraemer*, ruling such covenants unconstitutional.[25] The covenants outraged Kennedy. On July 31, Senator Kennedy stated: "I think both those [restrictions] are significant," he said during a recess. "The basic issue is [Rehnquist's] sensitivity to civil rights." Kennedy, a lawyer, must have known that the covenants were inserted in the chain of title long before Rehnquist purchased it, and that the need to expunge the covenants has not been necessary for 38 years.

On August 2, however, it was discovered that John F. Kennedy's house in Georgetown, owned while he was a Senator, had a restrictive covenant against blacks. Except to defend the civil rights record of his brother, the senior senator from Massachusetts did not raise the issue again. Later, the Washington-based Center for Judicial Studies disclosed that Biden also lived in a house with a restrictive covenant. James McClellan, President of the Center, noted: "We believe that the American people have a right to know about the existence of these documents in judging the worth and sincerity of accusations that have been raised concerning Mr. Justice Rehnquist's property holding."[26] Subsequently, restrictive covenants were discovered on houses of former Democrat presidential nominees Hubert Humphrey and George McGovern.[27]

Restrictive covenants are not a proud part of this nation's history, but the covenants, inserted into the chain of title in the distant past, are difficult to remove. Whatever the intent of the parties to the original transactions, they did not reflect the state of mind of later purchasers, such as John Kennedy, Hubert Humphrey or William Rehnquist. The removal of the covenants, of course, is unnecessary because they have no legal effect. This topic quietly, but embarrassingly to the Democrats who sought to make it an issue, disappeared from the confirmation hearings.

LAIRD V. TATUM

Laird v. Tatum came before the Supreme Court in 1972 after a favorable ruling for plaintiffs from the District of Columbia Federal Court of Appeals. Plaintiffs—a group of civil rights activists and anti-war demonstrators—filed a class action against the U. S. Army alleging that its Domestic Surveillance Program was unconstitutional. The program had been authorized in the 1960s by a Defense Department Directive on civil disturbances. The program's emphasis, at least in part, shifted to concern over the disruptive effects of antiwar demonstrations. Rehnquist headed the Office of Legal Counsel at the Justice Department at a time when discussions between the Army and Justice were underway. After public disclosure of the surveillance, the Senate Judiciary Committee's Subcommittee on Constitutional Rights under Senator Sam Ervin (D-NC) held hearings in 1971. The Justice Department tapped Rehnquist as its witness. In the course of his testimony before the Subcommittee, he mentioned the *Tatum* case which was already underway.

The plaintiffs requested that Rehnquist recuse himself—that is, disqualify himself from consideration of the case—because of his prior participation in an agreement between the Army and the Justice Department, prepared through Rehnquist's Office of Legal Counsel. After Rehnquist delivered a lengthy opinion expressing why it was appropriate for him to hear the case with the rest of the Court, the result was a 5-4 decision for the government dismissing the suit for lack of standing to bring the action. Without Rehnquist's vote, the 4-4 tie would have permitted the appellate decision in favor of the plaintiffs to stand. (The High Court's decision was based on the lack of standing of the plaintiffs to bring the suit.)

This action, which involved claims about politically sensitive issues of the era, outraged some Senators who accused the nominee of deliberately attempting to conceal illegal activities. Kennedy's conclusions were the most extreme, indicating Rehnquist was the architect of the policy[28] and claiming that the nominee's motivation in not recusing himself was precisely because he knew about "illegal intelligence activities going on inside the Nixon administration . . . and did not want the American people to know about them."[29]

In 1972, the federal statute governing recusal stated:

> Any justice . . . shall disqualify himself in any case in which he has a substantial interest, has been of counsel, is or has been a material witness, or is so related to or connected with any party or his attorney as to render it improper, in his opinion, for him to sit. . . .[30]

Rehnquist's record evidences no reluctance to recuse himself in appropriate situations: he did so nearly 100 times, including situations in which he had a minimal advisory role at the Justice Department.[31] In this case, his involvement with executive branch surveillance was, in the words of Senator Hatch, "extremely minimal." Hatch continued:

> He helped to prepare an initial draft of a plan dealing with civil emergencies, including a section concerning information about potential instigators of unrest. This was simply a planning memo; the Justice did not participate in its implementation. The planning memo says nothing about surveillance underway nor about any specific event of the sixties or seventies.[32]

Rehnquist's opponents buttressed their position with a memorandum from Professor Geoffrey Hazard, who was principally involved in rewriting the judicial ethics requirements in 1972 (subsequent to *Tatum*).[33]

Hazard's report would prove interesting if it was indeed a study of ethics considerations—a strict memorandum of law. Hazard's report, however, is filled with factual assumptions and conclusions as to what Rehnquist knew and did. His ultimate conclusions on the necessity for recusal rest squarely on those assumptions. If those were right, he would make a persuasive argument against the propriety of Rehnquist's actions. But the assumptions have no foundation except for general considerations of what was "likely" to have occurred. As such, the report reads as an advocate's brief, not a considered legal memorandum. (It is not unfair to note, at this juncture, that Hazard squarely fits into the camp of judicial activism antithetical to Rehnquist's judicial restraint.)

Hazard assumes that Rehnquist was involved to a substantial extent. Among Hazard's assumptions, he assumes "it appears that Mr. Rehnquist ... had a relationship to the surveillance program beyond that disclosed in his opinion ... or revealed in his testimony." This assumption is based on the disputed testimony of others, primarily that of Robert Jordan, General Counsel of the Army. Based on this testimony, Hazard concluded there were heavy negotiations: "The *circumstances strongly suggest* that Mr. Rehnquist was personally and substantially involved" in the negotiations. The circumstances cited by Hazard are that the "subject was highly important," the Office of Legal Counsel was small in size, and Rehnquist sent a *transmittal letter* to President Nixon.

Hazard concludes:

> In a matter of substance and complexity, it is implausible that the head of the government office responsible for development of its legal aspects would not be personally involved in considerable detail concerning the facts and issues going into the policy and its formulation.[34]

This is a conclusion of fact—and a fact hotly contested. As Senator Hatch correctly noted, *Hazard "resolved" every issue of fact against Rehnquist*.[35] From this basis, Hazard is able to conclude the failure of Rehnquist to recuse himself was unethical. An additional problem is that Hazard fails to describe adequately the ethical standards in existence in 1972, as opposed to now. Rehnquist's opinion justifying his failure to recuse himself relied on an article "Disqualification of Judges: In Support of the Bayh Bill,"[36] which Hazard concedes was an accurate statement of the law in 1972.[37] In attempting to drive home his point, Hazard quotes from that article:

> Justices disqualify in Government cases in which they have been directly involved in some fashion in the particular matter, and not otherwise.

Hazard omits, however, a later sentence from the *same* paragraph:

More important, Justices who have come from the Government do not disqualify merely because the particular matter involves a policy which, when in the Government, they may have helped to form.[38]

Rehnquist's substantive involvement, to the extent it existed, would have to be characterized as policy formulation.

Being involved in policy formulation in some way is not grounds for subsequent judicial disqualification. Justice Hugo Black, as Senate Labor Committee Chairman, voted for the constitutionality of the Fair Labor Standards Act which he helped write.[39]

VOTER CHALLENGE PROGRAM

Critics also charged that Rehnquist improperly engaged in voter challenges in black wards in Maricopa County in the early 1960s.[40] In the rhetoric of some, such as Senator Riegle, voter challenges were transformed into a "voter intimidation program."

Voter challenges, however, were (and are) not illegal. Indeed, both political parties were actively involved in challenging individuals. Challengers were appointed to represent each party, and their responsibility was to watch for irregularities at the polling places.[41] Rehnquist's role during this period was legal advisor to the Republican Party and he did occasionally travel to a precinct. But his role was advisory. He did not challenge voters. Nevertheless, some individuals testified that they saw him challenge voters in 1962 and 1964.

According to Senator Hatch, one of the low points in Rehnquist's confirmation was the opposition bringing in witnesses to testify on events that happened 24 years—events of a single day which most people could not recall. The issue was investigated in the 1971 nominations and the chairman, Democrat Senator McClellan, concluded: "Voter harassment charges against Mr. Rehnquist are found by this committee to be wholly unsubstantiated. Viewed in its entirety, the incident suggests at the very most a case of mistaken identity."[42] This conclusion came 9 years after the incident, not 24 years. Senator Hatch's conclusion best expresses the testimony:

Much of their testimony is consistent with Attorney Rehnquist's role as legal advisor who visited precincts to settle voting disputes. Of the seven who claimed to have seen attorney Rehnquist challenge voters, five did not know him at the time and only identified him on the basis of 1971 newspaper photographs. . . . All of those purporting to have seen Attorney Rehnquist challenging are committed Democrat or liberal activists, whereas six Democrats—including four State or Federal Judges—refute the harassment or challenging charge.[43]

James J. Brosnahan proved the most forceful witness. A former United States attorney, he served as an Assistant U.S. Attorney in the early 1960s. Prior to the Committee hearings, he stated that he went *to the Bethune precinct* in 1962 with an FBI agent to investigate complaints about Republican voter challenges. While there, Rehnquist was pointed out as the instigator of the problems. Brosnahan's memory, surprisingly fresh after 24 years, quickly blurred at the Judiciary Committee hearing a few weeks later. He was no longer certain at what precinct he spotted Rehnquist. His supervisor, Carl Muelke, only mentions sending Brosnahan to Bethune, not to any other precinct.[44] Senator Hatch did not let this "lapse of memory" slip by unnoticed.

If Brosnahan had continued to identify Bethune as the precinct where Rehnquist was spotted, he would have seriously undermined his own testimony. In contrast to Brosnahan's statement, there were several, unambiguous accounts of the disturbance at that site.[45] At Bethune in 1962, a person did challenge voters. While challenging voters was lawful, the aggressive manner in which the person in question challenged the voters caused problems. Following the actions of the challenger, a scuffle ensued, and the police escorted the individual away from the polls. The miscreant, however, was identified as Wayne Bentson, according to contemporaneous materials, including police and FBI reports and news accounts in the Arizona *Republic*. This is corroborated by the then U.S. Attorney Carl Muecke, a Democrat, who investigated the 1962 harassment charges, and by others. For example, Charles L. Hardy, attorney in charge of the Democratic Party Election Advisory committee and an arbitrator for voter challenges and disputes during the 1960s, Rehnquist's Democratic counterpart at the time, also supported this.[46] Hardy, now a federal judge, indicated that he "can state unequivocally that Mr. Rehnquist did not act as a challenger a the Bethune precinct . . . challenging voters was not a part of Mr. Rehnquist's role in 1962 or subsequent election years."[47]

Vincent Maggiore, former Democratic party chairman for Maricopa County, testified that he was the one who called the U.S. Attorney's office—as well as the sheriff and police—in 1962 to complain about the Bethune challenges. Indeed, he admits that he may have instigated the scuffle by sending some of his aides to "help out." He testified:

> [A]t no time did anybody come to me and state that Justice Rehnquist had committed any of the acts that I have heard for 2 of 3 days [of the confirmation hearings]. I feel that I was the party leader . . . and, for sure, all of these things should have come to me.[48]

He even noted stopping Rehnquist on the street some days after the Bethune incident and complaining that some voters were deprived of their rights, a conclusion with which Rehnquist agreed!

Thomas Murphy, 1964 Democratic Party chairman for Maricopa County, now a judge in American Samoa, indicated he personally investigated election day complaints in 1964 and that the allegations against Rehnquist were unfounded.

Incredibly, one witness actually identified Rehnquist as the person who challenged him with clinched fists. Anyone familiar with the Justice's demeanor can only scoff at such allegations. This charge illustrates a disheartening reality about the recent confirmation process. Individuals who did not even know Rehnquist in the early 1960s and who never reported the incident to authorities at the time could—nine years later in 1971— identify the then Associate Justice nominee through a *picture in the papers*. They found national recognition in 1971 and again in 1986.

To what extent do such implausible claims deserve national exposure before the Judiciary Committee? Continued and deliberate character assassination, emanating time after time from the same opponents to both judicial and Justice nominations, is quite disturbing. The effect upon the nomination was little more than an attempt to tarnish the image of the nominee through unsubstantiated events 24 years old. In sum, the confirmation process was transformed into a forum for character assassination and personal vindictiveness.

BROWN V. BOARD OF EDUCATION

Another controversy involved a memorandum written by Rehnquist for Supreme Court Justice Robert Jackson while serving as his law clerk in 1952. The memorandum dealt with the issue of "separate but equal educational facilities" in the famous case, *Brown v. Board of Education*. Under the separate but equal doctrine, the government could provide segregated schools, so long as the facilities were "equal". The memorandum urged support for the separate but equal doctrine ruled constitutional in *Plessy v. Ferguson*, the case *Brown* eventually overturned. Some questioned whether the memorandum's support of the separate but equal doctrine was not, in fact, the personal view of the nominee. Rehnquist explained, in both the 1971 and 1986 hearings, that the memorandum was written at the behest of Jackson to express Jackson's, not Rehnquist's, views. Jackson, of course, eventually joined the unanimous decision overturning *Plessy*. Support for Rehnquist's testimony came from former Justice William O. Douglas, a participant in *Brown*. According to Bob Woodward & Scott Armstrong's *The Brethren*, a behind the scenes look at the inner workings of the Court:

> [Douglas, t]he only remaining member of the Court that had decided the Brown cases, examined a copy of Rehnquist's testimony [in 1971]. Rehnquist was correct, he told clerks. The views [on the separate but equal doctrine] were, in fact, Jackson's.[49]

Donald Cronson, also a Jackson clerk at the time, cast further doubt on those attempting to discredit the nominee. According to Cronson, the memorandum, although signed with Rehnquist's initials, was more a collaborative effort and, according to his recollection, was more his product than that of Rehnquist.[50]

STILL, THE PROCESS "WORKED"

The Judiciary Committee hearings began July 29, continuing

through August 1 with approximately 40 hours of hearings. The Committee voted on August 14, 1986, approving the nomination by 13-5 vote.

Steadily, Rehnquist moved toward confirmation. On September 17, after a floor battle, cloture was invoked by a 68-31 vote. The new Chief Justice was confirmed later that afternoon by a 65-33 vote.[51]

Scalia. Antonin Scalia was nominated to fill Rehnquist's Associate Justice seat. Scalia's nomination, coming after his service as appellate judge on the District of Columbia Federal Court of Appeals, ran into no problems. With hearings and floor debate progressing at approximately the same time as Rehnquist, he sailed through without a single negative vote in the Judiciary Committee. The vote was 18 to 0.

The opponents of judicial restraint and the Reagan Administration's nominations made the conscious choice not to oppose Scalia, committing their capital on Rehnquist. In the absence of material from which they could fashion arguments with at least some plausibility, they would not oppose the conservative jurist. The decision to leave Scalia alone seemed clearly predicated on a concern that they would jeopardize whatever perception of impartiality their criticism still merited. By voting against yet another nominee on what observers increasingly recognized as ideological grounds, opponents of judicial restraint would have hurt their own cause. Scalia won easy confirmation.

What is surprising is that opponents, such as Kennedy, claimed they saw none of the extremist views found in Rehnquist. Extremist views, as Kennedy understood it, included a reliance upon judicial restraint. Scalia was perhaps blessed that he had served on the bench for such a short time. Scalia, however, was in the spotlight over the years through his teaching at several law schools. It was clear that his jurisprudence was similar to Rehnquist's.

CONCLUSION

The confirmation process endured by Chief Justice Rehnquist is illustrative of the problems found in today's understanding of what tactics are considered "acceptable" in the confirmation process. Let there be no misunderstanding. Every judicial nominee should be worthy to don his robes. The confirmation process is an important responsibility of the Senate and should never be lightly undertaken.

But when process turns into character assassination, it becomes an event abused by those bearing that responsibility. That abuse is felt in many ways. First, many candidates will find the process not worth the effort. It is difficult enough to convince lawyers of good stature to accept judicial positions. Surely, there is a special satisfaction associated with serving one's nation in this special way, while the power itself attracts some men and women. But most potential judicial candidates, because they have risen to the top of their profession, make far more than a judge's salary. The reduction in income is substantial and can be a disincentive to public service. There is no need for further disincentives through minute and conclusory characterizations of all parts of an individuals's life.

This devolution into abuse of the process can occur regardless of which political party is in power. The most dangerous part of such activity is that it will, regrettably but understandably, produce reciprocal thrust when others, politically and ideologically, occupy the White House. It is too dangerous for this to continue. All politicians must begin to understand this before "The Judges War" becomes the domestic, political equivalent of the Iran—Iraq War.

REFERENCES

Rehnquisition: Rite of Passage for a Chief Justice by Jeffrey P. O'Connell and Patrick B. McGuigan

1. 132 *Cong. Rec.* S12762 (daily ed. September 17, 1986).
2. 132 *Cong. Rec.* S12383 (daily ed. September 11, 1986) (statement of Sen. Hatch).
3. See 132 *Cong. Rec.* S12379 (daily ed. September 11, 1986) (statement of Sen. Thurmond).
4. 132 *Cong. Rec.* S12468-9 (daily ed. September 12, 1986).
5. *Id.*
6. 132 *Cong. Rec.* S12389 (daily ed. September 11, 1986).
7. *Id.*
8. 132 *Cong. Rec.* S12773 (daily ed. September 17, 1986).
9. *Id.*
10. Gary Born, "Senate Should Give Prompt Approval to Rehnquist," Tuscon *Citizen*, reprinted in 132 *Cong. Rec.* S12416-7 (daily ed. September 11, 1986).
11. 132 *Cong. Rec.* S12468 (daily ed. September 12, 1986). Kerry asserted that Rehnquist dissented alone over 50 times. 132 *Cong. Rec.* S12773 (daily ed. September 17, 1986).

12. 132 *Cong. Rec.* S12403. (daily ed. September 11, 1986) (statement of Sen. Hatch).
13. 132 *Cong. Rec.* S12773 (daily ed. September 17, 1986).
14. 132 *Cong. Rec.* S12777 (daily ed. September 17, 1986).
15. 132 *Cong. Rec.* S12415 (daily ed. September 11, 1986).
16. 132 *Cong. Rec.* S12627 (daily ed. September 16, 1986).
17. *Id.*
18. 132 *Cong. Rec.* S12773 (daily ed. September 17, 1986).
19. 132 *Cong. Rec.* S12776 (daily ed. September 17, 1986).
20. 132 *Cong. Rec.* S12384 (daily ed. September 11, 1986) (statement of Sen. Hatch), quoting the *Legal Times.*
21. Gary Born, "Senate Should Give Prompt Approval to Rehnquist," Tucson *Citizen, supra* n. 10.
22. 132 *Cong. Rec.* S12384 (daily ed. September 11, 1986) (statement of Sen. Hatch).
23. 132 *Cong. Rec.* S12382 (daily ed. September 11, 1986).
24. *Marbury v. Madison,* 5 U.S. 374, 1 Cranch. 137 (1803).
25. *Shelley v. Kraemer,* 334 U.S. 1 (1948).
26. Center for Judicial Studies Press Release, August 7, 1986, p. 3.
27. See 132 *Cong. Rec.* S12446 (daily ed. September 11, 1986) (statement of Sen. Simpson).
28. 132 *Cong. Rec.* S12412 (daily ed. September 11, 1986).
29. 132 *Cong. Rec.* S12388 (daily ed. September 11, 1986).
30. 28 U.S.C. 445 (1972). See 132 *Cong. Rec.* S12404 (daily ed. September 11, 1986) (statement of Sen. Hatch).
31. 132 *Cong. Rec.* S12472 (daily ed. September 12, 1986) (statement of Sen. Hatch).
32. 132 *Cong. Rec.* S12404 (daily ed. September 11, 1986) (statement of Sen. Hatch).
33. Letter of Geoffrey Hazard dated September 8, 1986 to Sen. Charles Mathias, reprinted in 132 *Cong. Rec.* S12412-13 (daily ed. September 11, 1986).
34. *Id.*
35. 132 *Cong. Rec.* S12404 (daily ed. September 11, 1986).
36. 35 *Law and Contemporary Problems* 43 (1970).
37. Letter of Geoffrey Hazard, *supra* n. 33.
38. 132 *Cong. Rec.* S12763 (daily ed. September 17, 1986) (statement of Sen. Hatch).
39. See 132 *Cong. Rec.* S12404 (daily ed. September 11, 1986) (statement of Sen. Hatch). Other situations involving a potential conflict on the part of Supreme Court Justices include Felix Frankfurter who wrote a labor law and was a force in the Norris-Laguardia act; Frankfurter wrote the opinion sustaining the constitutionality of that Act. Justice Robert Jackson dealt with an immigration matter, the policy which he formulated as Attorney General. Chief Justice Fred Vinson reviewed legislation he formulated while in the House of Representatives. Chief Justice Charles Hughes wrote a book critical of a case, then when on the bench he overruled the case. These show that Justices were predisposed to an issue of law coming into the role. But it would be a poor nominee who did not have a view of major legal issues. Justices are not supposed to have a blank mind.
40. 132 *Cong. Rec.* S12760 (daily ed. September 17, 1986).
41. See 132 *Cong. Rec.* S12413 (daily ed. September 11, 1986) (statement of Sen. Thurmond).
42. 132 *Cong. Rec.* S12406 (daily ed. September 11, 1986) (statement of Sen. Hatch).
43. *Id.,* p. 407. (emphasis added)
44. 132 *Cong. Rec.* S12407 (daily ed. September 11, 1986) (statement of Sen. Hatch).
45. *Id.,* p. 408.
46. 132 *Cong. Reg.* S12414 (daily ed. September 11, 1986).
47. 132 *Cong. Rec.* S12486 (daily ed. September 11, 1986) (statement of Sen. Hatch).
48. 132 *Cong. Rec.* S12414-5 (daily ed. September 11, 1986).
49. 132 *Cong. Rec.* S12628 (daily ed. September 16, 1986).
50. See 132 *Cong. Rec.* S12470 (daily ed. September 12, 1986) (statement of Sen. Hatch).

51. Rehnquist's confirmation did not deter some opponents from planning additional attacks on him. A group called the Rehnquist Watch was formed. The three page invitation to the Rehnquist Watch's organizational meeting stated that the group's intent was to "weaken the moral authority of the chief justice when he issues opinions' and "diminish the impact and enforcement power of Rehnquist decisions." One goal was to "deny to the chief justice the special trappings of his office, such as the ability to speak in lofty, moral terms at American Bar Association conventions on the dignity and impartiality of the law." The invitation's proposal seemed nothing less than intimidation, because the group's actions were designed to "give pause to other Supreme Court Justices about being closely associated with Rehnquist opinions." At the same time, the Rehnquist Watch founders hoped selectively to diminish precedent because it intended to "embolden liberal and neutral federal and state judges to narrowly construe Rehnquist opinions." See Al Kamen, "Rehnquist Watchdogs' Rough Start," Washington *Post*, December 4, 1986, p. A21. Subsequent investigation helped complete the profile of these who participated in the effort to trash Rehnquist. *See* Kristin R. Blair, "Biden's Term at Judiciary Helm Begins as ABA Criticism Mounts and Liberal 'Rehnquist Watch' Group Forms," *Judicial Notice*, January/February 1987, pp. 1-5.

3

THE JUDICIALIZATION OF THE
AMERICAN REPUBLIC

by James McClellan

The subject of this grim little essay is the judicial takeover of America. Among the nations of the world, both slave and free, government by judiciary is peculiar to the United States. It is alien to the republican tradition of representative democracy, and wholly unprecedented in the history of government. That it is also fundamentally at odds with the intent and purpose of the American Constitution is a matter we shall address later. We shall also be considering ways in which the Constitution might be recaptured, repaired, and returned to the true sovereigns— the states and the people thereof. Our immediate inquiry, however, is to determine the nature and origin of this peculiar form of government.

A NEW FORM OF GOVERNMENT

So new is this creature that the political scientists have yet to coin a word for it. Government by the few under the classification of the ancient Greeks is an aristocracy, which in its perverted form becomes an oligarchy. But the Greeks were strangers to judicial oligarchy and had no word to describe it. They did, however, have judges of a sort called *archons*, who presided over the Assembly of citizens and the courts and exercised a judicial-like function. Ordinary citizens, chosen by lot, possessing no special knowledge of the law, archons had neither the power nor the inclination to compel the jurors to decide in accordance with the law. They were administrators of a judicial system that was incapable of principled jurisprudence or rule of law. In a number of ways, it would seem, the archons were the ancient forerunners of today's judges on the Supreme Court.

In the interest of accuracy, it behooves us to update the classification of our political system so that it may properly reflect the
commanding role of the American judiciary. In recognition of
the fact that federal judges, to say nothing of their state counter-
parts, are making the key policy decisions in the United States,
and have become, in reality, the repository of sovereign power,
is it not fatuous to continue this charade of describing ourselves
as a democratic federal republic?

Democratic government is government by majority rule.
How can ours honestly be called democratic if the interests of
the minority, in the name of civil rights, are preferred to those of
the majority, and the people are governed by unelected judges?

Federal government, as contrasted with a unitary state, is that
system in which two levels of government function independently, each sovereign within its own sphere of powers. The
one, which is national, possesses delegated and enumerated
powers, and the other, which is state, exercises reserved powers.
The distribution of powers requires a written constitution explicitly defining the division of powers. This constitution must
be supreme as well, lest the powers distributed will be arbitrarily
redistributed. Legislative supremacy, executive supremacy, and
judicial supremacy are all fundamentally hostile to federalism
and limited constitutional government. But what person of
sound mind would claim today that our states are more than
conquered provinces?

Republican government, as Thomas Cooley correctly defined
it in his *Principles of Constitutional Law*, "is understood as government by representatives chosen by the people; and it contrasts on the one side with a democracy, in which the people or
community as one organized whole wield the sovereign powers
of government, and, on the other side, with the rule of one man,
as king, emperor, czar or sultan, or with that of one class of
men, as an aristocracy [or judicial oligarchy]."[1] In what respect
can we boast that our system is republican, however, in light of
the practices of the Supreme Court? Hundreds, perhaps thousands of state laws and local ordinances, all duly enacted by representatives of the people, have been declared unconstitutional,
either on their face or as applied, by the Supreme Court in just
the past few decades.

In what respects, then, does the term "democratic federal republic" accurately reflect political reality in the United States today? Perhaps it is time we acknowledge the judicial oligarchy that governs our affairs and update the classification of our political system by recognizing it for what it is: an *archonocratic* form of government. This government is as novel as the word to describe it, as uniquely American as the Constitution from which it illegitimately sprang.

Its apologists will object, of course, that we have overstated the case against the judges; that such an unorthodox interpretation reflects a misunderstanding of our political system; that there are too many exceptions to justify the claim that such a radical transformation has occurred; that there is nothing particularly exotic or unconventional about the modern Court because it marches forward in the style and tradition of John Marshall; and that this is still a democratic federal republic in all of its esential attributes.

THE DESPOTIC TREND AND SUPREME
JUDICIAL POWER

Not even the Court's most frenzied admirers will deny, however, that the modern Court is an activist one, or that federalism has been in a state of decline for a number of years. The question is one of degree. Was it *Garcia*[2] that killed federalism or was it already dead? If so, at what point in time did it expire? Or is it not true that States' Rights, despite its weakened condition, lives on, and that republicanism is safe and sound?

There is no sure answer to these questions, for we cannot measure with scientific precision the heartbeat of political principles that give life to our Constitution and fix the perimeters of public policy and the decision-making process. If it be said that our assessment of the situation is merely conjectural because we cannot know for certain the extent to which these principles are still operative, the answer is we can only show the overwhelming tendency toward centralization of authority in the hands of these modern-day archons sitting on the High Court. Neither jurisprudence nor government is a science.

Certainly there is no shortage of examples to illustrate judicial subversion of the federal principle. The Court, in fact, has given us some real dillies, decisions so preposterous in their reasoning and results as to suggest that we are dealing with fools or knaves. One thinks, for example, of *Wickard v. Filburn* (1942),[3] in which the Court held that the power of Congress to regulate commerce among the states meant that the Department of Agriculture had the right to punish a small Ohio farmer for exceeding the market quota established on his farm for winter wheat. The wheat never passed the front gate. So small was his crop that he used it for home consumption—to make bread for his table and to feed his cows and chickens.

A *unanimous* Court reasoned nevertheless that Filburn's wheat was moving mystically through space, like an ethereal flying bakery. Actually, you see, it was a part of interstate commerce even though it was not part of interstate commerce. That is, these grains of wheat were in interstate commerce because they had "a substantial economic effect" on interstate commerce, the assumption being that everything, sooner or later, in some way or another, down to the last crumb, affects interstate commerce. Therefore, reasoned the Court, Farmer Filburn's home consumption had a "substantial economic effect" on interstate commerce in two ways: first, he was consuming wheat that he otherwise would have had to buy; and second, his consumption, *if* added to that of other defiant farmers, meant that he would be contributing to the evil of surplus wheat, even though standing alone the effect of his crop was so small as to be immeasurable. "That appellee's own contribution to the demand for wheat may be trivial by itself is not enough to remove him from the scope of federal regulation," the Court announced triumphantly, "where, as here, his contribution, taken together with that of many others similarly situated, is far from trivial."[4] It is worthy of notice, by the way, that among the delegated and enumerated powers of Congress the word "agriculture" does not appear. Surely the Founders never imagined such a grotesque interpretation of the Constitution.

Another old favorite is *United States v. Appalachian Electric Power Co.* (1940),[5] which sent the Commerce Clause on a fantastic voyage down the white water rapids of the New River, a wild mountain stream that flows through Virginia and West Virginia. The case is a classic example of how the modern Court has, again and again, distorted the opinions of John Marshall, in the name of John Marshall, in order to justify the federal takeover of state affairs.

In *Gibbons v. Ogden* (1824),[6] Marshall held that the power to regulate commerce necessarily included power over navigation, the "avenue of commerce." From this modest beginning the Chase Court advanced to the proposition that the power to regulate commerce comprehends the control of navigable waters—but only if they are navigable "in fact."[7] In the *Appalachian* case, however, the Court paddled around these precedents, applying the droll theory that the New River was navigable because it was "capable of being made navigable"—a bizarre notion in this instance, thought Justice Roberts, who pointed out in dissent that the cost alone of blasting out hundreds of miles of mountains, reefs and shoals for channels, canals, dams and locks to make the New River "fit for some sort of commercial use" would be astronomical.[8]

The extension of federal power resulting from this decision is, of course, staggering. It gives the general government absolute control, potentially as well as in fact, over the production and distribution of all hydroelectric power in the United States, and authority to protect any future interest it may someday wish to assert concerning such matters as flood control and watershed development.

The case also underscores the validity of the thesis we have been developing in this essay. The federal district court earlier took the position that the New River was not navigable. The U.S. Court of Appeals said the river was not navigable. Forty-one state attorneys general, including Earl Warren of California, joined Virginia as *amici curiae* in challenging the jurisdictional claims of the federal bureaucracy. Together, they spoke for nearly the whole population of the United States. Six men, five of them freshly scrubbed Roosevelt appointees exercising supreme archonic power, rose to the occasion and turned thumbs down. Exceptions do not necessarily disprove general rules, of course, and if *Appalachian* were out of the ordinary we would be hard pressed to draw a lesson from it. Unfortunately, it is part of a consistent pattern of decisions down to the present that make a mockery of federalism, republican government, and the Constitution.

THE AGGRANDIZEMENT AND USURPATION
OF POWER

But enough of this. We might go on forever citing cases to show that members of the Supreme Court have been rewriting the Constitution. For present purposes, it will be more instructive to examine the powers of the Court to determine their general scope and substance, and to proceed from here to the overarching question: to what extent does the sovereign power in the United States now reside in the private chambers of the Supreme Court?

A comparison between the powers of the Court and those of the President sheds some light on these matters. The history of the American presidency, observed the late Edward S. Corwin, is a history of aggrandizement.[9] In striking contrast, the history of the Supreme Court is a history of *usurpation*. Whereas the growth of executive power has been achieved almost exclusively at the expense of Congress, that of the Supreme Court has come at the expense of Congress, the President, and especially state and local governments—even the private citizen. Judicial review looks to a comprehensive and wholesale embrace of the entire political system of the United States. Much the same can be said of Congress, of course, but with this important exception: Congress has rarely asserted its authority over the Court, whereas the Court has frequently overturned or altered the meaning of laws passed by Congress. Among the three departments of the federal government, therefore, only the Supreme Court, in reality, claims and exercises total control over the federal, state and local governments. "Usurpation" is a more useful and accurate term than "aggrandizement" to describe this phenomenon, because it suggests more than the growth of power in one branch. When we refer to the aggrandizement of power by the Chief Executive, we have in mind the accumulation and concentration of power in the executive office. But usurpations of power by the Supreme Court are more far-reaching.

First, they are not so clearly dependent upon the personality traits of the incumbent, as seems true of the presidency. Strong-willed and weak-willed Presidents alternate from one administration to the next. Political precedents established by one President may lay dormant in succeeding administrations for decades. Once invoked, they are vulnerable to constitutional attack from the Supreme Court and political assault from the legislature. President Nixon's retreat and surrender on the question of executive privilege seems to be a case in point.

Usurpations by the Supreme Court, however, are not personal but institutional in nature. Almost invariably they are fixed in concrete as permanent *legal* precedents, immune to legislative and executive reversal. This is because the Court, unlike the other branches, is the judge of its own powers—as well as everybody else's. Though there are ways to emasculate or overturn a judicial precedent, they are almost never used. We can count on the fingers of one hand the number of times during the past two centuries that Congress has withdrawn the appellate jurisdiction of the Supreme Court to dislodge an unwanted judicial precedent, or the states have amended the Constitution to nullify a decision of the judges. The Court's usurpations, in other words, are for all practical purposes amendments to the Constitution.

Second, the Court's usurpations not only add power to the federal judiciary by enlarging its jurisdiction, but may also add power as well to the entire federal government—to Congress, in particular, which in turn passes it along to independent regulatory commissions and executive agencies. If the issue is one of civil liberties, the Court assumes an interventionist posture, seizes jurisdiction, and pulls the powers of the states and Congress to its breast, thereby enhancing its own power. If the issue is one of commerce or some other matter that is not on the Court's civil liberties agenda, the Court again assumes an interventionist stance, but this time may well be content to affirm a congressional usurpation of state power, whence the power is apt to end up on the desk of some nameless bureaucrat. The important point is that the Supreme Court is making all of the decisions as to where the powers of government shall be lodged: keeping some for itself, letting some remain with Congress, leaving the scraps to the states. The Court is thus a federal magnet, a power broker for the federal government. It functions as a centripetal force in the American political system.

JUDICIALIZATION AND SELECTIVE JUDICIAL REVIEW

This exercise of sovereign power by the Supreme Court has resulted in a massive transfer of power, either to the Court itself or to the federal government at large. This is the judicialization of the American republic. It is more than a judicial veto over laws passed by representative assemblies. Until the twentieth century, the Court had little discretion over cases that arrived at its doorstep by appeal. Under the old writ of error, appeals were, in effect, thrust upon the Court and it had little choice but to decide the case. This system necessarily limited the Court's ability to shape and direct constitutional development. Even if the Court wished to move in a particular direction, it had to wait for the "right" case.

In 1925, however, Congress changed the appellate process by authorizing the Court to grant *writs of certiorari*[10]. Most cases decided by the Court today reach the Justices by this method. Instead of being a passive recipient of disputes working their way through the lower courts, the judges on the High Court may now survey the entire field, and, at their discretion, pick the cases they wish to hear. With so many thousands of cases on the dockets—and the number is increasing every year—it is not that difficult for the Court to find the perfect case it needs to develop systematically the constitutional doctrine it desires. The net effect is a growing body of case law that is so comprehensive in certain fields as to force elected officials to follow Supreme Court policies at virtually every step of the law making process.

Notwithstanding the stated principle that ours is a government of limited powers, the Court nevertheless also has unlimited remedial power. Federal judges are free to impose upon elected officials any remedy that the laws of nature permit. So sweeping is this power that it allows the federal courts, in effect, to initiate laws in state legislatures, compelling them to appropriate public funds in order to satisfy a Court order. Taken together, the power of judicial review and the corresponding equity or remedial power of federal judges make for a judicial takeover of the American political process.[11]

The Court employs two doctrinally inconsistent methods of judicial review in order to accomplish its self-appointed task.

The first, sometimes mislabeled "negative judicial review," is a doctrinaire form of selective review. This is the "hands-off" face of judicialization, and it applies only to certain provisions of the Constitution, the commerce clause being the most egregious example. The provisions selected are basically exempted from the review process, giving Congress complete freedom to adopt whatever policy suits its fancy. In the case of Congress, the Court simply places its official stamp of approval on federal laws and regulations that strip the states of their autonomy, independence, and reserved powers. The Court, in this instance, acts as an accessory to the centralization of authority, aiding and abetting the congressional majority.

During the past fifty years, that majority has almost invariably been the Democratic Party. This practice has been in existence since 1937, when the Court succumbed to the immense pressures of the Roosevelt Administration, suddenly began reversing a long line of cases dating back to the turn of the century, and then promptly underwent a complete change of court personnel, thereby sealing the fate of the states. The Court's involvement in this partnership with the Democratic Party and Congress has resulted mostly in sweeping endorsements of Congress' broad interpretations of its own powers under Article I, Section 8, particularly the welfare and commerce clauses, giving Congress plenary authority to redistribute the wealth, satisfy the material wants and needs of that portion of the electorate which sustains the Democratic Party, and in general determine the whole range and substance of social, economic and regulatory policy in the United States. With one minor exception, which was subsequently overruled, the Supreme Court has not overturned a single act of Congress based on the commerce power since 1937.[12]

That same year, in *West Coast Hotel v. Parrish*, the Court also made an about-face respecting the power of the States to regulate the economic life of its citizens, again reversing a plethora of cases dating back to the turn of the century. Prior to 1937, the Court had subjected state regulatory measures to careful scrutiny under the Due Process Clause of the Fourteenth Amendment. In *Parrish*, however, the Court abruptly changed its position, praised the virtues of democracy, and announced that henceforth it would no longer substitute its judgment for that of a state legislature in cases involving economic and business regulation. Abandoning the field to the state assemblies, it has never returned except for an occasional visit or two. This was the end of what had once been known as "economic due process."

In fact, insofar as the commercial life of the nation is concerned, Congress has a free hand to regulate every form of economic activity. In this respect, the Court adheres to the doctrine of legislative supremacy, not the supremacy of the Constitution. Under the scheme of *hands-off* judicialization, the Court reserves the right of re-entry, but otherwise gives Congress *carte blanche* authority to dictate the terms of American economic policy. What has not been pre-empted by Congress is left to the states, leaving economic minorities, property holders, and entrepreneurs to defend themselves in the political arena at both the state and federal levels. Though a silent partner, the Court is the real source of power here; for it is the Court which stripped the parties of their constitutional protection and threw them to the wolves. The judges set this policy and they keep it in place.

The flip side of selective judicial review is judicial activism. This is the obtrusive, interventionist face of judicialization that is better known and more easily recognized than its passive counterpart. Once again, only selected portions of the Constitution are involved. If a case presents a question of political or civil liberty, the Court does not defer to the judgment of elected representatives, but spontaneously pre-empts the field and defines the policy for the assembly. Any law touching civil liberties is presumptively invalid, and the burden is on the popular assembly to prove that it is reasonable. Whether it is or is not is a mattter to be decided solely by the Court; for the determination of what is reasonable, say the judges, is the exclusive prerogative of the judges. Usually, of course, the representatives are found by the Court to be unreasonable under some latitudinarian construction of the Bill of Rights and the Reconstruction Amendments.

Since the New Deal, members of the Supreme Court have exercised this prerogative without restraint, swatting down state and local laws like so many flies on a summer's day. So pervasive, so all-encompassing is the Court's power over civil liberties that in recent years it has extended its reach beyond the public sector to private institutions—schools, businesses, clubs, associations, and even the family.

Although the states and their political subdivisions are the usual target, Congress is also sure to lose if it dares to depart from the Court's civil liberties ideology. Thus, almost every federal law restricting the activities of Communists has been invalidated or rendered useless,[13] whereas virtually every federal law enlarging some ersatz political or civil right, such as the Voting Rights Act and its amendments, has passed judicial scrutiny with flying colors.[14]

What we have, then, is a Janus-faced Court, marked by conflicting double standards of judicial review. There is no basis in the constitutional text, the founding documents, or in the American political tradition even remotely sanctioning such arbitrary exercises of judicial power. Neither conceptually nor in practice has the power of judicial review ever been understood to mean that its exercise is dependent upon the kind of right or constitutional provision at issue. Selective judicial review has no place in a system of government based on constitutional supremacy. Indeed, by habitually deferring to Congress, as the Court is wont to do in cases involving the federal commerce power, the Court is actually enshrining legislative supremacy and abandoning its responsibility to uphold the supremacy of the Constitution. Likewise, when the judges clothe all state and federal laws with presumptive invalidity if they restrict civil rights, inexorably rule that the reasonableness of such legislation is solely within their discretion, and proceed on this basis to censor and suppress virtually any law or policy that is personally objectionable, then the Court is placing itself above the Constitution. This is judicial supremacy, which is no less violative of the Constitution than legislative supremacy. Put another way, a dogmatic adherence to judicial activism or judicial restraint cannot be reconciled with the supremacy of the Constitution.

Judicialization, then, is the predisposition, or what might better be called the uncontrollable passion, of the judges to impose their own values and policies upon those expressed or implied in the Constitution or in the laws. When they succeed—and it seems they always do—the illegality of their behavior is plain enough. Having taken an oath to uphold the Constitution, they uphold instead their own arbitrary notions of fairness and justice. Should the judge happen to be part of the controlling majority on the Supreme Court, his action may also be unlawful if the Court usurped the powers of the states and thereupon expanded its own jurisdiction. Only Congress, we should bear in mind, is authorized to enlarge or contract the appellate jurisdiction of the Supreme Court. Where the judge's action is unconstitutional, it is also anti-democratic because he has imposed his will upon that of the people. If it is a statute, he has ignored the will of the people as expressed by their delegates. If it is the Constitution he has intentionally distorted, he has ignored what the Founders referred to as "the permanent will of the American people". In either case, he has ceased to be a judge and has become an enemy of the people.

JUDICIALIZATION IN RETROSPECT

Our Constitution, it would seem, has been corrupted in proportion to the advancement of the Supreme Court toward omnipotence. The question naturally presents itself: how did a free people, intensely loyal to the constitutional system they inherited from their ancestors, allow as few as five individuals to change the purpose and meaning of its basic precepts and substitute their will for that of the true sovereigns? More importantly, can the decline of constitutional government be arrested in these United States?

These are difficult questions. While we cannot know for certain all of the causes of our current predicament, it is possible nevertheless to discern some of them, to become aware of the mistakes of the past and to learn from them, and to take corrective action once we know how and where to repair our constitutional fabric.

It is a common mistake among conservatives to point an accusing finger at the late Chief Justice Earl Warren, whose name alone alarms friends of the Constitution. But Earl Warren was a symptom, not a cause. That he cared no more about the real meaning and integrity of the Constitution than a socialist respects the rights of property should not detract us from the realization that he was part of a collective effort, and only seemed more outrageous than his colleagues because he lacked their skill and finesse.

The causes, then, lie deeper and are far more complex than the mind and jurisprudence of this California politician. Some of them, notwithstanding the diatribes of Justice Thurgood Marshall, may be traced to the Constitution itself. The Framers were wise and learned men, but they were not soothsayers or clairvoyants, and could not predict or anticipate the entire course of human events that was to follow.

FROM LEAST DANGEROUS TO MOST DANGEROUS: SOME INHERENT FLAWS

Struggling through a transitional phase of political and legal development, when courts of law were just beginning to emerge as independent and separate entities, the Framers underestimated the powers of the Supreme Court and took too few precautions to protect the states and the people against an overbearing minority of entrenched judges. They provided no general guidelines for the interpretation of the Constitution, ignoring the warning of Anti-Federalists that the power to interpret is the power to govern. They failed to define the power of judicial review and thereby lost an opportunity to limit its exercise. The uncertainty attending Congress' responsibility under the separation of powers scheme to check judicial encroachments, particularly upon the reserved powers of the states, suggests further that the Framers should have spelled out more clearly the legislative power to regulate the jurisdiction of the federal courts. Notwithstanding the protests of the Anti-Federalists, they also elected not to place any limits on the equity powers of the judges, giving them plenary authority to take whatever remedial action they pleased—action, in modern times, that has resulted in the judicial administration of state educational and correctional institutions and the unrestricted use of the injunctive power.[15]

The silence of the Constitution respecting the size and composition of the Supreme Court and the qualifications of its members, and the unsure meaning of the term "good behavior" that conditions their tenure, have exacerbated our difficulties with the Court. The Framers did not specify any qualifications for the office, and left it to chance that knowledgeable and virtuous men, well-versed in, and loyal to, the principles of the Constitution, should occupy the office. This oversight has come back to haunt us in a number of ways. Most appointees have been run-of-the-mill lawyers who have disappeared into well-deserved obscurity after leaving the Court. Most have been appointed because of their political connections or standing in the "old boy" network of the legal establishment, not because they had demonstrated any particular knowledge or interest in the Constitution before coming on to the Court. For too many, tenure on the Court has been on-the-job training, limited to the reading of judicial precedents.

Then too, the Framers neglected to consider the possibility and consequences of "court-packing," when a President, serving a number of terms, is able to appoint the entire bench from existing vacancies (or seeks to multiply the number of judges and increase the size of the Court), as occurred under Franklin Roosevelt.

The Framers even forgot to give the states a presence on the Supreme Court—an extraordinary oversight when we recall the prolonged struggle in the Federal Convention over the issue of how to structure the legislative and executive branches to allow for a state presence. Until 1875, this omission had no effect because of the Judiciary Act of 1789. This Act established the circuit riding system, which required members of the Supreme Court to travel throughout the judicial circuit to which they were assigned and sit with a district judge in federal trials. This necessarily limited the President's choice of Supreme Court nominees to residents of the judicial circuit over which they would preside, for much of the country was a vast wilderness and transportation was slow and difficult. As a result of this practice, the Supreme Court was a cross-section of the young nation, and all regions were represented in the Supreme Court. Thus before 1860 roughly one half of the Court drew its members from south of the Mason-Dixon line and the other half from north of it. Although the judges frequently complained of circuit riding (Justice John McKinley of Kentucky, covering the west, estimated in 1838 that he traveled 10,000 miles a year!),[16] many members of Congress believed that it enabled the Justices to become "acquainted with local facts, the character of our people, and the various interests in different parts of the country."[17]

But circuit riding was abolished by the Judiciary Act of 1875,[18] and the Court has not since been a representative body. Since the War Between the States, for example, only thirteen Justices of the Supreme Court have claimed a Southern State of the old Confederacy as their home state[19]—which is only three more than the number of Justices from the state of New York alone. The western states have fared even worse: seven, which is only one more than the state of Ohio has had on the court.[20] For more than a century, the northeast has enjoyed a disproportionately large share of judges on the Supreme Court—and, it would seem, of influence as well. The states are taken into account in the composition of both houses of Congress, and in the executive branch through the electoral college, but not in the Supreme Court. Perhaps it is more than coincidental that the branch of the federal government that is least amenable to States' Rights is the only branch in which the different sections of the country are not fairly represented.

CONGRESS AND THE COURT: THE ODD COUPLE

The rise of political parties and the growth of ideology in modern America have altered the constitutional structure in ways that the Framers could not have foreseen. Factions in the Federal Convention of 1787 centered mostly around States' Rights issues, not party politics or ideological disputes. There were no political parties; and there were no liberal versus conservative divisions, no socialist splinter groups, no doctrinaire libertarians, no rabid egalitarians. Ideology was born in Paris with the French Revolution, not in Philadelphia with the American rebellion against British rule.

The political parties that arose in the United States, as in England, were to some extent responses to French revolutionary doctrines. As these doctrines took hold and political parties organized around them, the separation of powers principle underwent the slow transformation that has brought it to its present state. Gone today are dominant factions in Congress based on the kinds of conflicting interests with which the Framers were familiar—agricultural versus commercial, property owners versus the propertyless, North versus South, large states versus small states, nationalism versus States' Rights. Instead, these issues have been subsumed under a broader division that follows party and ideological lines, the former often overshadowed by the latter.

This realignment and recomposition of factions—often liberal against conservative—has resulted in a dilution of the check and balance system that was designed to restrain the powers of government and maintain the separation of powers. Instead of institutional loyalty, inter-branch rivalry, and tension betwen Congress and the Courts, we find harmony and cooperation, both branches pulling together to implement and protect liberal values, policies and programs. Both branches habitually invade and usurp the reserved powers of the states, but neither branch checks the encroachments of the other. What we have, in effect, is a complete breakdown of the separation of powers system as it applies to congressional-judicial relations.

The Seventeenth Amendment, it should be noted, figures prominently in this scheme of things. The Senate, the one body that was tied to state government, is now made up of individuals who, like the Representatives, claim to speak for "the people." The change from the indirect to the direct election of Senators, in other words, has tended to encourage the illicit intimacy that best describes legislative-judicial relations in the United States for the past half-century. The states have no constituency either in Congress or in the Supreme Court. It is little wonder they have been reduced to administrative subdivisions of the central government.

THE ROAD FROM APPOMATTOX

Another important turning point in American constitutional development—and many would argue convincingly that it very nearly marked the end of the Constitution of 1787—is the Civil War and the Reconstruction Amendments. The surrender of General Lee at Appomattox Courthouse in 1865 meant more than the defeat of the Confederate States and the end of slavery. It also meant the end of a powerful constitutional tradition, the tradition of States' Rights that had dominated American politics from the birth of the Republic.

Nowadays, we tend to associate the doctrine of States' Rights exclusively with the South and the slavery controversy. At its inception, however, and for many decades thereafter, the States' Rights theory of the Constitution enjoyed wide support throughout the Union; and the question of slavery did not cloud the debate on the nature of the Union until much later. At the Federal Convention of 1787, in fact, most of the leading opponents of a strong central government were men of the North— Elbridge Gerry of Massachusetts, Robert Yates and John Lansing of New York, and William Paterson of New Jersey, to mention only a few. The Virginia and Kentucky Resolutions of 1798, representing the first instance of organized resistance to federal authority among the states, were based not on the issue of slavery, but on the ground that the Alien and Sedition Acts were unconstitutional because the federal government had no authority to regulate First Amendment freedoms.[21] The first movement toward secession occurred not in South Carolina, but in New England, at the abortive Hartford Convention of 1814.[22] The earliest full-scale treatise on the Constitution was written in 1825 by William Rawle, a Pennsylvania jurist. Though an anti-slavery Federalist, he rejected the view that the Union was irrevocable and defended secession as a fundamental right.[23]

The tradition of States' Rights, then, was national in origin, transcending the interests of a particular region or the policy objectives of a single group. It was an integral part of the American political tradition favoring limited constitutional government. Technically, it was based on a theory of the nature of the Union. More fundamentally, however, it was rooted in a deep suspicion of centralized power and an abiding belief that freedom requires cultural diversity, local autonomy, and government close to the people. These are enduring political values that a federal system is designed to protect. To dismiss the doctrine of States' Rights as a mere subterfuge for the oppression of minorities is to misunderstand its history and meaning and distort the motivating forces behind it.

But it is true that as the nineteenth century progressed, the States' Rights school of thought found its most loyal supporters and eloquent spokesmen in the ante-bellum South. Around this tradition there developed a great legal culture of its own, illuminated by the writings, speeches, and constitutional treatises of Thomas Jefferson, James Madison, Henry St. George Tucker,

John Randolph of Roanoke, John Taylor of Caroline, Spencer Roane, Abel Upshur, John C. Calhoun, and many others. Their works filled an entire library and their teachings permeated the mind of the South—long before States' Rights became a convenient excuse to defend slavery. Southerners of the antebellum period were born and bred in the Jeffersonian tradition of strict construction. As a civilization, the Old South stood like a rock in defense of limited constitutional government; and its leaders, quick to detect the slightest intrusion upon state sovereignty or departure from principle, were united in their determination to resist consolidation and preserve the independence of their states—at any cost.

On the eve of secession, then, a mighty force, stretching from the Potomac River to the Gulf of Mexico, stood poised for battle in defense of "States Rights." The world had seen nothing like it before, and will not likely see anything like it again. For here was an entire civilization prepared to go to war in defense of its constitutional principles and the ideal of limited government. This was the "lost cause" of the Confederacy, a cause which Jefferson Davis would later insist was "not that of the South only, but the cause of constitutional government."

The defeat of the Confederate States brought about the collapse and destruction of the last major barrier to centralization in the United States, thus preparing the way for the judicialization of the American Republic. The American political and legal tradition that had produced lawyers committed to principles of strict construction and statesmen of the caliber of Webster, Clay and Calhoun was gone. When the Populists and Progressives commenced their assaults upon the Constitution toward the end of the nineteenth century, there was therefore no enlightened force to offer spirited and informed resistance within the legal profession or the halls of Congress. Similarly, when Franklin Roosevelt and his judges were remaking the Constitution at will during the New Deal, the conservative legal response was virtually non-existent.

With a few notable exceptions, the period between 1865 and 1965 is an intellectual wasteland from the standpoint of conservative constitutional scholarship. Significant and enduring constitutional works of the conservative persuasion in these years are as rare as Gutenberg Bibles. Cheapened and distorted by the slavery controversy, the doctrine of States' Rights is only now regaining its respectability. The States' Rights legal tradition was a conservative force in American politics that might have impeded consolidation or prevented its worst aspects. In any event, resistance to centralization has been scattered and feeble since the fall of the Confederacy, and it is here we mark the great turning point in American constitutional history that has led us to the present crisis. The conclusion seems inescapable that the annihilation of the States' Rights school of thought in American law contributed mightily to the decline of limited constitutional government in the United States.

The crushing military defeat of the Confederacy and the ensuing decade of political radicalism also ushered in an amendment that has changed the face of the Constitution and substantially altered the frame of government. This is the Fourteenth Amendment, which long ago outlived its usefulness and now threatens to pull down the remaining pillars of the original Constitution. During the Reconstruction period, when this Amendment was forced upon the prostrate South, the Radical Republicans governed this country. Congress was king, and legislative supremacy was the law of the land. The Enforcement Clause of the Fourteenth Amendment, a strange and unique provision that promised to subvert the separation of powers by making Congress the judge of its own powers, was designed to serve as the vehicle for legislative supremacy.[24] But Congress soon fell prey to internal difficulties and partisan bickering, and by 1875 the Supreme Court had taken full charge of the Fourteenth Amendment and its proper interpretation.

Although the Court magicians have performed some rather remarkable feats with the Equal Protection Clause of the Fourteenth Amendment, their principal source of supernatural power has been its Due Process Clause. As written, it provides simply that no state shall deny any person "life, liberty or property without due process of law." The concept of due process, as originally understood, applied only to court proceedings. If the individual was to lose his life, his liberty or his property, such deprivation had to be in accordance with the process that was due him. Rooted in Magna Carta, it was designed to give the individual a "fair trial"—to ensure that the defendant would be properly served, given an opportunity to appear in court, and be charged with a violation of some existing law. It was directed, then, against abuses of the judicial process.[25] No sooner was the Fourteenth Amendment adopted than the Supreme Court transformed the Due Process Clause into a judicial power to test the "reasonableness" of state laws and curb the "abuses" of the legislative process.

The first rabbit out of the Due Process hat was "economic due process," a clever trick to prohibit a state legislature from interfering with economic liberty. The legislative procedure followed was quite irrelevant, and the words "due" and "process" became part of a disappearing act. The Court was not interested in process, but in end results, in the substance of the law. Thus was created what later came to be known as "substantive due process." If a state law, in the opinion of the judges, constituted an "unreasonable" abridgement of economic liberty, then, presto!—it violated liberty without due process of law and was unconstitutional. The most memorable act performed by the Court in the heyday of economic due process occurred in 1905, in the case of *Lochner v. New York*.[26] On stage was a state "sweatshop" law limiting the working conditions of bakery employees to sixty hours per week. Seems reasonable enough, but the Court thought otherwise. Such a law, said the Justices with a wave of the wand, interferes with "liberty of contract" and is in violation of the Due Process Clause of the Fourteenth Amendment. From the late nineteenth century until 1937, the Supreme Court invalidated countless state laws on similar grounds.

It has been observed by apologists for this era of judicial policy-making that the judges were well-intentioned conservatives struggling desperately to save laissez-faire capitalism from the wave of "socialism" sweeping across the nation. While it is true that many were motivated by a desire to limit the regulatory powers of the states in the name of free enterprise, it is no less the case that such result-oriented jurisprudence is the very antithesis of federalism and the conservative constitutional tradition of strict construction. Added to that, laissez-faire capitalism is rooted in liberalism and is associated with the egocentrism of Darwinian economics. Though supportive of property rights and a free market economy, the conservative tradition has customarily opposed absolute liberty of any sort, much preferring to balance it with other values, particularly the moral and religious. An unfettered economy is by definition a libertarian goal that conservatives have ordinarily rejected.

Thus the charge that it was the conservatives who first distorted the meaning of due process and subverted the Fourteenth Amendment is not entirely accurate. In truth, the conservative tradition of American law and politics was eclipsed in the late nineteenth and early twentieth centuries by superior forces. Demoralized by the Civil War, and half-dazed by economic depression and Reconstruction, the South struggled simply to survive, its conservative voice silenced. The Republican Party of the North had become the party of plunder and grasping opportunism. The corruption that engulged the nation might be cured, it was believed, by more democracy. And so, an unprecedented tidal wave of democratic reform swept the nation, resulting in many foolish constitutional changes at both the federal and state levels, including the election of state judges and the direct election of Senators. There was no coherent conservative response to these radical changes. As Russell Kirk has observed, "when we speak of 'conservative thought' which existed in the Gilded Age, really we mean a set of principles very like English Liberalism, which honest and confused men were trying to apply to conservative ends."[27]

In the period between the administration of Abraham Lincoln and that of Woodrow Wilson, twenty-six of the appointees to the Supreme Court were Republicans, principally from the northeast, and only eleven were Democrats, five of whom were also from the North. It was Rufus Peckham, a New York Democrat, however, who wrote the Court's opinion in *Lochner*; and it was Edward Sanford, a Tennessee Republican, who wrote the fateful opinion in *Gitlow v. New York* (1925),[28] to which we shall turn presently. Indeed, the line separating the conservative wing of the Court from the liberal wing does not correspond much with party divisions. There really was no identifiable conservative wing in these years, nor any notable conservative leadership on the Court.

It was a period of constitutional erosion, political confusion, and judicial mediocrity. Democrats as well as Republicans joined in the assault upon the Constitution. After the First World War, the Court moved progressively to the left, until Franklin Roosevelt packed the high bench with liberal Democrats who adhered uniformly and consistently to a particular set of political and legal ideas; and at no time has the party of Lincoln produced a Supreme Court that is faithful to the tradition of strict construction.

Whoever is to blame for giving birth to economic due process, the significant point to bear in mind is that it helped to prepare the way for the judicial takeover of the American republic. The judicial construction of this doctrine represents the first instance in American constitutional history where the Supreme Court, as an institution, knowingly defied or ignored the intent of the Constitution on a grand scale in order to achieve the public policy it favored. There were isolated instances of judicial abuse in the Marshall and Taney Courts, to be sure, but they pale considerably before the pattern of judicial activism that has come to symbolize the modern Court.

We are still paying for the constitutional mistakes of the Gilded Age, for the judicial precedents established during this period laid the foundation for subsequent and more far-reaching judicial usurpations. In 1937, the same year the Court abandoned the Commerce Clause to Congress, it simultaneously jettisoned economic due process and gave back to the states all of the regulatory power it had usurped through the Fourteenth Amendment. This was the case of *West Coast Hotel Co. v. Parrish*,[29] which is still the law today. The Court's about-face did not, however, represent a return to the traditional standards of constitutional interpretation but only a change of values. Property rights and economic rights were thought to be second-class rights. What was now important were civil liberties, or what the Court described in *Palko v. Connecticut* (1937)[30] as the "preferred freedoms" of the First Amendment. Freedom of thought and speech, said Justice Cardozo, "is the matrix, the indispensable condition of nearly every other form of freedom."[31] This would be the new focus of the Court, at least until 1940, when the Court would begin creating new freedoms for the honor roll. That the Court's new theory of freedom was historically inaccurate, philosophically questionable, and constitutionally unsound did not receive much notice at the time, even within the legal profession.

This brings us to the Court's second rabbit in the due process hat, the extraordinary sleight-of-hand in *Gitlow v. New York*

(1925) that made *Palko* possible. Standing on its mountain of precedents established under substantive or economic due process rulings, the Court in *Gitlow*, without so much as a supporting argument, arbitrarily announced that, "For present purposes we may and do assume that freedom of speech and of the press—which are protected by the First Amendment from abridgement by Congress—are among the fundamental personal rights and 'liberties' [sic] protected by the Due Process Clause of the Fourteenth Amendment from impairment by the States... ."[32] With these words, the fate of the Constitution was sealed—maybe forever—and we entered upon a new era of wholesale constitution-making and judicial activism that has continued unabated down to the present, changing the character of the American republic in ways that will probably never be undone.

Gitlow was the origin of the so-called doctrine of incorporation, a radical theory of interpretation—stumbled upon by accident, it would seem—that has since resulted in the nationalization of almost every provision of the Bill of Rights. Through this interpretive device, the Court has "incorporated" various provisions of the Bill of Rights into the word "liberty" of the Due Process Clause, thereby making the Bill of Rights applicable to the States. It is by these means that the members of the Supreme Court have seized jurisdiction over almost every civil liberties dispute in the United States during the last fifty years. By reading the Bill of Rights into the Fourteenth Amendment, the Court has read federalism out of the Constitution and superimposed its own Constitution upon that of the Framers, accomplishing a constitutional revolution of awesome proportions. The upshot is near total concentration of power in the hands of nine or fewer individuals—the very essence of tyranny, as Madison pointed out in *The Federalist*.

As originally conceived, the Bill of Rights had a *twofold* purpose. The first and obvious was to protect each individual from encroachments upon his liberty by the federal government. The first three amendments are clearly directed toward Congress, and all but the last of the remaining seven are to a large extent limitations upon the federal judiciary. Thus the First Amendment provides that *Congress* shall make no law abridging the free exercise of religion, and by inference leaves the question of religious freedom within the states to the states themselves. The Fifth Amendment, on the other hand, instructs Congress and the federal courts to follow various procedures that are consistent with due process and Anglo-American principles of justice.

The second purpose of the Bill of Rights was to assure the states that they would retain *exclusive* jurisdiction over all civil liberties disputes within their borders, except in those instances where they had agreed to submit to a uniform national standard, as exemplified by Article I, Section 10. By exempting the states from its provisions, the Bill of Rights thus guaranteed to each state the right to decide for itself, under its own constitution, bill of rights, and statutes, all matters of public policy regarding the rights of speech, press, religion and other personal freedoms that its citizens claimed against the state. The Bill of Rights, in order words, was a States' Rights document, the bulwark of American federalism. It rested on the assumption that personal freedom was too important to entrust to a central government, and that individual liberty would best be protected at the local level, where the citizens had a larger say in public affairs and public officials were near at hand and probably shared the same cultural background.[33]

Acknowledging the sovereignty of the states and the intent of the Framers in such matters, a unanimous Supreme Court, speaking through Chief Justice Marshall, held in *Barron v. Baltimore* (1833)[34] that no provision of the Bill of Rights applied to the States. The record shows, to the satisfaction of nearly every observer who has inquired into the subject, that the authors of the Fourteenth Amendment did not intend by its due process clause to overthrow *Barron* or to "incorporate" the Bill of Rights and thereby enlarge the jurisdiction of the Supreme Court.

Thus, the doctrine of incorporation is utterly inconsistent with the original meaning and fundamental purpose of the Bill of Rights. The Court has indeed converted the Bill of Rights into an instrument of federal judicial power, putting it to the very use it was intended to prevent. So far-reaching is this perverse judicial doctrine that it presently extends beyond the Bill of Rights to unexplored space. For the Court is now busily at work divining new rights, such as the supposed right of privacy, which appear nowhere in the Constitution. These, too, are thrown into the incorporation hopper, to be transformed into "constitutional" rights that the states are forbidden to restrict. Because the number and variety of human wants and desires (read "rights") are infinite, so too are the incorporation powers of the Supreme Court.

In sum, this rule of interpretation concocted by the Court has produced a massive shift of power from the states to nine individuals on the Supreme Court. It is an incredible power—the power to define the scope and meaning of every expression of individual liberty for a nation of some 250 million souls. The doctrine of incorporation, it may thus be seen, is the great wellspring of federal judicial power today. It is devoid of any constitutional foundation, conflicts with republicanism (the most fundamental of all rights in the American political tradition), and renders federalism meaningless. Its very presence makes limited constitutional government difficult, if not impossible.

PROSPECTS FOR CONSTITUTIONAL REFORM

The preceding account of important turning points in the history of the American Constitution, while hardly comprehensive, nevertheless points to the conclusion that the judicialization of the American republic has been an evolutionary rather than a revolutionary process. Its roots may be traced back to inherent flaws in the Constitution itself, to the decline and ultimate disappearance of the conservative legal tradition in American constitutional law, to the reallocation of power between the national and state governments brought about by the Civil War and Reconstruction, and to the almost total centralization of power arising from the doctrine of incorporation.

The common thread of these tangled precedents is the gradual accumulation of power in the Supreme Court. The fundamental problem is that the federal judiciary has too much power and the states have too little. The collapse of federalism is thus a major factor in understanding the cause of our present dilemma. Judicial activism is largely a result of centralization. It necessarily follows that any attempts at lasting reform must deal with the problem of power and the need to strengthen the states.

Toward that end, basic changes in the constitutional structure are necessary in order to correct the mistakes of the past, provide for a permanent restoration of limited government, and make the Constitution a living document that actually functions as a constitution. It is a Herculean task, to be sure, given more than a century of constitutional confusion and apoplexy in conservative circles, as well as the enormous accumulation of liberal precedents, the radicalization of the legal profession, the entrenchment of the Supreme Court, and the widespread ignorance of matters constitutional among our political leaders and the general population; but anything less than a formal amendment that is designed to check the growth of the judicial power will bring only temporary relief.

How can this be accomplished? By removing the *causes* of judicialization? This would entail an actual reduction of judicial power and curtailment of the Court's jurisdiction. Congress has plenary authority to regulate and thus limit the jurisdiction of the federal courts, but has generally declined to do so. Would an amendment clarifying its appropriate use increase the likelihood that the power will be exercised? But this assumes that Congress might wish to protect the states—a questionable assumption, at best. Might not Article III, Section 2 be amended to give the *States* a share of power concerning the regulation of Supreme Court jurisdiction? The thought is intriguing.

The repeal of the Fourteenth Amendment would, of course, eliminate the chief cause of judicialization. Certainly the Fourteenth Amendment outlived its original purpose years ago; but repealing an amendment is surely more difficult than adopting one, and probably the time has passed when repeal would have been politically feasible. The mere thought of having to explain to the public why this Amendment and its incorporation apparatus should be banished from the Constitution is enough to confound the statesman and stagger the most sober of lawyers. We may indulge our fantasies, but we cannot contemplate with much hope of success a popular movement to drive a stake through the heart of this monster.

If we cannot remove the causes of judicialization, perhaps, then, we can at least control its *effects*. This is the kind of protection that the Framers scrupulously crafted in designing the legislative and executive departments, but neglected to provide in our jerry-built judiciary. That is to say, the Supreme Court lacks any real *internal* checks that might serve to moderate its behavior. The only restraint it knows is self-restraint, which has increasingly declined with each succeeding generation of new judges. In effect, the Supreme Court is a superlegislature because it operates beyond the pale of our checks and balances system and is subject neither to external nor internal controls.

Acknowledging the fact that the Supreme Court is not about to lose its power, either voluntarily or by political force, perhaps our wisest course of remedial action is internal reform. If the Court is to be, in effect, a third house of Congress, then let us ameliorate the oversight of the Framers by making it a body in which the states are represented or at least have some influence. This could be achieved by establishing a residency requirement for the office that takes into account the various regions or states of the nation. An appropriate amendment in this regard would be one which divided the nation into nine, roughly equal circuits (based upon both state boundaries and the decennial census) returned the Justices to circuit-riding, and stipulated that each Justice must be a resident of the circuit over which he presides at the time of his appointment.

This amendment would be all the more meaningful if it further provided that all federal judicial appointments be subject to confirmation by the state legislatures located within the circuits, as well as the U.S. Senate. At present, the states have no influence in the selection of Supreme Court Justices or federal judges at large, thanks in part to the Seventeenth Amendment, which abolished the direct election of Senators by state legislatures and thereby weakened the influence of the states in determining the composition of both the Senate and the federal judiciary.

The amendment contemplated here would restore, to some extent, the role of the states and reintroduce the missing element of federalism into the third branch. This complete disregard for federalism in the composition of the federal judiciary naturally extends, with predictable results, to the decision-making process of the federal courts, particularly at the Supreme Court level. In striking contrast to the first one-hundred years or more of Supreme Court history, the modern court overturns state laws and reverses state Supreme Court decisions with impunity. Between 1789 and 1860, the Supreme Court held a state constitutional provision, law or ordinance unconstitutional in only thirty-six instances. This number was quickly matched in the period from 1861 to 1873; and from 1861 to 1937, the number climbed to

515, about a 1,400 percent increase. Since then, the Court has followed a hands-off policy with respect to laws passed by Congress, but has stepped up its attack on the reserved powers of the States. During the reign of Earl Warren, the Supreme Court held 166 state constitutional provisions, laws or ordinances invalid. But the worst Court in American history from the standpoint of federalism was the Burger Court, which held 310 state constitutional provisions, laws or ordinances to be unconstitutional. Since 1789, the Supreme Court has overturned 1,140 state laws, ordinances or constitutional provisions on the ground that they conflicted with the Supreme Court's interpretation of the Constitution—and this does not include the work of the present term. Considerably more than half of these decisions have been delivered in the past fifty years.[35]

What lawyers and scholars today euphemistically call "constitutional law" is, in reality, the *Court's* constitution, as distinguished from the *People's* Constitution of 1787. As similarities between the original document and the actual law of the land become increasingly warped and obscure, so, too, is the putative notion that ours is a marvelously short and simple constitution with only twenty-six amendments. The manner and frequency of amendment by judicial decree suggests, indeed, that our Constitution is so arcane, complicated and prolix as to defy human understanding.

This precarious state of affairs was not anticipated by the Framers. To protect the Constitution from the vagaries of constant and radical change, they devised a cumbersome amendment process requiring extraordinary majorities representing a broad geographical distribution of the American people—three-fourths of the states across the land, not three-fourths of the people limited to a particular section. Yet, as few as five individuals, representing only themselves and certainly not a national consensus, add as many amendments to the Constitution in a single term of the Supreme Court as the nation itself has added in two centuries. The current practice of unrestricted judicial amendment-making not only runs counter to the basic philosophy of change embodied in the Constitution, but also undermines the political, social and economic stability of the nation, and the principle of rule of law.

Much of this could be avoided by the addition of an amendment to the Constitution which simply required a three-fourths majority on the Court before any state constitutional provision, law or ordinance could be invalidated on constitutional grounds. This would restore balance to the system by making the amendment process cumbersome across the board, and give us greater assurance that state laws would be nullified only when they clearly and unquestionably violated the Constitution. Such an amendment would probably do more to restore constitutional government in the United States than any change that has previously been proposed.

In addition to the formal amendments that have been submitted for consideration here, there is much that can be done to alleviate the burden of judicialization through corrective legislation. Although it never got the hearing it deserves and has already been relegated to the dust-bin of history, the Judicial Reform Act of 1982 sponsored by the late Senator John P. East is still the most comprehensive, thoughtful and promising legislative cure for our constitutional ills that has been proposed in this century. We are not wanting for ideas. What is needed are statesmen who possess the courage, determination and understanding to put the Constitution ahead of politics and their careers—the kind of men who did just that two hundred years ago, or the kind before that who pledged their lives, their liberty, and their fortunes to give us self-government—the most basic freedom we possess and the one today that is least observed.

No less fundamental is the need to restore constitutional literacy at every level of the educational process. In the colleges, political science departments have even stopped teaching constitutional law; and in the law schools the students receive only a smattering of that, with no attention paid to the meaning and purpose of the original design. A profession of 650,000 lawyers whose legal education and constitutional understanding reach back no further than the decisions of the Warren-Burger Courts—which is all that is offered in most law schools under the abysmal case method of teaching—is a profession that endangers the freedom and safety of the republic, particularly when it occupies the federal bench. We recall Alexander Pope's admonition that a little learning is a dangerous thing. Something drastic must be done soon to bring the Constitution back to constitutional law, and to put legal history and legal philosophy back into the law school curriculum. Another generation of culturally rootless pettifoggers administering the law . . . and the Constitution is gone.

In the final analysis, we must be mindful that the Constitution is too important to be left to the lawyers alone. Constitutional misinterpretations, distortions and even amendments may often be attributed to ignorance of constitutional theory and political principles implicit in the structure, or to the uncritical acceptance of alien doctrines that have crept into the law and captured the imagination of untutored minds. Just as every American believes he has an informed political opinion, so, too, do law professors and judges commonly act upon the dubious assumption that they have an informed philosophical grasp of the law. But lawyers are not political philosophers.

Yet the Supreme Court Reports are bristling with judicial opinions, most especially since 1937, which read like the revolutionary tracts of John Lilburne and the Levellers. Platoons of law professors fall quickly in line, armed with books and heavily footnoted law reviews to justify the Court's latest usurpation under the rubric of some higher moral philosophy. Despite a confused and often contradictory record, the judge who wrote the opinion may even be persuaded by his obsequious flatterers that he is a philosopher-king, and that his judicial utterances rise to the level of a coherent doctrine consistent with the Constitution. Not a few legal writers refer audaciously to the "philosophy" of this or that judge, as though he were a deep thinker struggling with the great philosophical questions of Western Man. He is likely to be none of these things, but only a simple lawyer who appreciates neither his own limitations nor those of the political ideology that unconsciously colors his opinions and influences his interpretations.

The great difficulty lies in getting the legal profession to open its eyes to the world of constitutional scholarship—much of it developed by political scientists and historians—that derives not merely from the opinions of judges, but more fundamentally from the original documents themselves and from an informed understanding of political philosophy and legal history. It seems that every modern lawyer is familiar, to some extent at least, with major opinions written by Justices Holmes, Brandeis, Cardozo, Douglas, and Black. But how many have read Walter Berns' devastating repudiation of Holmes' jurisprudence?[36] Or Harry Clor's *Obscenity and Public Morality*,[37] which effectively demolishes the Court's rationale for pornography? Or F.A. Hayek's *magnum opus, The Constitution of Liberty*, which teaches the reader more about freedom, equality and rule of the law than he will learn from all of the Supreme Court Reports ever published?[38]

For that matter, how many law professors teach constitutional law from *The Federalist* or Story's *Commentaries on the Constitution*, as well as from the opinions of the Warren-Burger Courts? How many federal judges do you suppose have a copy of Madison's *Notes*[39] in their library, or have ever held in their hands a single volume from Elliot's *Debates in the Several State Conventions on the Adoption of the Federal Constitution?*[40] One need only turn to the opinions of the judges and the references they cite to see what they are reading—each other's opinions and the most recent law review articles by their former clerks. Ignorance of the law, the lawyers tell us, is no excuse. But neither is ignorance of the intellectual tradition which created it, gives it meaning, and puts it in perspective.

The problem is one of education, or emancipating the lawyers from the crabbed learning of their peers. This is not a new problem, but it is a more serious one today because the law has been captured by ideology. This is the civil liberties/civil rights ideology that took hold in the Roosevelt Court and has now become an integral part of our jurisprudence. The civil liberties side of the equation is rooted in the libertarianism and the political thought of John Stuart Mill and his progeny. The driving force behind this theory of freedom is the belief that all freedoms, rights, and political values must give way to freedom of speech and press, a theory that does not hold water, as J.F. Stephen, F.A. Hayek and many others have amply demonstrated, but one which nevertheless has held sway in the Supreme Court for the past fifty years and has governed the Court's First Amendment decisions. Since the 1960s, libertarianism has spread to other sections of the Bill of Rights respecting criminal procedure, but this represents a perversion of Mill's thought and the ascendancy of a nondescript humanitarian impulse.

The civil rights side of the equation, on the other hand, is rooted in egalitarianism, the racial struggles of black Americans, and in more recent times the feminist movement. Once ennobled by the great American principle of equal opportunity, it has since degenerated into affirmative action and equal results and is now at odds with liberty and equality before the law—the very foundation of Anglo-American jurisprudence.

The combined effects of the civil liberties/civil rights assault on the Constitution are manifested in the decisions of the modern Court. So deeply embedded is this framework of legal analysis in American law that it has taken on the characteristics of rigid ideology. Like medieval monks contemplating the number of angels dancing on the head of a pin, there are many lawyers today who live in a world of law that is divorced from reality, a world consumed by an insatiable lust for absolute liberty or total equality. Every legal dispute is approached with the single-minded objective of pressing either liberty or equality beyond its natural limits, with no thought in mind that disorder and injustice lie around the corner, or that other values, whatever their importance, must be sacrificed to *liberte', egalite' et fraternite'*.

And so we witness the ultimate triumph of Jacobinism on our own shores, and the insidious constitutionalization of the French Declaration of Rights. Yet too much freedom is as dangerous as too little. It is noteworthy that the American people also grasp this basic truth. The impetus for a libertarian Bill of Rights has come not from any popularly based political movement but from the lawyers and judges holding custody of our Constitution. Our egalitarian Fourteenth Amendment may be traced to the same source. At bottom, it would seem, we are governed by a foreign ideology that is imposed by the unwitting disciples of Jean Jacques Rousseau. No doubt the Founding Fathers would call them tyrants. We call them "Justices."

The obstacles to constitutional reform are formidable. The unholy alliance between the Supreme Court and Congress has become almost an American political tradition. What strengthens the alliance considerably is the House of Representatives. As a result of political gerrymandering, the Democratic Party is now the permanent majority in this body—and it is an incredibly lopsided majority that is out of tune with the national majority. No doubt there are more "safe seats" for Democrats today than there ever were "pocket boroughs" for privileged members of the House of Commons in eighteenth century England. Once the most democratic of our representative institutions, the House is now the property of the political party least likely to favor reform. We shall get no relief from this quarter.

Nor can we expect much in the way of educational reform in the law schools. Almost without exception they function as instruments of judicial supremacy, supplying the legal profession with ever increasing numbers of lawyers trained in the doctrines of the Court, while providing intellectual ammunition for judicial usurpations of authority through faculty publications and law reviews. The conservative presence in these institutions is so slight as to be immeasurable. To be sure, the liberal takeover of the law schools has been complete, and until some semblance of balance is achieved there will be no pressure from the bar for constitutional reform. This is surely a serious obstacle to reform.

This leaves only two alternatives: state-initiated amendments to the Constitution, bypassing Congress and the Courts, or control of the presidency. While the former offers permanent reform, the latter presents an opportunity for some temporary relief. Both means should be pursued, but conservatives should be alert to their limitations.

During the past two hundred years, only one method of amending the Constitution has been successfully attempted. This is the method by which an amendment is proposed by Congress. But amendments may also originate in the states. The time has come for conservatives to examine closely this alternative route, for it holds great promise as the ultimate and final act of sovereignty that makes it possible for the American people to recapture their Constitution. At present, the main obstacle to the implementation of this device has been fear—fear cultivated by interested liberals (and some confused conservatives) that this amendment method should never be tried because it will produce a "runaway" convention that will rewrite the Constitution and make things worse. This is a theory that does not stand up under analysis, but one which does stand in the way of what may be our only route to salvation. False prophecy succeeds only where ignorance prevails.[41]

Moreover, there can be no meaningful constitutional reform until conservatives gain an understanding of the proper use of the amendment process. We cannot control the Court with amendments responding to policies. As the late Senator Sam Ervin (D-NC) wisely observed, we cannot amend the Constitution fast enough to keep pace with the usurpations of the Court. If remedial legislation cannot succeed, then we should look to amendments that will cure the cause of the problem. Our purpose, then, should be constitutional restoration—to restore the division of *power* between the federal government and the states—not quick-fix amendments to achieve a specific policy.[42] One thinks, for example, of the conservative resources wasted on the fruitless prayer amendment, which, even if passed, would have left the federal courts in full control of church-state relations. No less foolish is that old conservative favorite that keeps showing up on our household shopping list: the amendment to limit the terms of Supreme Court Justices. Such an amendment, of course, would accomplish nothing from the standpoint of reducing judicial power, and seems to rest on the bizarre assumption that judges would be less tyrannical if they served for a limited number of years rather than for life. By rotating tyrants and increasing their number, however, such an amendment might actually worsen our situation. Amendments should go to the heart of the problem, with a view toward limiting the power and jurisdiction of the Court, either directly, by getting at the cause, or indirectly, by controlling its effects.

This brings us finally to the presidency, the only branch of the federal government where conservatives still enjoy opportunities for success. It is also the only branch in the separation of powers system that still functions as a check on both of the opposing branches. Its importance today is suggested by the fact that, were liberals to capture the White House in 1988, we could expect a sufficient number of new appointments to the Court, through death or resignation, as to pack the Supreme Court with liberals and put it out of reach by 1992 for the remainder of this century. Whether the Constitution could survive another Roosevelt Court is a troubling question.[43] The next presidential election could be one of the most important turning points for the Constitution in our history.

Persuading Republican Presidents to take the Constitution seriously has to date been a serious obstacle to reform of the judiciary. Most Supreme Court Justices appointed by Republican Presidents since Franklin Roosevelt have turned out to be votaries of Rooseveltian constitutional principles and precedents, Warren and Brennan being merely the most extreme examples. Even the Reagan Administration has betrayed itself, despite all of the hoopla about Reagan's judicial appointments. His first appointment to the Supreme Court was based on political rather than constitutional considerations. William French Smith, his first Attorney General, frequently challenged Republican Senators seeking to limit the jurisdiction of the federal courts, and Rex Lee, his Solicitor General, struggled mightily to strengthen and perpetuate liberal precedents.[44]

Today, we witness his Attorney General, on the one hand, vigorously and courageously assailing the doctrine of incorporation, while his new Solicitor General, on the other hand, scrupulously avoids challenging the Court's jurisdiction. At no time since taking office has President Reagan demonstrated sufficient interest in constitutional reform to launch a legislative program that would serve to educate Americans about the nature and extent of judicial activism, and would also put the liberals in the untenable position of having to defend and explain the Court's misdeeds. These capitulations to political and constitutional compromise should be a sufficient warning to those conservatives who look to the presidency to save the Constitution and cling to the single-minded strategy of reforming the Courts and the Construction with new judges devoted to judicial self restraint.

We do not denigrate the accomplishments of the Reagan Administration toward improving the quality of the federal bench when we recognize the fact that this is a risky strategy. Conservatives should have learned by now that we cannot trust the judges, and that well-intentioned Presidents often misjudge the people they appoint. Already we have seen the President's two most recent appointees to the Court, Rehnquist and Scalia, voting with Justices Brennan and Marshall to apply the Fifth Amendment's Takings Clause to the states in the name of property rights.[45] This is the kind of result-oriented jurisprudence that has made a wreck of federalism and the Bill of Rights, and driven the Constitution aground. That some short-sighted conservatives hailed the decision as a great victory raises the question of whether we have lost our capacity for principled jurisprudence and our ability to learn from the mistakes of the past.

Perhaps, then, conservatives need to re-evaluate the current constitutional crisis. If the three branches of the federal government cannot be trusted to stop the judicialization of the American republic—and who can be trusted to surrender power voluntarily?—what, then, is our wisest course of action? Getting state legislators and the American people to take the Constitution seriously may, in the final analysis, be our only recourse. If this be true, then conservatives should also be rethinking their political strategy, with a view toward concentrating their efforts on state governments and state legislative contests. With reapportionment looming on the horizon, there is much at stake in the immediate future and much to be done in laying the groundwork for the amendment struggle that lies ahead. In anticipation of our present predicament, the Framers of our Constitution gave us the tools with which to reassert the sovereignty of the states and of the American people. If we fail, it will be because we lacked will and understanding, not because we lacked the means. The Constitution can be saved, and 1987, the year of its bicentennial, is surely a fitting time to begin the arduous task of restoring that grand old structure.

REFERENCES

The Judicialization of the American Republic, by James McClellan

1. Thomas M. Cooley, *Principles of Constitutional Law* (Boston: Little, Brown & Co., 1898), pp. 213–14.
2. In *Garcia v. San Antonio Metropolitan Transit Authority*, 469 U.S. 528 (1985), the Supreme Court ruled that, under its commerce power, Congress may regulate the wages and hours of state and local government employees—a radical intrusion upon the reserved powers of the states. If the states wish to protect their rights and interests, reasoned the judges, they should look to Congress and the political process for relief, not to the Court and the Constitution.
3. 317 U.S. 111 (1942).
4. *Id.* at 127–28.
5. 311 U.S. 377 (1940).
6. 9 Wheat.1 (1824).
7. *The Daniel Ball*, 10 Wall. 557 (1871).
8. 311 U.S. at 434.

9. Edward S. Corwin, *The President: Office and Powers, 1787-1957* (New York: New York University Press, 1964), p. 307.

10. The Judges Bill of 1925 eliminated all but one type of *obligatory* review of circuit court of appeals decisions and made review almost wholly *discretionary*. *See* 28 U.S.C. §1254. The Court's discretionary jurisdiction is invoked by filing a petition for a writ of certiorari. If four members of the Court vote to grant the writ, the case is reviewed. Attorneys who lost a case below routinely petition the Court to grant the writ, except in cases where a right of appeal lies.

11. Since *Brown v. Board of Education of Topeka*, 347 U.S. 483 (1954), the Supreme Court has found it necessary to implement many of its equal protection rulings in two stages. The first is to declare the existence of a right, and the second is to order state officials to take whatever action the judge deems necessary to implement the right. New rights call for new remedies. To achieve this result, the federal judiciary has used its equity powers to circumvent state assembles and formulate public policy on its own authority.

    Thus the federal judiciary has been using its equity powers not simply to grant relief to individuals, as occurs in "hard bargain" cases involving mistake or fraud, but also to satisfy the wants and needs of whole classes of people. The equity power, it may thus be seen, is a major source of judicial activism. For an excellent study of the problem, *see* Gary McDowell, *Equity and the Constitution* (Chicago: University of Chicago Press, 1982). As Professor McDowell observes, the Court "is exercising not merely judgment: it is making policy choices: it is exercising its own will. It is exercising a power that the Constitution denies it. The Court, under the guise of its 'historic equitable remedial powers,' has been endeavoring to formulate public policies for which it lacks not only institutional capacity, but, more important, the constitutional legitimacy." (p. 11) The cure, he argues, is congressional regulation of the equity jurisdiction of the Supreme Court and lower Federal courts. (p. 122)

12. For a profound analysis of the Supreme Court's misinterpretations of the commerce and welfare clauses, *see* Raoul Berger, *Federalism: The Founders' Design* (Norman, University of Oklahoma Press, 1987). The Supreme Court, he concludes, has reduced the Tenth Amendment to an "empty promise."

13. *See, e.g., Aptheker v. Secretary of State*, 378 U.S. 500 (1964) [§6 of the Subversive Activities Control Act unconstitutional on its face because it too broadly and indiscriminately restricts the "right" to travel]; *Albertson v. Securities Activities Control Board*, 382 U.S. 70 (1965) [registration requirement for members of the Communist Party under §4(a) of the Subversive Activities Control Act violates privilege against self-incrimination]; *United States v. Robel*, 389 U.S. 258 (1967) [§5(a)(1)(D) of the Act making it a crime for a Communist to work in a defense facility unconstitutionally restricts the "right" of association]; *United States v. Brown*, 381 U.S. 437 (1965) [§504 of the Labor-management Reporting and Disclosure Act of 1959, making it a crime for a Communist to be an officer of a labor union, constitutes a bill of attainder]; *Lamont v. Postmaster General*, 381 U.S. 301 (1965) [Federal law authorizing postal authorities to screen and detain Communist propaganda from abroad until delivery requested violates First Amendment "right" to receive information and ideas].

14. *See, e.g., Katzenbach v. Morgan*, 384 U.S. 641 (1966) [Congress' power to enforce the Fourteenth Amendment includes the power to override state laws requiring ability to read and write English language as prerequisite to voting. Congress may enlarge the guarantees of the Amendment but it may not restrict them]. In response to Justice John Harlan's powerful dissent in *Oregon v. Mitchell*, 400 U.S. 112 (1970), in which he argued from original sources that the Fourteenth Amendment was never intended to authorize Congress to set voter qualifications in either state or federal elections, Justice Brennan replied for the Court: "We could not accept [Justice Harlan's] thesis even if it were supported by historical evidence far stronger than anything adduced today. But in our view, [his] historical analysis is flawed by his ascription of twentieth century meanings to the words of nineteenth century legislators." 400 U.S. at 251. The evidence that the Framers and backers of the Fourteenth

Amendment never intended that it be applied to voting and reapportionment is overwhelming. *See* Justice Harlan's dissent in *Reynolds v. Sims,* 377 U.S. 533 (1964) and Raoul Berger, *Government By Judiciary* (Cambridge: Harvard University Press, 1977), pp. 69–98.

15. Particularly insightful were the prognostications of "Brutus" and "The Federal Farmer" on the Judiciary, reprinted in Herbert Storing, ed., *The Complete Anti-Federalist* (Chicago: University of Chicago Press, 1986), Vol. 2 pp. 214–452. "It is a very dangerous thing," warned The Federal Farmer, "to vest in the same judge power to decide on law, and also general powers in equity; for if the law restrains him, he is only to step into his shoes of equity, and give what judgment his reasons or opinion may dictate." October 10, 1787, *id.* at p. 244.

16. James McClellan, *Joseph Story and the American Constitution* (Norman: University of Oklahoma Press, 1971), p. 42 n.146.

17. 41 *Cong. Globe* 1487 (1869) (remarks of Senator Charles Buckalow, a Pennsylvania lawyer).

18. In addition to relieving Supreme Court Justices of circuit-riding duty, the Act of March 3, 1875 also greatly expanded the jurisdiction of the lower federal courts by giving them original and removal jurisdiction "for vindicating *every right* given by the Constitution, the laws, and treaties of the United States." (emphasis supplied). It has been observed that "This new jurisdiction for the federal courts reflected a somewhat more general subordination of state to national authority following the Civil War, and had the effect of creating 'a flood of totally new business for the federal courts.'" Stephen B. Presser, *Studies in the History of the United States Courts of the Third Circuit* (Washington, D.C.: Judicial Conference of the U.S., 1982), p. 8.

19. Woods (Ga.), Lamar, L. (Miss.), Jackson (Tenn.), White (La.), Lurton (Tenn.), Lamar, J. (Ga.), McReynolds (Tenn.), Sanford (Tenn.), Black (Ala.), Byrnes (S.C.), Clark (Texas), Fortas (Tenn.), Powell (Va.).

20. Field (Cal.), McKenna (Cal.), Van DeVanter (Wyo.), Sutherland (Utah), White (Colo.), Rehnquist (Ariz.), O'Connor (Ariz.).

21. Thomas Jefferson was the author of the Kentucky Resolutions of 1798. Much to his disappointment, Leonard Levy acknowledges that, although the Resolutions are often praised by liberals as a libertarian statement, they are nothing of the sort. Of the nine resolves, only one dealt with freedom of the press, declaring that the Constitution and the First Amendment deprived the federal government of an authority over the press. "The bulk of the other resolves affirmed the principle of *federalism* as the reason for the unconstitutionality of the Sedition Act...States' Rights were the prime message of the Kentucky Resolutions. The Sedition Act was not void because a free, republican government could not punish the press for verbal crimes. It was void because the power to punish the crime reached by the act is reserved, and of right appertains, solely and exclusively, to the respective states, each within its own territory. It was void because the states retain to themselves the right of judging how far the licentiousness of speech, and of the press, may be abridged without lessening their useful freedom." *Jefferson and Civil Liberties: The Darker Side* (Cambridge: Harvard University Press, 1963), p. 56.

22. *See* James M. Banner, Jr., *To the Hartford Convention* (New York: Alfred A. Knopf, 1970). "The Federalist theory of interposition, so widely held after 1808, was rooted in the premise that the nation was a collection of 'several independent confederated republics,' a 'league' of equal and sovereign states which had surrendered only a portion of their authority to the central government under the Constitution. In constitutional arguments sharply reminiscent of the Virginia and Kentucky Resolutions...Federalists declared that the Constitution was variously a 'treaty,' 'contract' or 'association.'" *Id.* p. 118. The Convention Report asserted that, "In cases of a deliberate, dangerous, and palpable infraction of the constitution, affecting the sovereignty of a state, and liberties of the people, it is not only the right but the duty of such a state to interpose its authority for their protection." *Id.* p. 339. The movement centered in Massachusetts, and included such leading New England Federalists

as Harrison Gray Otis, George Cabot, Nathan Dane, Zephaniah Swift, William Sullivan, and Josiah Quincy. Gouverneur Morris, who supported the effort, favored an autonomous New England confederacy.

23. William Rawle, *A View of the Constitution of the United States of America*, 2d ed. (Philadelphia: Philip H. Nicklin, 1829), pp. 295-310. "The secession of a state from the Union," Rawle contended, "depends on the will of the people of such state. The people alone...hold the power to alter their constitution." *Id.* at p. 302.

24. Secton 5 of the Fourteenth Amendment states that "Congress shall have power to enforce, by appropriate legislation, the provisions of this article." This is the first but not the last appearance of an "Enforcement Clause" in an amendment to the Constitution. Its meaning is obscure. Does the empowering of Congress exclude the Supreme Court or do both branches "enforce" the Amendment together? Can the President "enforce" the Amendment? How is Congress to "enforce" the Amendment? If the purpose of the Enforcement Clause was to give Congress authority to enact legislation to provide for due process and equal protection, why did the authors not use the necessary and proper clause wording of the Constitution? Does the power to enforce include the power to define the meaning of the Amendment, or conversely, to reject the Court's definition? Or does it mean simply that Congress shall have the power to pass corrective laws against the operation of state laws? See *Civil Rights Cases*, 109 U.S. 3 (1883).

25. *See* Raoul Berger, "'Law of the Land' Reconsidered," in his *Selected Writings on the Constitution* (Cumberland, Va: James River Press, 1987), pp. 126-147.

26. 198 U.S. 45 (1905).

27. *The Conservative Mind* (Chicago: Henry Regnery Co., 1972), p. 295.

28. 268 U.S. 652 (1925).

29. 300 U.S. 379 (1937). "The judicial reaction against economic due process after 1937 is unique in the history of the Supreme Court...[I]t is hard to think of another instance when the Court so thoroughly and quickly demolished a constitutional doctrine of such far-reaching significance." Robert G. McCloskey, "Economic Due Process and the Supreme Court: An Exhumation and Reburial," 1962 *The Supreme Court Review* 24.

30. 302 U.S. 319 (1937).

31. 302 U.S. at 327.

32. 268 U.S. at 666.

33. The origin and purpose of the Bill of Rights and the doctrine of incorporation are discussed in McClellan, *supra* n.16, pp. 142-59.

34. 7 Peters 243 (1833).

35. *See, The Constitution of the United States of America: An Analysis and Interpretation* (Washington, D.C.: Library of Congress, 1973), 1623-1785. Statistics covering the Court's rulings against the states since 1973 obtained through personal interviews with Library of Congress staff. The Supreme Court, the Administrative office of the United States Courts and the Federal Judicial Center do not publish or maintain statistical records on the Supreme Court's invalidations of state constitutional provisions, laws, and ordinances.

36. Walter Berns, "Oliver Wendell Holmes, Jr." in *American Political Thought*, ed. by Morton Frisch and Richard Stevens (New York: F.E. Peacock Publishers, 1983), pp. 295-318.

37. (Chicago: University of Chicago Press, 1969).

38. Friedrich Hayek, *The Constitution of Liberty* (Chicago: University of Chicago Press, 1960).

39. The most comprehensive, up-to-date edition is James McClellan and M.E. Bradford, eds., *Debates in the Federal Convention of 1787 As Reported By James Madison* (Cumberland, Va: James River Press, 1987).

40. A new, revised and greatly enlarged edition of this work will soon be published by the Center for Judicial Studies, under the editorship of James McClellan and M.E. Bradford. Volume 3 of this now 7 volume work, containing James Madison's *Debates in the Federal Convention*, was published in the fall of 1987.

41. *See* Grover Rees, "The Amendment Process and Limited Constitutional Conventions," 2 *Benchmark* 66–108 (1986).

42. James McClellan, "Kicking the Amendment Habit," 1 *Benchmark* 1–3 (January–February 1984).

43. *See* Raoul Berger, "The Activist Legacy of the New Deal Court," in his *Selected Writings on the Constitution* (Cumberland, Va: James River Press, 1987).

44. *See* James McClellan, "A Lawyer Looks at Rex Lee," 1 *Benchmark* 1–16 (March–April 1984).

45. *First English Evangelical Lutheran Church of Glendale v. County of Los Angeles*, No. 85–1199 (June 9, 1987).

4

THE ROLE OF CONGRESS IN
CONSTITUTIONAL INTERPRETATION
by Bruce Fein

The Founding Fathers anticipated a prominent role for Congress in rectifying misuses of the Supreme Court's power of judicial review—namely, the power to nullify acts of Congress, the President, or the states on the ground of unconstitutionality, or to approve government action in excess of constitutional authority. Writing in *Federalist 81*, Alexander Hamilton observed:

> that the supposed danger of judiciary encroachments on the legislative authority . . . is in reality a phantom. Particular misconstruction and contraventions of the will of the legislature may now and then happen; but they can never be so extensive as to amount to an inconvenience, or in any sensible degree to affect the order of the political system. This may be inferred with certainty from the general nature of the judicial power, from the objects to which it relates, from the manner in which it is exercised, from incapacity to support its usurpations by force. And the inference is greatly fortified by the consideration of the important constitutional check which the power of instituting impeachments in one part of the legislative body, and of determining them in the other, would give to that body upon the members of the judicial department.

Hamilton misestimated the propensity of the Supreme Court to usurp legislative power in the guise of constitutional interpretation. By emasculating the constitutional requirement of "standing" to initiate a challenge to government action,[1] i.e., requiring a federal court plaintiff to allege and prove a material concrete harm traceable to asserted constitutional misconduct, the High Court has fostered a mushrooming of constitutional litigation. And the greater the occasions for judicial interpretations of the Constitution, the greater the power of the judiciary.

Additionally, federal courts assert jurisdiction over a much vaster array of constitutional issues than Hamilton anticipated. The ratifications of the Bill of Rights and Civil War Amendments dramatically enlarged the number of disputes between government and private parties that raised profound constitutional questions. Freedom of speech, press, and religion, police searches, seizures, and interrogation tactics, racial discrimination, capital punishment, abortion, and electoral districting are illustrative of the types of subjects routinely addressed by federal courts under a constitutional mantle.

Further, the Supreme Court's latitudinarian construction of federal power over interstate commerce and authority to spend for the general welfare injected constitutional and federal statutory power into oceans of economic grievances regarding state regulation.[2] And the growth of public interest class action litigation has transformed the typography of numerous constitutional decrees of the federal judiciary. It is commonplace for federal courts to supervise the detailed operations of jails, prisons, public schools, mental health institutions, public housing authorities, or police departments by virtue of remedial power triggered by a constitutional infraction.

The repeated invasion of legislative prerogatives by federal courts is substantially ascribable to the Supreme Court's disavowal of Hamilton's understanding that judges would have no license to interpret according to the spirit of the Constitution, but would be bound down by strict rules and precedents to avoid an arbitrary discretion in the courts.[3] Justices William Brennan, John Paul Stevens, and Thurgood Marshall, at present occupying seats on the High Court, have all openly repudiated in extrajudicial statements the idea that the intent of the authors of the Constitution and its Amendments are the touchstones for construction. But no interpretive standard other than intent can prevent judges from arrogating legislative authority.

Contrary to Hamilton's forecast, Congress has generally acquiesced in judicial usurpations. Its power to impeach federal judges for high crimes and misdemeanors is not used to check such abuses. Why?

The majority in Congress are career politicians. Perpetuation in office is their overriding aspiration. They seek to avoid responsibility for any controversial issue that might upset a portion of their constituents. To accept responsibility might occasion a loss of electoral support or popularity. Accordingly, the typical congressman silently rejoices when the federal courts decide vexing or contentious policy questions under a constitutional banner because he can then censure the judges for any result his constituents dislike. Congressmen generally detest making unequivocal policy decisions which a political rival might exploit in the next election campaign. If a congressman is responsible for nothing substantive, the benefits of incumbency ordinarily will prevail over political challengers and insure continuation in office.

There is a manifest need, however, for Congress to play a collaborative role with the Supreme Court in the evolution of enlightened constitutional jurisprudence. As Justice Robert Jackson pointed out, the Supreme Court is not final because it is infallible, but is often mistakenly believed to be infallible because it is final.[4] And any asserted infallibility of the High Court is disproved by its overruling of over 250 of its own decisions. These numerous judicial errors can largely be ascribed to the circumscribed mental acumen of the majority of judges. As Justice Oliver Wendell Holmes lectured, judges are prone to simple-mindedness and naivete, and need education in the obvious to overcome preconceived notions of what is good or enlightened in their judicial deliberations.[5]

That type of judicial mind was epitomized by Justice David Brewer. He boasted that:

[Judges generally] are as well versed in the affairs of life as any, and they who unravel all the mysteries of accounting between partners, settle the business of the largest corporations and extract all truth from the mass of sciolistic verbiage that falls from the lips of expert witnesses in patent cases, will have no difficulty in determining what is right and wrong between employer and employees, and whether proposed rates of freight and fare are reasonable as between public and owners . . .[6]

Criticism and challenge to Supreme Court decisions is thus imperative to rectify frequent interpretive errors and to check purposeful abuses of judicial power. Justices of the High Court have conceded that fact. Chief Justice William Howard Taft acknowledged:

Nothing tends more to render judges careful in their decisions and anxiously solicitous to do exact justice than the consciousness that every act of theirs is to be subject to the intelligent scrutiny of their fellow men, and to their candid criticism...In the case of judges having life tenure, indeed, their very independence makes the right freely to comment on their decisions of greater importance, because it is the only practical and available instrument in the hands of a free people to keep such judges alive to the reasonable demands of those they serve.[7]

And Chief Justice Harlan Fiske Stone reproved unthinking reverence of judicial decisions, declaring:

I have no patience with the complaint that criticism of judicial action involves any lack of respect for the courts. When the courts deal, as ours do, with great public questions, the only protection against unwise decisions, and even judicial usurpation, is careful scrutiny of their action and fearless comment upon it.[8]

Justice Felix Frankfurter urged a sustained and informed public critique of courts decisions,[9] and suggested the influence of trenchant criticism in a letter to his former law clerk Alexander Bickel:

I can assure you that explicit analysis and criticism of the way the court is doing its business really gets under their skin, just as the praise of their constituencies, the so-called liberal journals and well-known liberal approvers, only fortifies them in their present result-oriented jurisprudence.[10]

Congress is endowed with a broad array of powers employable to correct Supreme Court errors and to check its usurpations of policymaking authority. Constitutional pronouncements of the High Court may be repudiated through the amendment process prescribed in Article V. The Eleventh Amendment, generally shielding states from suit by private parties in federal courts, the Fourteenth Amendment's grant of both national and state citizenship to blacks, the Sixteenth Amendment's augmentation of the federal taxing power, and the Twenty-sixth Amendment's protection of the franchise for persons aged 18 or older in state or local elections all rejected decisions of the Supreme Court.[11] In each instance, the amendment process was initiated by a two-thirds vote of the House and Senate, with subsequent ratification by three-fourths of the States.

The amendment process, however, is generally protracted, and impotent to correct fundamental errors by the Supreme

Court in its approach to constitutional interpretation. To meet these concerns, a different congressional strategy is required. One alternative is the enactment of laws that challenge rulings that Congress believes are misinterpretations of the Constitution in the expectation that the Supreme Court will overrule the precedent. Former Congressman Cordell Hull of Tennessee expounded the constitutional legitimacy and imperative of such legislative challenges to the judiciary. In urging Congress to enact a federal income tax law in the teeth of adverse Supreme Court pronouncements,[12] Hull declared:

> I agree that Members of Congress are under oath to support the Constitution, and that it is the duty of the Supreme Court, under proper circumstances, to construe and expound the instrument; but I submit that where, in the judgement of Members of Congress a palpably erroneous decision has been rendered by the Supreme Court, stripping the coordinate legislative branch of the government of one of its strong arms of power and duty...every Member of Congress owes to himself and to the country the duty of exhausting every reasonable and legitimate means to secure review by the Court of the question erroneously decided.[13]

On several occasions, the strategy recommended by Hull has been productive. In 1857, for instance, the Supreme Court declared that Congress lacked power to proscribe slavery in territories of the United States.[14] Five years later, nevertheless, Congress enacted a statute establishing such a prohibition.[15] The constitutionality of the law was mooted by the ratification of the Thirteenth Amendment in 1865 banning slavery throughout the United States.

The Supreme Court held unconstitutional in *Adair v. United States* (1908)[16] a federal criminal statute prohibiting railroad common carriers from employment discrimination animated by union membership. Justice John Marshall Harlan, writing for a 6-2 majority, explained that the due process clause of the Fifth Amendment safeguarded the right to make contracts for the provision of labor. Any government regulation of that right could be sustained only if reasonably necessary to advance the common good. The questioned statute could not satisfy that test. It condemned voluntary arrangements between employers and employees that conditioned employment on non-union status or activity. Harlan elaborated:

> The right of a person to sell his labor upon such terms as he deems proper is in its essence, the same as the right of the purchaser of labor to prescribe the conditions upon which he will accept such labor from the person offering to sell it. So, the right of the employee to quit the service of the employer, for whatever reason, is the same as the right of the employer, for whatever, reason, to dispense with the services of such employee.[17]

Justice Harlan also denied that the statute might be justified as a proper congressional regulation of interstate commerce. He stoutly refused to indulge the assumption that labor disruptions on interstate rail carriers were more likely if wage-earners were not union members, or that Congress intended to prefer unionized over non-unionized workers.

In *Coppage v. Kansas*, (1915),[18] the Supreme Court invalidated a state criminal law prohibiting employment discrimination based on union membership. Justice Pitney, speaking for a 6-3 majority, reasoned that the *Adair* decision compelled the result. He noted:

> Included in the right of personal liberty and the right of private property—partaking of the nature of each—is the right to make contracts for the acquisition of property. Chief among such contracts is that of personal employment, by which labor and other services are exchanged for money or other forms of property. If this right be struck down or arbitrarily interfered with, there is substantial impairment of liberty in the long-established constitutional sense. The right is as essential to the laborer as to the capitalist, to the poor as to the rich; for the vast majority of persons have no other honest way to begin to acquire property, save by working for money.[19]

Pitney denied any legitimate public interest in strengthening private voluntary associations such as labor unions. He further rejected the assertion that inequality of bargaining power between employers and employees justified government intervention on behalf of the latter. Pitney demonstrated that "unless all things are held in common, some persons must have more property (or bargaining clout) than others, [and thus] it is from the nature of things impossible to uphold freedom of contract and the right of private property without at the same time recognizing as legitimate those inequalities of fortune that are the necessary result of the exercise of those rights."[20]

Despite the authoritative pronouncements in *Adair* and *Coppage* that government lacks any constitutionally legitimate interest in restricting an employer's freedom to discriminate against workers who join unions, Congress enacted the Norris-LaGuardia Act in 1932 challenging that judicial doctrine. Section 3 of the Act prohibited federal courts from enforcing any contract requiring any employee to decline membership in a labor organization. Congress declared in section 2 that the purpose of the limitation was to overcome the disadvantage in bargaining position of employees vis-a-vis employers that could be ascribed to government efforts authorizing property owners to organize in corporate and other forms of association. Overcoming private bargaining disadvantage, however, had been denounced as a constitutionally illicit purpose for granting employee rights in *Adair* and *Coppage*.

Section 3 of the Act was not assailed in litigation. Soon after its enactment, the Supreme Court repudiated the freedom of contract theories of *Adair* and *Coppage*, and upheld the power of government to regulate comprehensively employer-employee relations.[22]

In 1935, Congress passed the National Labor Relations Act. It prohibited employers whose business affected interstate commerce from discriminating against employees who joined or supported unions. In *NLRB v. Jones & Laughlin Steel Corp.* (1937),[22] the Supreme Court sustained the constitutionality of the Act. Writing for the Court, Chief Justice Charles Evans Hughes maintained that labor strikes or stoppages in manufacturing industries significantly depress the volume of interstate commerce. Additionally, the Chief Justice asserted:

> Experience has abundantly demonstrated that the recognition of the right of employees to self-organization and to have representatives of their own choosing for the purpose of collective bargaining is often an essential condition of industrial peace. Refusal to confer and negotiate has been one of the most prolific causes of strife. This is such an outstanding fact in the history of labor disturbances that it is a proper subject of judicial notice and requires no citation of instances.[23]

Accordingly, Hughes reasoned, Congress could constitutionally interdict discriminatory treatment of unionized employees to safeguard the flow of interstate commerce.

Hughes also scorned the idea that government lacked a legitimate interest in redressing inequality of bargaining power between employers and employees. Maintaining that workers are entitled to join labor unions, Hughes endorsed the argument:

> that a single employee was helpless in dealing with an employer; that he was dependent ordinarily on his daily wage for the maintenance of himself and family; that if the employer refused to pay him the wages that he thought fair, he was nevertheless unable to leave the employ and resist arbitrary and unfair treatment; that union was essential to give laborers opportunity to deal on an equality with their employer.[24]

The Court, in *Jones & Laughlin*, spurred by enactments of Congress, thus repudiated the factual and doctrinal underpinnings of *Adair* and *Coppage* — namely, that labor conflicts and burdens on commerce were not engendered by employer discrimination against unionized workers; and, that government lacked any constitutionally legitimate motivation for seeking to reduce bargaining inequalities between employers and employees. Through legislation, Congress collaborated with the Court in establishing the now half-century old constitutional principle that employers may be prohibited from discriminating against workers for engaging in union activity.

Congress played a similar partnership role with the High Court in shaping the constitutional law of labor injunctions. In *Truax v. Corrigan* (1921),[25] the Court held unconstitutional an Arizona statute prohibiting judicial injunctions against striking workers who through aggressive picketing and opprobrious language sought to destroy a business by inducing a curtailment of customer patronage. Speaking for the Court, Chief Justice William Howard Taft explained that an employer is constitutionally entitled to operate a business in a lawful manner free from private illegal conspiracies involving picketing or boycotting. Further, Taft declared, injunctive relief as opposed to damages was frequently necessary to save the business of an employer injured by unlawful picketing or boycotting. The Arizona statute violated the equal protection clause of the Fourteenth Amendment because it invidiously deprived only employers of the availability of injunctive relief in courts for illegal conduct typically engendered by labor disputes.

Despite the *Truax* ruling, Congress enacted a host of anti-injunctive provisions in the Norris-LaGuardia Act aimed at handicapping employers embroiled in labor conflicts. Section 1 of the Act generally proscribed federal court injunctions in litigation stemming from labor disputes, subject to narrow exceptions. It also prohibited injunctions against workers that might impede concerted activity designed to achieve union recognition or improved collective-bargaining contracts.

Section 4 of the Act enumerated nine specific types of actions precipitated by labor disputes that could not be enjoined by federal courts, including striking, peaceful picketing, informing the public of the facts regarding labor disputes, and assembling or organizing to promote worker interests.

The constitutionality of the congressional curbs on labor injunctions was upheld by the Supreme Court in *Lauf v. E.G. Shimer & Co.* (1938),[26] without discussion of the significance of *Truax*. That latter case manifestly cast a constitutional shadow on legislation like the Norris-LaGuardia Act whose purpose was to aid unions in disputes with employers by curtailing the remedial power of courts over concerted employee activity, such as strikes, picketing, or boycotts.

In addition to the enactment of laws at odds with prevailing Supreme Court decisions, Congress is endowed with independent power under Section 5 of the Fourteenth Amendment to define and to create rights that further the Amendment's objectives. Section 5 provides that "the Congress shall have power to enforce, by appropriate legislation, the provisions of this article." The foremost provisions are in section 1. It denounces any state law that deprives "any person of life, liberty, or property, without due process of law," or denies "to any person within [state] jurisdiction the equal protection of the law."

The Supreme Court expounded on the power of Congress to enact appropriate legislation to advance the objectives of the equal protection clause in *Katzenbach v. Morgan*[27] (1966). At issue was a congressional ban on the denial of the franchise by states based on a failure to read or write English as applied to voters who had successfully completed the sixth grade in a Puerto Rican school in which the language of instruction was other than English. Writing for the Court, Justice William Brennan declared that section 5 of the Fourteenth Amendment "is a positive grant of legislative power authorizing Congress to exercise its discretion in determining whether and what legislation is needed to secure the guarantees of this...Amendment."[28] The challenged restriction on state power to establish voter qualifications was constitutional, Brennan asserted, if it was plainly adapted to enforce the equal protection clause.

The questioned statute surmounted the plainly adapted test. It aimed at nondiscriminatory treatment of Puerto Ricans both in the imposition of voting qualifications and in the provision or administration of governmental services, such as public schools, public housing and law enforcement, secured by enhanced political power. Justice Brennan emphasized:

> It was well within congressional authority to say that this need of the Puerto Rican minority for the vote warranted federal intrusion upon any state interests served by the English literacy requirements. It was for Congress, as the branch that made this judgement, to assess and weigh the various conflicting considerations—the risk or pervasiveness of the discrimination in governmental services, the effectiveness eliminating the state restriction on the right to vote as a means of dealing with the evil, the adequacy or availability of alternative remedies, and the nature and significance of the state interests that would be affected by nullification of the English literacy requirement as applied to residents who have successfully completed the sixth grade in a Puerto Rican School.[29]

Brennan further maintained that Congress might rationally have believed that English literacy requirements were adopted with an invidious intent to discriminate against Puerto Ricans. It might also have disagreed with the use of franchise qualifications as a means of fostering fluency in English. And Congress might have rationally concluded that an intelligent exercise of the franchise was promoted as much by Spanish fluency as English fluency for Puerto Ricans with access to Spanish-language newspapers and Spanish-language broadcasting providing information regarding election issues and governmental affairs. For any of these reasons, the challenged statute could be upheld as a rational effort to prevent violations of the equal protection clause created by English literacy requirements for the franchise.

In *Oregon v. Mitchell*, (1970),[30] the Court held that section 5 of the Fourteenth Amendment empowered Congress to compel the states to permit voter registration in presidential elections until 30 days before the election date, and to permit persons changing state residence within that 30 day period to vote for president in the state of previous residence. Such congressional commands, the Court reasoned, were reasonable methods of safeguarding a constitutional right of interstate travel.

The Court returned to congressional power under Section 5 in *Mississippi v. Hogan*, (1982).[31] In that case, by a 5-4 vote, the Court held unconstitutional the exclusion of males from a state supported professional nursing school. Such a gender-based discrimination, the Court concluded, violated the equal protection clause of the Fourteenth Amendment. Furthermore, the Court declared, Congress by statute could not shield the discrimination from invalidity by invoking its power under section 5. That power could be exercised to enhance, but not to dilute Fourteenth Amendment rights, and could not legitimize laws otherwise offensive to the equal protection clause.

In the fields of abortion, church-state relations and libel law, prevailing constitutional pronouncements of the Supreme Court seem dubious. Congress can play a constructive role in these areas by compelling the High Court to reexamine its decisions through enactment of legislation and the exercise of its section 5 powers under the Fourteenth Amendment.

A parade of decisions have created broad constitutional rights to abortion under a false banner of privacy rights.[32] The Court has held that during the first trimester of pregnancy, the right to an abortion is virtually absolute, but for physician licensing requirements. During the second trimester, abortions may be restricted only by measures reasonably necessary to safeguard maternal health. And during the last trimester of pregnancy, or when the fetus becomes viable outside the womb, abortion may be prohibited unless the physical or mental health of the mother could be adversely affected.

States cannot constitutionally endow a father with power to prevent abortions,[33] or provide parents with authority to override the abortion decisions of daughters.[34] Further, states are forbidden to provide information or to require waiting periods that might cause a mother to prefer childbirth over abortion.[35]

Congress should hold hearings to establish the earliest time prevailing medical technology enables a fetus to survive outside the womb. The hearings also should explore the pain suffered by a fetus during an abortion, the pain suffered by a mother during childbirth, and the pain or lost companionship suffered when a father's objection to an abortion is ignored. In addition, the hearings should examine the emotional scars to a minor caused by abortions, and the availability of adoption or foster homes to insure proper nurture of unwanted children.

The information elicited at the hearings might enable Congress to find:

1) that fetuses are viable several weeks before the third trimester of pregnancy;

2) that a fetus senses physical pain during many abortions;

3) that pain suffered by a mother giving birth to an unwanted child is generally tolerable;

4) that fathers are deprived of intimate companionship with a child when their objections to abortions are overridden;

5) that many minors would be saved from emotional harm if required to obtain the consent of parents prior to an abortion; and

6) that restrictions on abortions do not burden society with uncared for children because of adoptions and the supply of foster homes.

These findings could be prefatory to legislation under section 5 of the Fourteenth Amendment declaring a national abortion policy at odds with prevailing Supreme Court decrees. The statute might declare that states are constitutionally authorized to enact laws restricting abortions that rationally balance the interests of the mother, father, fetus, minors, and parents. States would possess power to forbid abortions at the time identified in the statute when fetuses are viable outside the womb.

The suggested congressional statute would further an enlightened implementation of the Fourteenth Amendment prohibition on the taking of life or liberty without due process of law. And it would challenge the Supreme Court to reconsider its abortion rulings.

In expounding the establishment clause of the First Amendment, the Court has erected high barriers to government financial or other aid to non-public schools.[36] The Amendment proscribes laws respecting an establishment of religion. The Court has generally invalidated state statutes providing funds to schools absent proof of a secular purpose, a principal or primary effect that avoids advancing religion, and an administrative scheme that does not entangle government with religion. Additionally, the Court has frowned on government aid that creates an appearance of sponsorship of religion.

Congress should hold hearings to survey the educational contribution of religious schools, especially as they help the disadvantaged. The hearings should explore whether the public generally perceives government aid to religious schools as sponsoring or establishing religion. They should also address whether such aid fosters political strife. And the hearings should probe whether religious diversity and freedom are curbed by an absence of monetary or other resources from government.

The hearings might enable Congress to find:

1) that evenhanded government funding of non-public schools threaten none of the evils apprehended by the establishment clause;

2) that religious schools are a vital element of educational diversity and enrichment;

3) that the public neither perceives state funding of religious schools as sponsorship of religion, nor fractures along political or other lines where such funding occurs; and

4) that religious freedom is promoted, not retarded, by government assistance to religious schools.

These findings could be prefatory to a statutory declaration of congressional policy that evenhanded government funding of non-public schools should be encouraged to promote and to strengthen educational and religious pluralism. If pursued, the policy would occasion the enactment of laws that would present opportunities for the Supreme Court to reconsider its prevailing interpretations of the establishment clause. The laws would be plainly adapted to secure the freedom of religion protected by the due process clause of the Fourteenth Amendment.

The Supreme Court has interpreted the First Amendment to forbid public officials to recover damages for false and defamatory statements of fact absent clear and convincing evidence that the culprit acted with actual malice.[37] The so-called "actual malice" rule seems misconceived because it fosters the publication of falsehoods that misinform rather than edify the public. The High Court has staunchly maintained, however, that the rule is necessary to prevent self-censorship by the media engendered by a fear of expensive and protracted libel suits.

Congress should hold hearings to explore the validity of the self-censorship assumption behind the actual malice rule. Reporters and publishers should be questioned as to whether they scrutinized government officials more closely after the actual malice rule was announced. They should also be questioned as to whether a statutory ceiling on damages in libel actions or the availability of reasonably priced libel insurance would prevent self-censorship in reporting on public officials. And Congress should inquire whether declaratory judgement suits to determine the falsity of a published statement with no monetary recovery would eliminate any chilling effect on vigilant reporting and publication.

The hearings might enable Congress to find that the actual malice rule should be abandoned by the Supreme Court because it is unnecessary to prevent self-censorship, at least if damages are limited or unavailable in defamation suits initiated by public officials. The findings could be invoked by public officials embroiled in libel litigation in urging the High Court to overrule its actual malice decisions. Congress might also use the findings to justify a federal libel statute applicable to federal officeholders permitting defamation actions without proof of actual malice.

In conclusion, the opportunities for Congress to participate constructively in the evolution of constitutional law pronounced by the Supreme Court are legion. As Justice Louis D. Brandeis noted, trial and error in the judicial process is every bit as essential to progress as it is in the physical sciences.[38] By challenging and questioning Supreme Court decisions through hearings, findings, declarations of policy, and statutes, Congress can strengthen the intellectual roots of constitutional doctrines, accelerate the correction of constitutional errors, and check abuses of judicial authority.

REFERENCES

The Role of Congress in Constitutional Interpretation by Bruce Fein

1. See *United States v. SCRAP*, 412 US 669 (1972).
2. See *NLRB v. Jones & Laughlin*, 301 US 1 (1937); *Steward Machine v. Davis*, 301 US 548 (1937).

3. See *Federalist 81.*

4. *Brown v. Allen*, 344 US (1953) (concurring opinion).

5. Oliver Wendell Holmes, *Law and the Court*, Occasional Speeches, p. 172 (House Ed. 1962).

6. Quoted by A. Mason, *Brandeis, A Free Man's Life* 201 (1946) (quoted, in turn, in J. Paschal, *Mr. Justice Sutherland*).

7. W. Taft, *"Criticism of the Federal Judiciary,"* 29 *Am. L. Rev.* 641, 642-643 (1895).

8. Preface, Supreme Court Review (1961) p. 3, n. 22.

9. Frankfurter, "Press Censorship by Judicial Constitution," in *Felix Frankfurter on the Supreme Court, Extrajudicial Essays on the Court and the Constitution* p. 89 (P. Kurland ed. 1970).

10. Quoted by B. Schwartz, *Superchief* (New York University Press, 1983).

11. See *Chisholm v. Georgia* 2 US [2 Dall.] 419 (1793); *Dred Scott v. Sanford*, 60 US [19 How.] 393 (1857); *Pollock v. Farmers Loan & Trust*, 157 US 429 (1895); *Oregon v. Mitchell*, 400 US 112 (1970).

12. See *Pollock v. Farmers Loan & Trust*, *supra* n. 11.

13. *The Memoirs of Cordell Hull*, Vol. 1, p. 59 (New York 1948).

14. See *Dred Scott v. Sanford*, supra n. 11.

15. Ch. CXI, 12 Stat. 432 (1862).

16. *Adair v. United States*, 208 US 161 (1908).

17. *Id.* at 174-175.

18. *Coppage v. Kansas*, 236 US 1 (1915).

19. *Id.* at 14.

20. *Id.* at 17

21. See *West Coast Hotel v. Parrish*, 300 US 379 (1937).

22. *NLRB v. Jones & Laughlin Steel Corp.*, 301 US 1 (1937).

23. *Id.* at 42.

24. *Id.* at 33.

25. *Truax v. Corrigan*, 257 US 312 (1921).

26. *Lauf v. E. G. Shimer & Co.*, 303 US 323, 330 (1938).

27. *Katzenbach v. Morgan*, 384 US 641 (1966).

28. *Id.* at 651.

29. *Id.* at 653.

30. *Oregon v. Mitchell*, 400 US 112 (1970).

31. *Mississippi v. Hogan*, 102 S. Ct. 3331 (1982).

32. See *Roe v. Wade*, 410 US 113 (1973).

33. *Planned Parenthood of Missouri v. Danforth*, 428 US 52 (1976).

34. *Belloti v. Baird*, 443 US 622 (1979).

35. *Thornburgh v. American College of Obstetricians and Gynecologists*, 106 S. Ct. 2169 (1986).

36. See *City of Grand Rapids v. Ball*, 105 S. Ct. 3216 (1985); *Aguilar v. Felton*, 105 S Ct. 3232 (1985).

37. See *New York Times v. Sullivan*, 376 US 254 (1964).

38. *Burnet v. Coronado Oil & Grain*, 285 US 393, 407-408 (1932) (dissenting opinion).

5

AN HISTORICAL SURVEY OF SUPREME COURT APPOINTEES

by Bruce Fein

From the inception of the Constitution, the United States Supreme Court has engendered public controversy and political conflict. Anti-Federalist opponents of the Constitution worried that the High Court would employ its interpretive powers to strengthen national powers at the expense of the States. Alexander Hamilton, defending the judiciary in *Federalist 81*, denied that the Supreme Court would enjoy any latitude to interpret the Constitution according to its spirit; instead he maintained in *Federalist 78*, it would be bound by strict interpretive rules and precedents to avoid arbitrary decisionmaking.

The paramount reason for political concern over the Supreme Court was its power of judicial review—namely, the authority to nullify acts of Congress, the President, or states by holding them unconstitutional, with a corresponding power to sustain the acts of elected branches of government that flout constitutional limitations.

The power of judicial review was manifestly intended by our constitutional architects. During the constitutional convention, for instance, delegate Elbridge Gerry of Massachusetts opposed including members of the judiciary in a proposed Council of Revision with authority to veto laws of Congress. Gerry asserted that the judiciary could protect itself from legislative encroachments "by their exposition of the laws, which involved a power of deciding on their Constitutionality."[1] Gerry noted that state courts, with general approbation, had set aside laws as unconstitutional under state charters.

Hamilton confirms that the Founding Fathers intended federal courts to exercise the power of judicial review. In *Federalist 78*, for instance, Hamilton responds to the charge that the power of courts to declare legislative acts void implies a superiority of the judiciary to the legislative power. To the contrary, Hamilton explained, "the rights of the courts to pronounce legislative acts void, because contrary to the Constitution," simply acknowledged that the people, in adopting a Constitution that limited powers of government, were superior to their elected representatives.

Hamilton further denied that the Constitution intended the legislature to judge the constitutionality of their own action. "It is far more rational to suppose," Hamilton reasoned, "that the courts were designed to be an intermediate body between the people and the legislature in order . . . to keep the latter within the limits assigned to their authority."

The power of judicial review made the Supreme Court a potent policymaking instrument of government because checks against abuse of its interpretive authority have been ineffectual. Justices of the High Court are constitutionally guaranteed life-tenure, subject to impeachment and removal by Congress for high crimes and misdemeanors. The impeachment power, however, has been invoked against only one Supreme Court Justice, Salmon Chase in 1805, who was acquitted by the Senate. The power to amend the Constitution to overturn the effects of a Supreme Court ruling has been utilized on only four occasions. And the power of Congress to alter the number of Justices on the Supreme Court to change its constitutional decrees through additional appointments fell into disrepute with President Franklin Roosevelt's ill-starred court packing scheme.

Generally speaking, therefore, constitutional pronouncements of the Supreme Court fix public policy for the nation. Moreover, Justices cannot be compelled to interpret the Constitution according to its intent, as was expected by the Founding Fathers. Indeed, a majority of Justices have routinely smuggled their idiosyncratic notions of enlightened public policy into their judicial deliberations.

All Presidents have recognized the large political component that influences the constitutional interpretations of the Supreme Court. Accordingly, appointees to the High Court typically have been chosen from a politically partisan circle of former legislators, executive officials, judges, campaign managers, or advisers holding unambiguous political philosophies shared by the President, whether liberal, conservative, or moderate. The handful of exceptions—including the appointments of Earl Warren and William Brennan by President Eisenhower—prove the rule.

A survey of every Justice appointed to the Supreme Court illuminates the pronounced political and policy partisanship that has informed the appointing process. The survey discredits the criticism of some that President Ronald Reagan's efforts to appoint to the federal judiciary persons with distinctive judicial or political philosophies that he applauds fall outside the mainstream of American political traditions.

Article II of the Constitution endows the President with power to appoint Supreme Court Justices, by and with the advise and consent of the Senate. The first President, Federalist George Washington, was acutely aware of the importance of Supreme Court appointments to the public weal. Writing to nominee John Rutledge, he declared that "[r]egarding the due administration of Justice as the strongest cement of good government, I have considered the first organization of the Judicial Department as essential to the happiness of our Citizens, and to the stability of our political system."[2]

Washington adhered to several criteria in selecting candidates to the Supreme Court. Foremost was strong support and advocacy of the Constitution, the chief earmark of a Federalist. Also important were distinguished service during the Revolutionary War, active participation in national or state politics, prior judicial experience, and suitable geographic representation. The latter was significant to assuage jealousies among the states, to bolster national unity, and to insure an adequate knowledge of local conditions and local laws in the fulfillment of circuit duties of the Justices.

President Washington nominated an historical high of fourteen candidates to the Supreme Court, but only ten served. Twelve of Washington's candidates were confirmed by the Senate, but two (Robert H. Harrison and William Cushing) refused to serve after their confirmations.

John Jay of New York—lawyer, jurist, diplomat, soldier, and political leader—was Washington's choice for Chief Justice. A devoted Federalist, Jay was instrumental in New York's ratification of the Constitution.

John Rutledge of South Carolina was another of Washington's initial appointees to the United States Supreme Court. Rutledge was a former governor of South Carolina, judge of its Chancery Court, and was a delegate at the constitutional convention.

James Wilson of Pennsylvania, a signer of the Declaration of Independence and a foremost drafter and supporter of the Constitution, was also appointed by Washington to the first Supreme Court. Wilson had been a key architect of Pennsylvania's 1790 Constitution, and was renowned for his legal erudition.

John Blair of Virginia was chosen by Washington as a fourth Justice to the Supreme Court. Blair was a participant at the constitutional convention, who followed the lead of fellow Virginian James Madison.

William Cushing of Massachusetts received a fifth slot on the United States Supreme Court from President Washington. Cushing was Chief Justice of the Supreme Judicial Court of Massachusetts at the time of appointment. He had stoutly championed ratification of the Constitution in Massachusetts, and served as Vice President of its ratifying convention.

James Iredell of North Carolina completed the complement of six appointed by Washington to fill the statutorily designated number of positions on the first Supreme Court. Former Attorney General of North Carolina, Iredell had ardently campaigned for ratification of the Constitution in the state's ratifying convention.

Washington's seventh Supreme Court appointment was Thomas Johnson of Maryland. He was a former governor of that state, a federal judge at the time of elevation to the High Court, and a delegate to the constitutional convention.

William Paterson of New Jersey was chosen as Washington's eighth Supreme Court appointee. Paterson was then Chancellor of New Jersey. He had previously served as the Attorney General of New Jersey, as a U.S. Senator, and as a delegate to the constitutional convention.

Samuel Chase of Maryland, a signer of the Declaration of Independence, received the nod as Washington's ninth appointment to the High Court. Chase was the Chief Justice of Maryland when appointed by Washington. He had initially opposed ratification of the Constitution, but subsequently became one of its most zealous champions.

President Washington's last appointment to the Supreme Court was Oliver Ellsworth of Connecticut. Ellsworth was a devoted Federalist, who had been centerstage in the drafting and ratification of the Constitution. He had served as a state judge and U.S. Senator, and was the principal author of the landmark Judiciary Act of 1789.

Federalist President John Adams appointed three Supreme Court Justices, all devoted to furthering the policies of the Federalist Party: Bushrod Washington, Alfred Moore, and Chief Justice John Marshall. Washington enjoyed prior legislative experience in the Virginia House of Delegates, Moore had previously performed judicial service in North Carolina, and Marshall had served in Congress and was Adams' Secretary of State when his nomination was sent to the Senate.

Democrat-Republican President Thomas Jefferson championed a political creed contrary to that of his predecessor. His three appointments to the Supreme Court—William Johnson of South Carolina, Henry Livingston of New York, and Thomas Todd of Kentucky—were ardent Democrat-Republicans and strong political voices for Jefferson. Hailing from diverse states, the three had impressive records of public service. Johnson was crowned with six years of judicial experience and the Speakership of the South Carolina House of Representatives. Livingston had served in the New York State Assembly and on the New York Supreme Court. And Todd had served as Chief Justice of the Kentucky Court of Appeals.

Jefferson's hand-picked successor to the presidency, Democrat-Republican James Madison, appointed Joseph Story and Gabriel Duval to the High Court. Previously elected to Congress from Massachusetts, Story's political credentials were viewed with suspicion by Jefferson. He correctly feared that Story would be too adamant in defense of national powers and property rights under the Constitution.

Gabriel Duval, a faithful Democrat-Republican, had served six years on the highest court in Maryland. Duval was also Comptroller of the Treasury under Jefferson and Madison.

Democrat-Republican President James Monroe's solo appointee to the Supreme Court was Smith Thompson, his Secretary of Navy hailing from New York. Thompson was a faithful adherent of Monroe's Democrat-Republican party, and had a record of personal integrity.

Democrat-Republican President John Quincy Adams' single High Court appointee was Robert Trimble of Kentucky. Elevated from the U.S. District Court for Kentucky, Trimble held a Democrat-Republican political banner, but had displayed judicial devotion to the supremacy of national over states' rights.

Democrat President Andrew Jackson's six appointments to the Supreme Court altered its judicial complexion. Jackson generally opposed the assertion of broad national powers, epitomized by the Bank of the United States, and was less solicitous of property rights than many of his predecessors. But judicial philosophy was not controlling in Jackson's deliberations over Supreme Court vacancies.

Political loyalty, prior public service, and geography were the pivots that informed Jackson's six selections: John McLean, Henry Baldwin, James M. Wayne, Roger B. Taney, Philip P. Barbour, and John Catron.

A native of Ohio, McLean was Jackson's Postmaster General, but deemed politically untrustworthy. His appointment removed an obstacle to Jackson's use of the Post Office for patronage purposes.

A Congressman from Pennsylvania, Baldwin had been instrumental in guiding the state behind Jackson in the 1828 presidential contest.

James Wayne, former Judge of the Supreme Court of Georgia, was a strong advocate of national power, but politically cloaked in Jackson's Democratic party. Much to Jackson's chagrin, Wayne frequently voted on the bench to subordinate states' rights to the authorities of the federal government.

Roger Taney of Maryland had served as Jackson's Attorney General and Secretary of Treasury prior to appointment as Chief Justice of the United States. A staunch advocate of Jacksonian policy and a distinguished jurist, Taney led the Supreme Court in curbing private property rights and bolstering state powers.

Philip Barbour, a politically loyal Jacksonian on several contentious issues, was former Speaker of the House of Representatives. He also enjoyed eight years of prior judicial service.

A fellow Tennessean of Jackson's, John Catron, was a personal and prosperous friend of the president. Catron had earlier served as Chief Justice of the Supreme Court of Tennessee. Democrat President Martin Van Buren appointed two Justices to the United States Supreme Court. Van Buren's former presidential campaign manager and Democratic Senator from Alabama, John McKinley was his initial Supreme Court selection. The second fell to Peter Daniel, a Van Buren political loyalist, who was then serving as U.S. District Judge in Virginia. Daniel had earlier served in the Virginia state government as both legislator and Lieutenant Governor.

Whig President John Tyler, former Vice President, gained office when President William Henry Harrison unexpectedly died from pneumonia. Confronting a politically hostile Senate, five of Tyler's Supreme Court nominations were rejected, a presidential high. Tyler's sole successful nomination was Samuel Nelson, who earlier served as Chief Justice of the Supreme Court of New York.

President James K. Polk, a devoted Democrat, made two Supreme Court appointments. His first was Levi Woodbury, Democratic Senator from New Hampshire. Woodbury had also served as Governor of New Hampshire, Secretary of the Navy under President Jackson, Secretary of the Treasury under President Van Buren, and Judge on New Hampshire's Supreme Court.

Polk's second appointment was Robert C. Grier of Pennsylvania. A conservative Democrat, Grier was serving as a Pennsylvania state judge when he was tapped for the High Court.

President Millard Fillmore, a Whig, gave the nod to Benjamin R. Curtis as his sole appointment to the Supreme Court. A renowned and respected lawyer from Massachusetts, he earned Fillmore's gratitude in defending the constitutionality of the unpopular Fugitive Slave Act of 1850.

President Franklin Pierce, a Democrat, selected Alabamian John A. Campbell to the Supreme Court. A nationally respected legal expert, Campbell had served two terms in the Alabama state legislature and had twice declined nominations to the Alabama Supreme Court.

Democrat President James Buchanan's sole addition to the High Court was Nathan Clifford of Maine. An old political ally of Buchanan's with service as Attorney General under President Polk, Clifford had also been elected to the Maine state legislature and the U.S. House of Representatives.

President Abraham Lincoln, the first Republican president, elevated five persons to the United States Supreme Court. The necessities of the Civil War dominated Lincoln's judicial concerns. His first nominee was Noah H. Swayne from the border state of Ohio. Swayne's antislavery convictions, loyalty to the Union, and solidly conservative Republican credentials all commended themselves to Lincoln.

Samuel Miller of Iowa was Lincoln's second Supreme Court appointment. Holding both a medical and a law degree, Miller was a loyal Republican and staunch opponent of slavery.

Lincoln's third Supreme Court appointment, David Davis from Illinois, was a close personal and political friend of the president. Davis had been instrumental to the success of Lincoln's presidential quest, and served fourteen years as an Illinois state judge.

Democrat Stephen J. Field of California was tapped as the fourth Supreme Court appointee of Republican Lincoln. A strong Unionist and expert in property disputes in the West, Field had served in the California State Assembly and as Chief Justice of the California Supreme Court.

Lincoln's last appointment to the High Court was Salmon P. Chase as Chief Justice. An Ohioan, Chase was a founder of the Republican Party and Secretary of the Treasury in the Lincoln Administration. He had also served as Governor of Ohio and as U.S. Senator. Lincoln appointed Chase in the expectation that he would approve of military actions if assailed in court, and uphold the constitutionality of the 1862 Legal Tender Act passed to finance the Civil War. Regarding the latter statute, however, Chase voted in favor of invalidation.

Republican President Ulysses S. Grant appointed four Supreme Court Justices. The first two, William Strong of Pennsylvania and Joseph P. Bradley of New Jersey, were selected substantially because of their known sympathies for the constitutionality of legal tender laws. Shortly after their Senate confirmations, the two teamed with three other Justices to overturn a decision holding such laws unconstitutional, at least as applied to debts incurred before the statutory enactments.

Grant's last two appointments were Ward Hunt of New York and Morrison Waite of Ohio. Hunt had helped to organize the Republican Party in 1856 and enjoyed an abundance of legislative and judicial experience, including a seat on the New York Supreme Court.

Appointed to succeed Chase as Chief Justice of the United States, Waite had earned legal kudos as counsel for the United States before the Geneva Arbitration Commission considering claims against Great Britain for use of its ports in the construction and operation of the Confederate warship *Alabama*.

Republican President Rutherford B. Hayes appointed John Marshall Harlan and William B. Woods to the Supreme Court. A Kentuckian, Harlan had been a crucial ally of Hayes during the Republican Convention and the election campaign of 1876. Harlan also served on a Commission investigating disputed electrocal votes from Louisiana, and voted in Hayes' favor.

Woods, from Georgia, was a confirmed Unionist with service in the Federal Army. A Republican party member, Woods was serving as a U.S. Circuit Judge at the time of his elevation.

Republican President James A. Garfield made Stanley Matthews of Ohio his sole Supreme Court appointment. Matthews had previously been nominated to the Court by Hayes, but the Senate declined to act on the nomination. He had served in the Union Army, as a state legislator, and as counsel to the Republicans championing the election of Hayes before the Electoral Count Commission of 1876-1877.

Republican President Chester A. Arthur's twin appointments to the Supreme Court were Horace Gray and Samuel Blatchford. The former was a distinguished Republican jurist and scholar with lengthy service on the Supreme Court of Massachusetts. Blatchford had been a federal judge for fifteen years and was serving on the U.S. Court of Appeals for the Second Circuit when he was chosen for the higher judicial post. Like Arthur, Blatchford belonged to the Republican party.

Democrat President Grover Cleveland contributed four appointments to the Supreme Court: Lucius Quintus Cincinnatus Lamar of Mississippi, Melville Fuller of Illinois, Edward Douglas White of Louisiana, and Rufus Peckham of New York.

A Democrat, Lamar had served in the Confederate Army, had authored the Mississippi Ordinance of Secession, had served in the Confederate Congress, and had been the Confederate envoy to Russia. He also had been elected to the U.S. House of Representatives in 1872 and to the Senate in 1876. President Cleveland appointed Lamar as Secretary of the Interior in 1885.

Fuller was appointed Chief Justice by Cleveland to replace Waite. Fuller generally shared Cleveland's public policy views, and was an active Democrat, having attended four Democratic National Conventions.

White was the Democratic Majority Leader of the U.S. Senate and a Roman Catholic. His status assured him of unanimous confirmation by the Senate on the same day it received the nomination.

Peckham had served nine years as judge on the New York Supreme Court and the New York Court of Appeals, and seven years as District Attorney and corporation counsel for the state in Albany prior to ascending to the United States Supreme Court. His anti-Populist, conservative social and economic philosophy largely echoed that of President Cleveland.

Republican President Benjamin Harrison appointed a quartet to the Supreme Court during his single term in office. The first was David Brewer from Kansas, the conservative nephew of Justice Stephen J. Field. Brewer had served fourteen years on the Supreme Court of Kansas, and five on the U.S. Court of Appeals for the Eighth Circuit.

Harrison's second appointee was Henry Brown of Michigan. Selected when a U.S. District Judge for Eastern Michigan, Brown had previously served as a federal marshal, assistant United States Attorney, and state court judge.

George Shiras, Jr. of Pennsylvania was Harrison's third Supreme Court appointee. Unlike the typical Justice, Shiras lacked any background of sustained public service or involvement in political party affairs. As a private attorney, Shiras represented railroad, banking, oil, coal, iron and steel interests.

The final Harrison appointee—Howell Jackson of Tennessee—was elevated when serving on the U.S. Court of Appeals for the Sixth Circuit. A former collegue of Harrison's in the U.S. Senate, Jackson had also been an officer of the Confederate States during the Civil War.

Republican President William McKinley's solo appointee to the Supreme Court was Joseph McKenna of California. A close personal friend of McKinley's, McKenna had been elected to the U.S. House of Representatives on several occasions, had served five years as judge on the U.S. Court of Appeals for the Ninth Circuit, and was McKinley's Attorney General at the time of the appointment.

Republican President Theodore Roosevelt appointed a trio to the Supreme Court: Oliver Wendell Holmes of Massachusetts, William Rufus Day of Ohio, and William H. Moody of Massachusetts.

Holmes had served with bravery in the Union Army and was gracing the Supreme Court of Massachusetts with penetrating erudition when Roosevelt selected him for the Supreme Court.

Day had served as Secretary of State during the McKinley Administration, as well as on the U.S. Court of Appeals for the Sixth Circuit. Day had also toiled tirelessly for the election of President Benjamin Harrison.

Moody had served seven years in the U.S. House of Representatives, and as Secretary of the Navy and Attorney General in Roosevelt's Cabinet. His Republican party political credentials were impeccable, enjoying close social relations with Elihu Root, William Howard Taft, and Henry Cabot Lodge.

Republican President William Howard Taft made six Supreme Court appointments during his one term with exceptional care. Horace Lurton, a professor of law at Vanderbilt University, was Taft's maiden choice. Lurton had served with Taft on the U.S. Court of Appeals for the Sixth Circuit, but was a Confederate Army veteran and adherent to the Democratic party.

Taft's second choice fell to Charles Evans Hughes, Republican Governor of New York. Hughes was a learned attorney, and schooled in the complexities of public affairs.

Associate Justice Edward Douglas White was elevated by Taft to Chief Justice of the United States, largely a gesture of political conciliation with the staunchly Democratic South. White's generally conservative political philosophy largely mirrored that trumpeted by Taft.

Willis Van Devanter of Wyoming, sitting on the U.S. Court of Appeals for the Eighth Circuit, was Taft's fourth appointee to the Supreme Court. Van Devanter had served in various local and state legislative posts, and had donned robes as Chief Justice of the Supreme Court of Wyoming. He had also served as a U.S.

Department of Interior attorney specializing in public lands and Indian affairs.

President Taft's fifth appointee was Joseph Rucker Lamar, a Democrat from Georgia. Lamar had been a state legislator and had served on the Georgia Supreme Court.

Mahlon Pitney, a sitting Justice on the Supreme Court of New Jersey, was Taft's last High Court appointment. Pitney had been a U.S. Congressman for two terms, and had enjoyed the mantles of Republican Floor Leader and President of the New Jersey Senate.

Democrat President Woodrow Wilson appointed James Clark McReynolds, Louis D. Brandeis, and John Clarke to the United States Supreme Court. Wilson's Attorney General, McReynolds hailed from Tennessee and had actively campaigned for Wilson's election. He had earned political kudos for celebrated antitrust prosecutions.

Brandeis was a brilliant private attorney from Massacusetts and a close friend and political adviser to Wilson. He was the mastermind behind the Federal Reserve Act of 1913 and the Federal Trade Commission Act of 1914, two of Wilson's landmark legislative accomplishments. Brandeis' enthusiasm for so-called "progressive legislation" was manifest from his writings and involvement as a private attorney in public policy matters.

Clarke was elevated by Wilson from his post as U.S. District Judge for Ohio, and shared the progressive philosophy of the president.

Republican President Warren G. Harding placed four on the Supreme Court: William Howard Taft, George Sutherland, Pierce Butler, and Edward T. Sanford.

Taft was appointed to succeed Edward White as Chief Justice of the United States. A former President, Secretary of War, Governor of the Phillipines, and U.S. Circuit Judge for the Sixth Circuit, Taft's Republican politics and philosophy were unassailable.

Sutherland was a conservative Republican Senator from Utah who had served in the U.S. Senate with Harding. He had also served in the Utah Senate and the U.S. House of Representatives.

Harding's third appointment, Pierce Butler, was a conservative Cleveland Democrat from Minnesota. He was a political adviser of several Minnesota Governors.

The last of Harding's appointments, Edward Sanford, was raised from his seat on the U.S. District Court for Eastern Tennessee. Sanford had served as a special assistant to the U.S. Attorney General in an antitrust prosecution, and was subsequently appointed an Assistant Attorney General in Theodore Roosevelt's Administration.

Republican President Calvin Coolidge appointed Harlan Fiske Stone to the Supreme Court, his only appointment. Stone was Coolidge's Attorney General, with an impressive background in legal scholarship and private practice. Much to Coolidge's dismay, Stone charted a politically liberal course as a Justice, anathema to the politics of Coolidge.

Republican President Herbert Hoover contributed two giants to the Supreme Court bench: Chief Justice Charles Evans Hughes and Associate Justice Benjamin Cardozo.

Hughes had resigned from the Court in 1916 to run against Woodrow Wilson in the presidential sweepstakes. Hughes had also served as Secretary of State under Presidents Harding and Coolidge.

Cardozo, a New Yorker like Hughes, was plucked from the New York Court of Appeals where he had achieved national renown for his erudition and legal perspicacity.

Hoover's third Supreme Court appointee, Owen Roberts, had leapt into national prominence as an investigator of the Teapot Dome scandal. Hailing from Pennsylvania, Roberts had also served as a Special U.S. Deputy Attorney General during World War I to assist the prosecution of espionage and sabotage crimes.

Democrat President Franklin Roosevelt enjoyed nine Supreme Court appointments, and decisively changed the direction of constitutional jurisprudence.

Ardent New Dealer and Senator from Alabama Hugo Black was Roosevelt's maiden selection. A former state court judge and member of the Ku Klux Klan, Black became a celebrated defender of civil rights on the High Court.

Roosevelt's Solicitor General, Stanley Reed of Kentucky, was his second appointee. Reed had previously served as general counsel to the Federal Loan Board and the Reconstruction Finance Corporation, as well as special assistant to the Attorney General.

Felix Frankfurter, a Harvard Law School professor, was Roosevelt's third Supreme Court choice. A close personal and political confidant of the president, Frankfurter had been a prominent figure in civil rights and labor disputes. He had also served as an Assistant United States Attorney in the Southern District of New York.

Roosevelt's fourth appointment was a New Deal cohort, William O. Douglas of Washington. A close adviser of the president, Douglas was Chairman of the Securities and Exchange Commission when he was selected.

Roosevelt elevated his Attorney General, Frank Murphy of Michigan, as his fifth appointee. A crusading New Dealer, Murphy had previously served as a Detroit judge, Mayor of Detroit, Governor of the Phillipines, and Governor of Michigan.

Senator James F. Byrnes of South Carolina was Roosevelt's sixth appointee. A conservative Democrat, Byrnes had previously served the state of South Carolina in executive and judicial posts, and had been elected seven times to the U.S. House of Representatives.

Roosevelt selected Associate Justice Stone to replace the retiring Chief Justice Charles Evans Hughes as his seventh Supreme Court appointment. A Republican, Stone's selection symbolized national unity during the months preceding Japan's attack on Pearl Harbor.

United States Attorney General Robert H. Jackson of New York was Roosevelt's eighth appointment to the High Court. Jackson had also served as Solicitor General, Assistant Attorney General for Antitrust, and General Counsel of the Bureau of Internal Revenue. Jackson was a political ally of Roosevelt when the latter was Governor of New York, and campaigned for Roosevelt in the 1932 presidential battle with Herbert Hoover.

Wiley Rutledge, sitting on the U.S. Court of Appeals for the District of Columbia Circuit, was Roosevelt's last Supreme Court appointment. A spotless judicial liberal, Rutledge had served as Professor of Law at the University of Colorado, Professor of Law and Dean at Washington University, St. Louis, and Dean of Iowa Law School.

Democrat President Harry Truman made four undistinguished appointments to the High Court: Harold Burton, Fred Vinson, Tom Clark, and Sherman Minton.

A Republican Senator from Ohio, Burton was a former Senate colleague of Truman's and worked closely with the latter on the Special Senate Committee to Investigate the National Defense Program. Burton had also supported the Democratic foreign policy, and some domestic gambits, such as the Tennessee Valley Authority and agricultural subsidies.

Vinson, a Kentuckian, succeeded Stone as Chief Justice of the United States. He was Truman's Secretary of Treasury when appointed to the Supreme Court. Vinson had also served fourteen years in the House of Representatives and five years on the U.S. Circuit Court for the District of Columbia. He had also been Director of the Office of Economic Stabilization, Federal Loan Administrator, and Director of the Office of War Mobilization and Reconversion.

Truman's third appointment was his Attorney General, Tom C. Clark of Texas. Clark had earlier served as Assistant Attorney General for both the Antitrust and Criminal Divisions of the U.S. Department of Justice. He was also an enthusiastic campaigner for Truman in the 1948 presidential race against Tom Dewey.

Sherman Minton, then sitting on the U.S. Court of Appeals for the Seventh Circuit, was Truman's last appointee. Minton had served both in the Senate representing Indiana with Truman, and in the White House as an Administrative Assistant to President Franklin Roosevelt.

Republican President Dwight Eisenhower appointed five men to the Supreme Court: Earl Warren, John Harlan, William Brennan, Charles Whittaker, and Potter Stewart.

Warren was selected to replace Vinson as Chief Justice of the United States. Former Governor and Attorney General of California, Warren was Tom Dewey's running mate in 1948 and was instrumental in Eisenhower's capture of the Republican nomination for president in 1952.

Harlan, possessing a gifted legal mind, was sitting on the U.S. Court of Appeals for the Second Circuit when Eisenhower tapped him for elevation. Harlan had earned an impressive legal reputation during twenty-five years of private practice in New York.

Eisenhower's third appointee, William Brennan, was chosen when serving on the Supreme Court of New Jersey. A Democrat and Roman Catholic, Brennan's performance on the Supreme Court conflicted with virtually every political tenet of President Eisenhower.

Whittaker, Eisenhower's fourth selection, hailed from Kansas. He had served on the U.S. District Court there, and had been promoted to the U.S. Court of Appeals for the Eighth Circuit, from whence he was plucked for the Supreme Court.

Former Vice-Mayor of Cincinnati, Potter Stewart was Eisenhower's last appointee. A supporter of Eisenhower in the 1952 presidential race, Stewart had previously been appointed by him to the U.S. Court of Appeals for the Sixth Circuit.

Democrat President John Kennedy's two appointments to the High Court were Byron White of Colorado and Arthur Goldberg of Illinois. The former was Kennedy's Deputy Attorney General and organizer of the nationwide Citizens for Kennedy-Johnson in 1960. The latter was Kennedy's Secretary of Labor and former general counsel of the United Steel Workers, the Congress of Industrial Organizations, and the American Federation of Labor.

Democrat President Lyndon Johnson's Supreme Court appointees were Abe Fortas and Thurgood Marshall. Fortas was a close friend of Johnson's and had successfully represented him in contentious electoral litigation. He had also served during the New Deal in the Department of Interior, the Public Works Administration, and the Securities and Exchange Commission.

Marshall was the first and only black appointed to the United States Supreme Court. He was Solicitor General during the Johnson Administration, and had previously served as counsel for the NAACP in a landmark civil rights litigation, and on the U.S. Court of Appeals for the Second Circuit.

Republican President Richard Nixon appointed four to the Supreme Court: Warren Burger, Harry Blackmun, Lewis Powell, and William Rehnquist.

Warren Burger replaced Chief Justice Earl Warren. He had been Minnesota Republican state party chairman in 1952, and an Assistant Attorney General for the Civil Division in the U.S.

Department of Justice. Burger was sitting on the U.S. Court of Appeals for the District of Columbia Circuit when appointed by Nixon.

Harry Blackmun, also from Minnesota, was sitting on the U.S. Court of Appeals for the Eighth Circuit when Nixon appointed him to the High Court. Unlike Burger, Blackmun lacked long service in the political vineyards for the Republican party.

Lewis Powell of Virginia, Nixon's third appointee, was a former president of the American Bar Association, the American College of Trial Lawyers, and the Virginia State Board of Education. Atypically, Powell lacked federal legislative, executive, or judicial experience.

Nixon's last appointee, William Rehnquist from Arizona, had worked industriously for the Republican party. He was Assistant Attorney General for the Office of Legal Counsel in the U.S. Department of Justice when elevated to the High Court.

Republican President Gerald Ford's sole Supreme court appointee was John Paul Stevens of Illinois. Stevens was sitting on the U.S. Court of Appeals for the Seventh Circuit at the time of his appointment, and had been an antitrust expert in private practice.

Republican President Ronald Reagan has made three Supreme Court appointments. His initial appointment, Sandra Day O'Connor was the first woman to grace the High Court. Hailing from Arizona, O'Connor had served in the Arizona state Senate for five years, and was sitting on the state judiciary when she was appointed to the High Court.

Reagan's second appointment was the elevation of Associate Justice Rehnquist to Chief Justice. His third appointment was Antonin Scalia, a sitting judge on the U.S. Court of Appeals for the District of Columbia Circuit. Scalia had previously served as Assistant Attorney General for the Office of Legal Counsel in the U.S. Department of Justice during the Ford Administration, and as General Counsel to the Office of Telecommunications Policy in the Nixon Administration. He had also taught law and earned a nationwide reputation in the field of administrative law.

As Oliver Wendell Holmes observed, a page of history is frequently worth volumes of logic.[3] The foregoing historical survey of Supreme Court appointments authoritatively establishes that political service and loyalties and policy predilections have traditionally trumped legal lucubrations in the selection process. That fact is but a tacit recognition that the Supreme Court's power of judicial review is more an exercise of political power than of legal craftsmanship. Battles over Supreme Court appointments are battles to chart the destiny of public policy in the United States.

REFERENCES

An Historical Survey of Supreme Court Appointees by Bruce Fein

1. M. Farrand. *The Records of the Federal Convention of 1787*, Vol. I, p. 97 (Yale University Press)(1966).
2. Marcus and J. Perry, *The Documentary History of the Supreme Court of the United States*, 1789–1800, Vol. I, p. 20, (Columbia University Press)(1985).
3. *New York Trust Co. v. Eisner*, 256 US 345, 349 (1921).

6

JUDICIAL QUALIFICATIONS AND CONFIRMATION: THE CARTER YEARS

by George C. Smith

A recurrent theme in the criticisms of President Reagan's judicial appointments has been the charge that he has subordinated excellence to ideology. Much of this criticism has come from ideological advocates of the left, who have never reconciled themselves to the fact that Reagan was twice overwhelmingly elected *because* of the philosophical principles which would influence his selection of judges. Such recriminations are a natural feature of our political system and could be dismissed as such— except for the extraordinary prominence such partisan carping has been given by the major media and by Congress during the Reagan Era.

But some of the attacks on Reagan's judicial choices have come from sources less overtly linked with the hard ideological left. For example, a mixed coalition of law school deans joined in a letter urging the Senate to reject the nomination of Indiana conservative Daniel Manion to the U.S. Court of Appeals for the Seventh Circuit.[1] Although most of these deans had no first-hand knowledge of Manion or his actual accomplishments,[2] it took little prodding from the anti-Reagan legal activists to produce their lockstep condemnation of Manion's credentials. Lurking behind their overt criticism of Manion's unspectacular but solid background as a successful Hoosier practitioner was the Legal Establishment's endemic disdain for the honest conservative values he represented.

The Manion episode was but one well-publicized example of a broader effort to assault the qualifications and integrity of Reagan's judicial selections. The guardians of the liberal status quo on the federal bench recognized that they could not credibly oppose Reagan's judges on their conservatism alone. So the issues of "qualifications" and "professional excellence" have been used as fig leaves to conceal the true motives of their campaign. Where no plausible grounds for challenging qualifications exist, then allegations of racial "insensitivity," flimsy improprieties, or alleged lack of "judicial temperment" invariably surface in the hearings on conservative nominees.[3] The duplicitous nature of these efforts has been evident from the outset.

What has *not* been adequately recognized, however, is the blatant double-standard that has been applied to Reagan's nominees in comparison to those of his predecessor, Jimmy Carter. Claims that Reagan has departed from traditional norms of excellence have been taken at face value and selectively highlighted in the influential media. The ideologically-based assaults on such judicial nominees as J. Harvie Wilkinson, Alex Kozinski, Jefferson Sessions, Daniel Manion, and even William Rehnquist have invariably placed the Administration on the defensive, with the terms of the debate shrewdly determined by the most liberal opponents of judicial reform.

These debates have ignored an element of recent historical perspective which would reveal the fundamental hypocrisy of the assault on Reagan's judges. The missing element is the *alternative* policy of judicial selection which was followed by President Carter and advocated by both Carter and Walter Mondale in their failed presidential campaigns in 1980 and 1984.

Jimmy Carter gave the nation its first judge to be impeached in over 50 years (Harry Claiborne), and another judge (Alcee Hastings of Florida) who has been referred to Congress for impeachment consideration by his Circuit Judicial Council and the Judicial Conference of the United States.[4] Carter adopted and enforced a policy of unabashed race and gender quotas in the appointment of federal judges, and he sometimes compromised basic standards of qualification to sustain that policy.[5] And he allowed the selection and confirmation process to become infused with a spirit of political and ideological partisanship which made a mockery of his professed ideal of pure merit selection.

Jimmy Carter's record in selecting federal judges serves to remind us of what Ronald Reagan has so admirably accomplished in this crucial area of national policy. It also demonstrates that, far from injecting an unprecedented ideological emphasis at the cost of judicial excellence, President Reagan's selection process stands head-and-shoulders above that of his predecessor.

FROM "PURE MERIT" TO PURE POLITICS

Jimmy Carter's pre-presidential book, *Why Not the Best?*, professed his determination to abandoned political business-as-usual and instill a standard of pure merit in all segments of the federal government. In the flush of his early presidency, Carter persisted in stressing this lofty ideal. As for the federal judiciary, Carter firmly promised to select "all federal judges . . . strictly on the basis of merit, without any consideration of political aspects or influence."[6]

As with so many aspects of his presidency, Carter's actual record in judicial selection can only be viewed with irony when measured against his lofty promises.

The realities of Democratic interest group politics soon supplanted the pipedream of "pure merit" selection. Having promised the world to racial, ethnic, and feminist constituencies which were largely responsible for his narrow election, Carter announced that a sizeable portion of federal judgeships would be flatly allocated on the basis of race, gender, or ethnic group membership. In fairness, Carter was remarkably candid in stating his intentions in the matter:

> If I didn't have to get Senate confirmation of appointees, I could tell you flatly that 12 percent of my appointees would be Black and 3 percent would be Spanish-speaking and 40 percent would be women and so forth.[7]

There is a word for what Carter had in mind for staffing the federal judiciary: quotas. Americans had apparently become so accustomed to quotas in other contexts that Carter's plan to impose them on the federal judiciary did not seem as remarkable and improper as it was.

In fact, Carter's allocation of judgeships in some respects exceeded even his own numerical goals and quotas. Blacks constituted 16 percent of Carter's circuit court appointments and 14 percent of his district court appointments, while 3.6 percent and 7 percent, respectively, were Hispanic.[8] Not even the most uncompromising EEOC compliance office could take issue with the statistical rigor of this affirmative action plan for the federal judiciary.

While a more racially and ethnically diverse judiciary is doubtless a commendable goal, President Carter plainly exceeded any reasonable and responsible approach to achieving it. Race and gender quotas have no proper place in the selection of federal judges, yet Carter rigidly advocated and enforced them.[9] In several instances (discussed further below), he demonstrably allowed racial or gender criteria to override basic standards of qualification for the bench.[10] For example, Carter pressed forward with the nomination of two minority candidates who were overwhelingly rated "Not Qualified" by the American Bar Association Standing Committee on Federal Judiciary ("ABA Committee") and whose records were marred with improprieties that would have disqualified other candidates.

Concededly, President Carter's federal court appointments included a fair share of minority and female judges—Amalya Kearse of the Second Circuit, Cornelia Kennedy of the Sixth, and Ruth Bader Ginsburg of the D.C. Circuit are among those who come to mind—who command widespread and deserved respect across partisan lines. But in his inflexible commitment to meet his various judicial selection quotas, Carter too often sacrificed minimal standards of qualification and experience to the expediencies of interest group politics.

THE NOMINATING COMMISSIONS

Another much-vaunted aspect of the Carter Era was the use of the so-called Judicial Nominating Commissions to screen and propose candidates for federal judgeships. These panels were portrayed as a means to eliminate political influence from the process and to restore rational and objective merit criteria. In truth, however, the commissions were overwhelmingly partisan and riddled with leftist ideological influence. Not surprisingly, they produced nominees who were heavily predisposed to pursue the judicial activism favored by the liberal interest groups which so heavily influenced the Commission' composition and deliberations.

Studies show that some 87 percent of the members of Carter's Circuit Judge Nominating Commissions were Democrats, and

79 percent of the judicial candidates they recommended were Democrats.[11] But Carter's own final nominations were even more partisan; one report found that, as of October 1980, 97.8 percent of his judges were Democrats.[12] Yet when the nominees produced by this process were introduced before the Senate Judiciary Committee, they were described, with no hint of levity, as the choices of "bipartisan" nominating commissions.

More significant than the politically partisan character of this process—which was noteworthy only because of its pretensions to the contrary—was its domination by proponents of the ideological left. For example, one major study of the Carter Nominating Commissions process reports that:

> [A]pplicants had often been questioned [by judicial selection panelists] about nine contemporary social issues. ... The four areas which received most attention were the Equal Rights Amendment, affirmative action, first amendment freedoms and defendants' rights. Candidates were also asked about abortion, capital punishment, busing, economic regulations, and a number of pending Supreme Court cases.[13]

The same study revealed that the heavily feminist influence on the commissions resulted in the grilling of prospective nominees as to their views on liberal litmus tests such as abortion and the ERA. Some 41 percent of the members of Carter's Circuit Judge Nominating Commission responding to a survey indicated that candidates were asked their views on the abortion issue during Commission interviews.[14] Several commissioners later confirmed that the political slant and ideological emphasis of the process heavily influenced the deliberations and recommendations of the commissions.[15]

The significance of these practices can best be appreciated in comparison to the current experience of the Reagan Administration in dealing with liberal critics of its judicial selection practices. The slightest hint of any effort to explore the ideological inclinations of candidates for Reagan's judicial appointments has elicited indignant protests from Senate Democrats. Even efforts to determine a judicial candidate's relative firmness in upholding criminal prosecutions have been assailed as inappropriate and unseemly.[16]

The irony of this double standard is striking. The same liberals who zealously monitor the Reagan Administration's restrained and guarded inquiries for evidence of telltale conservative "litmus tests" were zealous participants in the *actual* litmus tests which permeated the entire selection process during the Carter years.

The ideological left's influence did not end with the recommendations of Carter's nominating commissions. Under the Carter system, the judicial candidate evaluations generated by ideological special interest groups were effectively given equal standing with the traditional evaluations performed by the ABA Committee on Federal Judiciary (which itself has reflected anticonservative bias in recent years).[17] When judicial nominees are introduced to the Senate Judiciary Committee, the traditional ritual is to announce that the senators from the nominee's state have approved his nomination and then to report that the ABA Committee has rated the nominee as qualified, well-qualified, etc. But during the Carter Administration, it also became necessary to recite the separate evaluations of the Federation of Women Lawyers' Judicial Screening Panel and the National Bar Association, an association of black lawyers.[18]

Far from being the kind of non-partisan, purely professional organization it was portrayed to be, the Women Lawyers' Panel was a coalition of some of the most radical elements of the ideological left. The members listed on its letterhead were affiliated with such groups as the National Lawyers Guild, the William Kunstler-led Center for Constitutional Rights, the NOW Legal Defense Fund, and the ACLU.[19]

The Women Lawyers' Panel purported to determine the adequacy of the nominee's "commitment to equal justice," while the National Bar Association decided the acceptability of their "attitude on racial and social issues."[20] The extraordinary twist of this procedure was that the ideological prejudices of these groups were given official status, comparable to the ABA's, and incorporated as an institutionalized component of the Judiciary Committee's "advise and consent" procedure. The official introduction of nominees came to feature the following standard recital, as reported from a typical confirmation hearing on three nominees during the Carter Era:

> The Federation of Women Lawyers' Judicial Screening Panel had reviewed the qualifications of the nominees and found that Professor Al-

drich has demonstrated an exceptional commitment to equal justice, Mr. Holschuh has demonstrated an adequate commitment to equal justice and Judge White has demonstrated significant commitment to equal justice.[21]

These "evaluations" of the Women Lawyers and the NBA were of course the purest of ideological litmus tests. They signaled whether the nominee had paid proper obeisance to such tenets of liberal orthodoxy as aggressive affirmative action, the virtues of *Miranda* and the exclusionary rule, the Equal Rights Amendment, busing, and liberalized abortion. Yet the charade proceeded as though these politicized special interest groups were performing a high public service of disinterested professional evaluation. In consequence, legitimate standards of qualification, competence, and integrity became hopelessly obscured and compromised.

CARTER'S JUDGES AND THE JUDICIARY COMMITTEE

President Carter's efforts to appoint hundred of federal judges sympathetic to the legal philosophies of the ideological left, the civil rights establishment, and feminist groups such as the National Organization for Women (NOW) owe much of their success to the compliant confirmation process followed by the Senate Judiciary Committee during the Carter Administration. The Committee of that era was chaired by Senator Edward Kennedy and included such forceful and energetic liberals as Birch Bayh (D-IN), John Culver (D-IA) and Howard Metzenbaum (D-OH). Not only were these senators in full sympathy with Carter's program to fill the federal bench with liberal judicial activists, but they were also vigilant in guarding against the appointment of judges considered unacceptable by their liberal constituencies.

The hard historical fact, documented in volume after volume of the Judiciary Committee's confirmation hearings, is that significant numbers of marginally qualified (and in some cases, demonstrably unqualified) lawyers were rushed through Committee and Senate confirmation with *no* questioning or inquiry, let alone voiced opposition. Most of these hearings involved little more than the ritual introduction of the nominees' families, the recital of boilerplate encomiums from the nominee's home state

Senate sponsors, and perhaps one or two questions on topical subjects unrelated to the nominee's fitness for the bench.

In a few isolated cases,[22] manifest shortcomings and documented improprieties were substantial enough to force extended hearings, but even then Senate confirmation almost invariably followed. The result was not merely to place the likes of the subsequently impeached Harry Claiborne and the subsequently indicted Alcee Hastings on the federal bench. It was to leave behind a double-standard of judicial selection and confirmation which is ingrained throughout the federal judiciary today.

THE CLEMON AND GRAY NOMINATIONS

In their search for grounds to oppose conservative judges nominated by Reagan, some Senate liberals and their allies have devised a new way of interpreting the ABA ratings system. In several of the more heated confirmation battles,[23] they have seized upon the fact that the nominees have been rated as only "qualified" (which compared to "well qualified" or "exceptionally well qualified") and cited that rating as one of the cumulative grounds for opposing confirmation. Significantly, more federal judges have received the "qualified" rating than any other during *all* Administrations going back to the Johnson Administration.[24] By a rhetorical sleight-of-hand best understood by themselves, the opponents of Reagan's judges have come to interpret the "qualified" rating as really meaning "*un*qualified" whenever it suits their purposes.

Given this exacting standard, one can only speculate upon how Reagan's critics would react were the President to submit a conservative nominee who had actually been rated "not qualified" by the ABA. The howls of senatorial indignation would undoubtedly reverberate from Capitol Hill to every network news program on the airwaves.

Curiously, however, a straightforward "not qualified" rating by the ABA did not have such dire consequences for the nominees of the Carter Era. Carter appointed three federal judges with that rating. That fact in itself would not be unduly alarming, inasmuch as many knowledgeable observers on both sides of the political divide believe that the ABA's institutionalized role in the advise and consent process is inappropriate and in many cases unfair (although in terms of ideological predisposition, there is little doubt that the ABA Committee is more hostile towards decidedly conservative nominees than it is towards their liberal opposites).[25] The more significant fact is the manifest disparity in how adverse ABA ratings have been interpreted and utilized as between Carter's nominees and Reagan's. A brief examination of two Carter nominees rated "not qualified" by the ABA is instructive in this regard.

U. W. Clemon, now a U.S. District Judge for Northern Alabama, was recommended for that position by the Alabama senators' nominating commission. Clemon had been a feisty civil rights activist with the NAACP Legal Defense Fund who was subsequently elected to the Alabama state Senate. After investigating a variety of troublesome allegations (some of which are summarized below), the ABA Committee rated Clemon Not Qualified by a vote of 12 to 2.[26] Nonetheless, President Carter pressed ahead with the nomination.

The Clemon hearings were lengthy and detailed. However, a sizeable portion of the inquiry was devoted more towards questioning the ABA's competence and integrity in finding Clemon unqualified than it was towards Clemon's well-documented shortcomings.[27]

One major charge against Clemon concerned his denial of the existence of federal and state tax liens against him; the denial was in direct response to a specific question on that point in the nominee's background questionnaire.[28] The existence of the tax liens, which resulted from a $14,000 delinquency in Clemon's federal tax payments, was not disputed at the hearing before the Judiciary Committee. Clemon's defense was that the tax liens had escaped his attention and that he had been careless in responding to the questionnaire. The hearing record also showed that Clemon had been apprehended for speeding at nearly 100 miles per hour en route to the State Senate. He then declared on the Senate Floor that he would continue to exercise his senatorial right to speed as long as white senators were also allowed to do so.[29] Other charges against Clemon concerned his removal from the board of the Birmingham Area Legal Services Corporation in connection with allegations of cronyism and other improprieties.[30]

143

But the 12-2 Not Qualified vote by the ABA and the other improprieties disclosed in Clemon's hearing proved insufficient to overcome the pressure to confirm a black civil rights activist who was strongly backed by the liberal legal community. While comparable shortcomings would surely guarantee Senate rejection of a conservative Reagan nominee today, Clemon was confirmed and seated.

Judge Clemon's hearings overlapped with those of Fred Gray, another black civil rights lawyer nominated by Carter for an Alabama federal district judgeship. Gray was also rated Not Qualified by the ABA, by a vote to 9 to 5,[31] and faced a variety of additional problems at his confirmation hearing.

Among the more significant charges involved in Gray's case were alleged conflicts of interest in connection with his representation of the Macon County government; a civil securities fraud complaint against him, which was resolved with the payment of a $40,000 settlement; and false certifications regarding a project site which did not exist, coupled with other breaches of professional duty, in connection with Gray's role as counsel in a mishandled municipal bond closing.[32]

The accumulation of evidence against the Gray nomination ultimately forced President Carter to withdraw it. Insisting on the confirmation of two "not qualified" judges in one fell swoop would likely have been too great an imposition on even the pliant Senate standards which prevailed at the time. Even so, the episode underscored the serious deficiencies which characterized Carter's judicial selection process.

RUBBER-STAMPING THE MARGINALLY-QUALIFIED

Another significant aspect of the Carter Era process—at least in comparison to the practice during the Reagan years—was the Senate's apparent lack of concern when confronted with nominees whose marginal qualifications were suggested by dissents on the ABA Committee against giving them a minimally qualified rating. Such mixed ratings have been frequently seized upon as grounds for sharply questioning the caliber of various Reagan court nominees. But during the Carter Administration—when no less than 22 district court nominees were considered "Not Qualified" by a minority of the ABA Committee—such ratings were rarely considered significant enough to justify even token scrutiny of the nominees in question. This was the case even when other shortcomings or problems in the nominee's record provided additional cause for concern.

Robert Aguilar, for instance, was among the large batch of nominees rushed through to confirmation in the final year of the Carter presidency. Selected for a seat on the U.S. District Court for Northern California, Aguilar was rated Not Qualified by a minority of the ABA Committee.[33] Beyond the fact that he had served less than one year in his position as a local trial judge in Santa Clara, there was one significant gap in Mr. Aguilar's resume. Aguilar had dropped out of Hastings College of Law before completing his degree requirements, and had never earned a law degree thereafter.[34] Since possession of a law degree might conceivably be considered a standard credential for appointment to the federal bench, some questioning as to Aguilar's off-setting qualifications would have seemed in order. But no such questions were raised. In fact, Aguilar was asked no questions at all by the Judiciary Committee, other than a personal query from Senator Heflin about the health of Senator Cranston's son (who had just been seriously injured in California).[35] Such were the standards of Senate scrutiny before the advent of Ronald Reagan stimulated the shift from cordial accommodation to hostile confrontation.

Another Carter nominee who received a "mixed/qualified" ABA rating was Anna Diggs-Taylor, selected for the U.S. District Court in Eastern Michigan. Taylor, who was formerly married to ex-Congressman Charles Diggs (D.-MI), presented several question-marks in addition to her marginal ABA rating.

First, her membership in the National Lawyers Guild (NLG), a notoriously radical organization of leftist lawyers, was raised ever-so-gently by Senator Kennedy as follows:

> You listed under the bar association memberships that you are involved with the National Lawyers Guild. In the past this organization has been identified as some [sic] with Communist connections. Those allegations were brought out in our consideration of the nomination of Mr. Levi, the Attorney General. He was also a member. Would you tell us a little bit about your association and participation with the guild.[36]

Taylor's response was remarkable in its straight-faced eva-

145

siveness. She responded to Senator Kennedy's question as follows:

> It [i.e., the Guild] is an association of very prominent judges and lawyers and active lawyers in the community in Detroit. In the mid-sixties, particularly in 1964, I was a board member of the Detroit Chapter.[37]

Remarkably, no Committee member followed up on this and Taylor's obfuscation of the NLG's true radical nature was allowed to stand uncorrected in the record. Blithely disregarded was the fact that the NLG had once been cited by a congressional investigating committee as "the foremost bulwark of the Communist Party (U.S.A.)"[38] No one explored exactly what kind of activities Diggs-Taylor had pursued or approved as a board member of the NLG's Detroit chapter.

The significance of this non-scrutiny is best understood by comparing it with the harsh criticism leveled against Daniel Manion when it was revealed that he had once said kind words about the John Birch Society in a piece of personal correspondence. Manion was pilloried for merely complimenting a conservative organization to which he had never belonged. The compliment was in the context of a courtesy letter sent to a Birch Society library in response to its condolences on the death of Manion's father, Clarence Manion. But Taylor's active leadership role in a radical organization of the left was politely ignored.

Taylor's confirmation hearing also revealed other significant problem areas. She had been the subject of an IRS tax lien after failing to pay her federal tax balance in the years 1974-76. Taylor explained that she had suffered a reduction in income complicated by a divorce during that period, had simply been short of money to pay her taxes, and had ultimately paid all balances due the IRS following a remarriage.[39] Further, in response to a question in the nominee's questionnaire as to whether her tax returns had ever been the subject of an audit, Taylor had answered "No."[40] Her statement proved to be untrue. There had been an audit of her joint returns filed during a previous marriage. However, Taylor's explanation that she had had no knowledge of the audit was uncontroverted and accepted by the Committee.

The full details of this inquiry remain a closed book, however. At Taylor's request, the inquiry was conducted in a closed session of the Committee.[41] One can only guess at the response that would occur today if a "controversial" Reagan judicial nominee, confronted with similar allegations, attempted to have them resolved in a secret session. But there was not a murmur of protest raised concerning the secrecy of the Taylor inquiry. She was soon confirmed without difficulty. (An example of the rulings she is now dispensing from the federal bench was a holding that it was unconstitutional for the City of Birmingham, Michigan, to display a Nativity Scene on public grounds during the Christmas Holiday Season.[42])

Carter's nomination of Judge Joseph Howard for the U.S. District Court in Maryland was another case where grave questions concerning the nominee's qualifications and suitability for the federal bench were politely ignored. A minority of the ABA Committee had found Judge Howard (then a Baltimore City Judge) not qualified. The Maryland Bar Association had also rated him as unqualified, based in part on a poll taken of its membership.[43] One significant aspect of that poll was explained during Judge Howard's confirmation hearings by Senator Heflin (who was chairing the hearing[44]):

> First, the poll the Maryland Bar Association conducted in conjunction with Baltimore Sun Newspaper, a poll which rated judges of the supreme bench of Baltimore City. Four hundred trial lawyers were asked unanimously to answer questions about judges. The results of the poll indicated that you were said to have displayed religious, racial, or ethnic bias "frequently" or "sometimes" by 59 percent of those polls [sic].

Howard also acknowledged during his hearings that, while he was serving as chief of the trial section in the State's Attorney's office in 1966, he had been "suspended from office for 4 months and referred to the grievance committee of Baltimore City for disciplinary action or perhaps disbarment." Howard's suspension from office (he was not disbarred) was based on public attacks he had made upon the City's alleged use of dual standards in the handling of rape cases.[45]

A further basis for the Maryland Bar Association's unqualified rating for Judge Howard had been his entering of two improper *ex parte* orders which were vacated by the Maryland

Court of Appeals in a controversial case between the State School Superintendent and the Baltimore City Board of School Administrators. In response to the charges regarding the unlawful *ex parte* orders, Howard was totally unrepentant:

> [I]t is my opinion that the decision I rendered, perhaps, was wrong or obviously was wrong legally, but it is one I think that was a result of my research and, again, I don't think there is anything I have to apologize for in that decision.[46]

Despite the grave doubts concerning Howard's qualifications and fitness that were so obviously presented by these facts, he was asked a total of two questions by the Judiciary Committee before it favorably reported on his nomination. He was then routinely confirmed by the Senate.

Numerous other Carter nominees were whisked through easy confirmation hearings despite dissents on the ABA Committee as to their qualified rating and other grounds for closer scrutiny. These included Veronica Wicker, nominated for the Eastern District of Louisiana, although 11 of her 13 years legal experience had been spent as a judge's law clerk;[47] Raul Ramirez, nominated for the Eastern District of California, who had only nine years experience as a lawyer (although two of them had been spent as a Municipal Court Judge in Sacramento[48]) and was only 35 years old; Alcee Hastings, whose subsequent criminal indictment and judicial misconduct charges revealed a striking lack of judicial temperament and propriety which somehow completely escaped detection during his nomination and confirmation procedures;[49] and Dorothy Nelson, who was nominated and confirmed for the Ninth Circuit Court of Appeals despite her minority Not Qualified rating and a near total lack of courtroom experience at either the trial or appellate level.[50]

Another noteworthy aspect of the Carter selection process was the almost complete absence of concern regarding length of legal experience before elevation to the federal bench. The point here is not so much the actual qualifications of the younger nominees—an ironclad rule against appointing judges whose abilities and accomplishments belie their relative youth would clearly be counterproductive—but again relates to the disparate approaches to this factor reflected during the Carter Era as opposed to the Reagan years.

Thus, when Carter nominated Myron Thompson to a federal district judgeship in Alabama, Thompson was only 33 years old and had been in practice for less than eight years. A good portion of his practice had been as a Legal Services Corporation activist and as a small town sole practitioner.[51] Despite some perfunctory inquiry as to the scope of his experience, there were no serious concerns expressed by any senators and he was easily and routinely confirmed.

Thompson's treatment stands in stark contrast to the exhaustive grilling of Reagan nominee J. Harvie Wilkinson by the Judiciary Committee. Wilkinson was 39 years old when nominated. Despite his superb credentials as a Supreme Court law clerk, a Deputy Assistant Attorney General of the United States, and a Full Professor of Law at the University of Virginia, Wilkinson's allegedly limited experience occasioned a lengthy onslaught of harsh criticism and opposition which nearly killed his nomination.[52]

This aspect of the double-standard was revealed explicitly by an ABA representative during the Wilkinson hearings. Referring to one of the reasons he had voted to find Wilkinson "not qualified," ABA Committee member Stewart Dunnings stated as follows:

> Also his admission to the bar did not comply with our rules, where we have announced that they should have at least 12 years.
>
> Now, we in the past, of course, have waived that, when you have an affirmative action candidate—and certainly he [i.e., Wilkinson] did not fall within that category.[53]

In short, the ABA had an established policy of applying one standard of qualification for "affirmative action" nominees— i.e., they waived the minimum experience requirement altogether—and another, more stringent standard for white male nominees. This double-standard enabled President Carter to obtain routine, rubber-stamp confirmation of many nominees whose limited experience would have elicited harsh opposition under the more exacting standards applied to the nominees of the Reagan era.

IDEOLOGICAL SCRUTINY

In achieving his goal of placing as many minority and female judges as possible on the federal bench, President Carter inevitably appointed a disproportionate number of judges who had devoted much of their careers to achieving liberal policy objectives through the courts. The pool of experienced and prominent minority lawyers from which Carter drew most of his minority judges had gained much of that experience and prominence in pursuing the legal agenda of groups such as the NAACP, the NAACP Legal Defense Fund, and the National Lawyers Guild. Many of the female nominees had similarly been active in the various causes of feminist and civil liberties groups. Carter's white male appointees also included longstanding liberal activists, such as former Illinois Congressman Abner J. Mikva.

The nomination of so many liberal activists to the bench raised obvious questions regarding the principles of restraint and impartiality which are critical to the integrity of the federal courts. Yet review of the Judiciary Committee hearing records reveals that nominees with activist backgrounds that raised genuine questions in this regard were asked nothing whatsoever about the issue; indeed, in many cases they were asked no genuine questions at all. Frequently, a nominee's background as a committed liberal-activist was the chief accolade on his record, and the probable basis for his nomination.[54]

However, the rare Carter nominee who displayed signs of independence from the prevailing norms of liberal orthodoxy would be subjected to harsh criticism and probing scrutiny before the Judiciary Committee. One such nominee was Cornelia G. Kennedy, undoubtedly one of the most outstanding appointments of the Carter administration. Kennedy was nominated for the Sixth Circuit Court of Appeals, having already served with distinction as a federal district judge in Michigan since 1970 (where she was Chief Judge). She was rated "well qualified" by ABA Committee[55], and her prompt and enthusiastic confirmation would have seemed assured.

But under the strangely skewed standards of the Carter Era, Judge Kennedy was subjected to a prolonged and bitter confirmation challenge foreshadowing what was to occur more frequently during the Reagan years. Ultra-liberal Congressman John Conyers (D-MI), the NAACP Legal Defense Fund, and other liberal luminaries were allowed to orchestrate a prolonged ideological assault on Judge Kennedy's record which seriously endangered and delayed her confirmation.[56] The chief source of opposition was the fact that Judge Kennedy's judicial decisions were not satisfactory to the NAACP Legal Defense Fund in race discrimination cases, *pro se* prisoners' complaints, and cases alleging police misconduct.[57] Her admirable adherence to the Federal Rules of Civil Procedure in dismissing frivolous and contrived cases was also roundly criticized as improper preoccupation with legal "technicalities." The Democratic-controlled Judiciary Committee found these criticisms so disturbing that it was considered necessary to secure the opinions of some 24 legal experts and groups, naturally including representatives of the ACLU and the Federation of Women Lawyers Panel.[58] Having first appeared before the Committee on July 18, 1979, Judge Kennedy was required to return nearly two months later to confront the liberal assault on her superb record.

Although Kennedy's nomination was ultimately reported out of the Judiciary Committee and confirmed by the Senate, her ordeal serves as graphic testimony to the ideological bias of the Carter Era. Nominees whose credentials and accomplishments paled in comparison to Judge Kennedy's were swiftly and compliantly confirmed amid inflated testimonials to their records as civil libertarians or civil rights activists. But a truly seasoned and accomplished jurist such as Judge Kennedy saw her confirmation placed in serious jeopardy because of her principled adherence to judicial restraint. Rarely, if ever, have considerations of raw partisanship and ideological prejudice so thoroughly dominated and distorted the judicial selection and confirmation process.

CONCLUSIONS

The judicial selection and confirmation process of the Carter Era was structured at every stage to satisfy the political, ideological, and special constituency objectives of those who designed and dominated it.

151

President Carter himself set the prevailing theme with his blunt declaration that a substantial portion of federal judgeships would be flatly allocated on the basis of race, gender, or ethnicity. And they were.

The Carter nominating commissions, proclaimed to be the instrument of bipartisan and merit-based selection, were instead dominated by both political and ideological partisanship of extraordinary dimensions. Ideological "litmus tests", now falsely ascribed to the Reagan Justice Department, were the *modus operandi* of the Carter process.

Traditional standards of qualification were bent, and sometimes broken, to assure the achievement of Jimmy Carter's affirmative action plan for the federal bench. Overwhelmingly negative ABA ratings, which would have conclusively doomed a conservative nominee of the Reagan era, were simply disregarded. And the ABA itself later acknowledged that it "waived" minimal experience standards applied to other nominees to accommodate affirmative action appointments.

Those who have devoted themselves to assaulting the integrity of President Reagan's judicial selection process—and those who have defended it as well—would do well to ponder the precedents of the Carter Era to enlarge their frame of reference. The validity and necessity of Reagan's search for sound strict constructionists and proponents of judicial restraint can only be appreciated in its historical context. Jimmy Carter and his liberal constituencies radically restructured the procedures and standards of judicial selection to pack the federal bench with judges who would perpetuate and expand the orthodoxies of liberal activism.

Ronald Reagan's fundamental opposition to those same orthodoxies was a central and well-understood component of the program which was overwhelmingly endorsed by the electorate in his two landslide elections. His democratic mandate lends full legitimacy to a policy of selecting judges whose commitment to judicial restraint will ameliorate the excess of the activists appointed by his vanquished predecessor. In attempting to achieve that end, however, the Reagan Administration has stopped far short of the crude methods employed by the Carter administration to achieve *its* ideological agenda for the courts. In a very significant sense, Reagan's judicial selection process has demonstrated the very kind of restraint and prudence he seeks in his judges.

It is high time for these realities to be recognized.

REFERENCES

Judicial Qualifications and Confirmation: The Carter Years by George C. Smith

1. "Manion given a Bum Rap, Backers Say," Los Angeles *Times*, July 13, 1986, pp.17-18. [Editor's note: The views expressed in Mr. Smith's article are solely those of the author, and do not reflect the views of any member of the Senate Judiciary Committee.]
2. *Id.* p. 18. Dean Arthur N. Frakt of Loyola Law School in Los Angeles signed the deans' letter "based on materials sent by a law professor and a liberal activist in Washington," according to this *LA Times* report. Frakt later confessed to "feeling a little sheepish" about being roped-in. *Id.*
3. *See, e.g.*, "Senators turn down Sessions for bench," Washington *Times*, June 6, 1986, pp. A1, A8. Among the chief grounds for the Senate's rejection of Jefferson Sessions III for an Alabama federal district judgeship was his perfectly legitimate criticism of such liberal sacred cows as the NAACP and ACLU.
4. For a full summary of the Claiborne impeachment, See *Congressional Quarterly*, Vol. 44, No. 41, Oct. 11, 1986, pp. 2568-2570. For the facts on the Judicial Conference recommendation that Judge Hastings be considered for impeachment by the House, see "Congress Asked to Consider Impeachment of U.S. Judge," *Congressional Quarterly*, March 21, 1987, pp. 528-29.
5. See text accompanying notes 26-32, *infra*.
6. L. Berkson and S. Carbon, *The United States Circuit Judges Nominating Commission: Its Members, Procedures, and Candidates*, p. 1 (1980) (hereafter cited as "Berkson & Carbon").
7. Abraham, *Judicial Process*, 5th Edition, Oxford University Press, Ch. 2, pp. 31-32 (1986).
8. S. Goldman, "Reagan's Second Term Judicial Appointments: the Battle at Midway", *Judicature*, April/May 1987, pp. 325, 328 (Table 1), 331 (Table 3).
9. *See* Abraham, *supra* n. 7. President Carter refused to nominate a judge for the U.S. District Court in Virginia until the District Nominating Commission produced a black nominee. He insisted on the nomination of a black candidate who was not selected as among the best qualified by the District Judge Nominating Commission. Hearings before the Senate Judiciary Committee, 96th Cong., 2d Sess., Serial No. 96-21, Part 8, pp.3-5 (Aug. 26, 1980, pp. 3-5) (remarks of Sen. Byrd).
10. See text accompanying notes 26-32, *infra*.
11. Berkson & Carbon, *supra* n. 6, pp. 97-99.
12. Fein, "The Silent Minorities?", *National Law Journal*, Jan. 12, 1981, p. 15.
13. Berkson & Carbon, pp. 97-99.
14. *Id.*, pp. 46, 98, 162-63.
15. *Id.*, pp. 162-63.
16. 1987 DOJ Auth. Hearings, *supra* n. 9, pp. 22-27 (questioning of Attorney General Edwin Meese III by Senator Joseph Biden).
17. The ABA Standing Committee's signal that it would likely give "not qualified" ratings to distinguished conservative law professors Lino Graglia of Texas and William Harvey of Indiana effectively killed their proposed nominations to U.S. Court of Appeals posts. Graglia's conservative positions on forced busing and Harvey's criticisms of abuses at the Legal Services Corporation have been widely cited as influencing the ABA's negative ratings. See "ABA Judge-Screening Panel Criticized," Washington *Post*, Dec. 24, 1985, p. A13.

18. Hearings before the Senate Judiciary Committee, 96th Cong., 1st Sess., Serial No. 96-21, Part 3, pp. 1, 3-4 (July 13, 1979).
19. *Id.*, Part 4, p. 319 (Sept. 6, 1979).
20. Senate Judiciary Committee Hearings, *supra* n. 18, pp.1,4.
21. Senate Judiciary Committee Hearings, 96th Cong., 1st. Sess., Serial No. 96-21, Part 6, p. 1 (Apr. 21, 1980).
22. See text accompanying notes 26-32, *infra.*
23. E.g., the confirmation hearings on Alex Kozinski (9th Circuit), Daniel Manion (7th Circuit), and Jefferson Sessions III (District Court, Alabama, not confirmed). See n. 3, *supra.*
24. Goldman, *supra* n. 8, p. 328, Table 1.
25. See n. 17, *supra.*
26. Senate Judiciary Committee Hearings, *supra* n. 21, p. 164, 202 (May 19, 1980).
27. *Id.*, pp. 180-203; 267-318.
28. *Id.*, pp. 267-68.
29. *Id.*, pp. 184, 335-36, 452.
30. *Id.*, pp. 194-95, 405-06.
31. *Id.*, p. 527. The ABA Committee originally voted Mr. Gray "not qualified" by a margin of 12-1. *Id.*, p. 528.
32. *Id.*, pp. 525-803.
33. Hearings before the Senate Judiciary Committee, 96th Cong., 2d Sess., Serial No. 96-21, Part 6, p. 71 (May 15, 1980).
34. *Id.*, p. 93.
35. *Id.*, pp. 78-79.
36. Senate Judiciary Committee Hearings, 96th Cong., 1st Sess., Serial No. 96-21, Part 4, p. 436 (Sept. 21, 1979).
37. *Id.*
38. H. R. Rep. No. 3123, House Committee on Un-American Activities, Sept. 21, 1950.
39. Senate Judiciary Committee Hearings, *supra* n. 36, pp. 467-71.
40. *Id.*, p. 471.
41. *Id.*, p. 470.
42. *ACLU v. City of Birmingham,* 588 F. Supp. 1337 (E. D. Mich. 1984), *aff'd.,* 791 F. 2d 1561 (6th Cir. 1986), *cert. denied,* U.S. (1987).
43. Senate Judiciary Committee Hearings, 96th Cong., 1st. Sess., Serial No. 96-21, Part 4, p. 368 (Sept. 20, 1979).
44. *Id.*
45. *Id.*, pp. 368-69.
46. *Id.*, p. 370.
47. Senate Judiciary Committee Hearings, *supra* n. 18, pp. 240, 251-53, 270 (July 23, 1979).
48. Senate Judiciary Committee Hearings, *supra* n. 33, pp. 41-45, 55 (May 1, 1980).
49. Senate Judiciary Committee Hearings, *supra* n. 36, pp. 457, 463-64 (Oct. 17, 1979).
50. Senate Judiciary Committee Hearings, 96th Cong., 1st Sess., Serial No. 96-21, Part 5, pp. 259, 265-66 (Dec. 12, 1979).
51. Senate Judiciary Committee Hearings, 96th Cong., 2d Sess., Serial No. 96-21, Part 8, pp. 149-58 (Sept. 22, 1980).
52. Senate Judiciary Committee Hearings, 98th Cong., 2d Sess., Serial No. 98-372, Part 3, pp. 5, 70, 225-417 (Feb. 22 and Aug. 7, 1984).
53. *Id.*, p. 352.
54. *See, e.g.,* the hearings on the nomination of NAACP General Counsel Nathaniel R. Jones for the Sixth Circuit Court of Appeals. Senate Judiciary Committee Hearings, 96th Cong., 1st Sess., Serial No. 96-21, Part 4, pp. 421-439 (Sept. 21, 1979).
55. Senate Judiciary Committee Hearings, 96th Cong. 1st. Sess., Serial No. 96-21, Part 3, p. 36 (July 18, 1979).
56. *Id.*, pp. 43-132.
57. *Id.*, pp. 43-94, 99-102.
58. *Id.*, Part 4, pp. 1-2 (Sept. 6, 1979).

7

QUALIFICATIONS AND CONFIRMATION OF REAGAN'S JUDGES

by Peter J. Ferrara

Liberal critics of President Ronald Reagan's judicial appointments have pressed their attack under the cover of concern over the qualifications and quality of the President's judicial nominations. They have contended that the Reagan Administration measures prospective judicial nominees on the basis of various ideological litmus tests, sacrificing quality for philosophical purity.

But the evidence demonstrates that Reagan's judicial appointments have been at least as well qualified as those from President Jimmy Carter and other recent Presidents before him. Indeed, a number of Carter judges have been cited for misconduct, but this has not been true of a single Reagan judicial appointee. Moreover, while the Reagan Administration has carefully chosen nominees who reflect the President's philosophy of judicial restraint, no litmus tests automatically disqualifying a candidate have been used in the selection process. During the Carter Administration, by contrast, strict ideological litmus tests were used, irretrievably disqualifying candidates who failed to toe the line on a number of issues.

BACKGROUND OF REAGAN'S JUDICIAL APPOINTEES

Through 1986, 38 percent of Reagan's appointees to the federal district courts were already judges at the time of appointment, higher than for Presidents Ford, Nixon or Johnson. In addition, 77 percent had prior experience as a judge or prosecutor, higher than for all recent Presidents back to Johnson, including Carter.[1] Of Carter's district court appointees, 72 percent had prior judicial or prosecutorial experience, and 45 percent were judges at the time of appointment.[2] Noting the increasing numbers of district court appointees during Reagan's second term with judicial or prosecutorial experience, University of Massachusetts Political Science Professor Sheldon Goldman, one of the nation's foremost authorities on judicial selection, states:

> If we consider previous judicial or prosecutorial experience significant preparation for a federal district judgeship, then the second term Reagan appointees were the best prepared group of appointees of all the administrations surveyed.[3]

Almost all remaining Reagan district court appointees were in private practice with considerable trial experience when appointed, amounting to virtually the same proportion of district court appointees with such experience named by Carter.[4]

Among Reagan's circuit court appointees, 51 percent were already judges when appointed, and 57 percent had judicial experience, higher in both instances than for the appointees of Carter and similar to the appointees of Nixon.[5] Another 21 percent of Reagan's circuit court appointments were law professors, uniformly recognized as among the best legal minds in the country, including Antonin Scalia, Robert Bork, Richard Posner, Frank Easterbrook and Ralph Winter.[6] Appointments from academia, where individuals study and teach the broader aspects of the law, are particularly appropriate for the circuit courts which are charged with the responsibility to consider issues of law and are not involved in the district court's fact finding process. The percentage of Reagan appointees who were professors is substantially higher than for the appointees of Presidents Carter (14 percent), Ford (0 percent), Nixon (2 percent) or Johnson (3 percent).[7] Almost all of the rest of Reagan's circuit court appointees were in private practice when appointed.[8]

As for Reagan's Supreme Court appointments, William Rehnquist, promoted to Chief Justice, already had 15 years experience on the Court. Antonin Scalia was serving as a circuit court judge at the time of his Supreme Court appointment, after a highly distinguished academic career. Sandra Day O'Connor was an Arizona state judge when appointed as the first woman ever to serve on the Supreme Court. Justice O'Connor had reportedly finished second only to William Rehnquist in her law school class at Stanford.

Overall, therefore, Reagan's judicial appointments have solid legal backgrounds quite similar to the appointees of previous Presidents. Indeed, Goldman states in regard to Reagan's judicial appointments,

> Again, with few exceptions, appointees to both the district and appeals courts have been men and women of accomplishment, and although there are some distinctive differences in the attribute profile of the second term appointees compared to those from the first term, they generally compare favorably with the appointments of previous administrations.[9]

Similarly, former ABA President William Falsgraf states concerning Reagan's judicial appointments, "Ideology is always a factor for a President. Putting that aside, the appointments have been of the highest caliber."[10]

Besides appointing the first woman Supreme Court Justice, Reagan has appointed 20 women to the district court bench, five times the total appointed to such courts by Ford, Nixon and Johnson combined in a period twice as long.[11] Reagan has also appointed four women to the circuit courts, compared to one for Ford, Nixon and Johnson combined.[12] Reagan has named 11 Hispanics to the district courts, compared to six for Ford, Nixon and Johnson combined.[13] One Hispanic and one black have been appointed by Reagan to the circuit courts, compared to no Hispanics and two blacks for Ford, Nixon and Johnson combined.[14] While Reagan has appointed four blacks to district court judgeships, however, Ford, Nixon and Johnson together appointed 14, accounting for a higher percentage of the total district court appointments of each.[15]

Carter appointed many more women, blacks and Hispanics than Reagan, but his Administration openly used racial and sexual quotas and preferences, which Reagan has quite properly refused to do. The Reagan Administration has adhered closely to the principle of choosing the best candidate regardless of race or sex.

Catholics have comprised a much higher percentage of Reagan's district court appointees (30 percent) than of the appointees of other recent Republican presidents, even exceeding the proportion of Catholics among Carter's appointees (28 percent) and roughly equaling the proportion among Johnson's appointees (31 percent).[16] Over a third (37 percent) of Reagan's circuit court appointees were Catholic, substantially more than for the appointees of Carter, Nixon or Johnson.[17] Jewish lawyers have also been more heavily represented among Reagan's judicial appointments than among those of other Republican presidents. During Reagan's second term, the proportion of appointees who were Jewish has been equivalent to the proportion in recent Democratic administrations.[18]

QUALIFICATIONS RATINGS

Reagan's judicial nominees are often assailed on the basis of qualifications ratings by the Standing Committee on the Federal Judiciary of the American Bar Association ("ABA").[19] But Reagan's nominees overall score as well on such ratings as those of Carter and other recent Presidents.

The ABA Committee rates each judicial nominee in one of four categories: Exceptionally Well Qualified, Well Qualified, Qualified and Unqualified. The ABA defines a rating of Qualified as certifying that the nominee would be able "to perform satisfactorily as a federal judge with respect to competence, integrity, and temperament."[20]

Through 1986, 52 percent of Reagan's district court appointments were rated Exceptionally Well Qualified or Well Qualified, a higher percentage than for Carter, Ford, Nixon or Johnson.[21] At the highest rating—Exceptionally Well Qualified—Reagan also bested Carter, Ford and Nixon.[22] The ABA ratings of Reagan district court appointees have also shown an improving trend, with 54 percent during the second term receiving one of the top two ratings compared to 50 percent during the first term.[23] Sheldon Goldman states concerning Reagan's district court appointees:

> If the top two ratings are combined, and if the ABA ratings are considered a rough measure of "quality", the second term appointees can be seen as marginally surpassing the first term appointees, as well as surpassing the appointees of Carter, Ford, Nixon and Johnson. Assuming that the ABA ratings are a reasonably accurate assessment of the credentials of appointees, the second term appointments, on the whole, may well turn out to be the most professionally qualified group of appointees over the past two decades.[24]

Among Reagan's Circuit Court appointments, 56 percent have been rated Exceptionally Well Qualified or Well Qualified.[25] The percentage rated Exceptionally Well Qualified (16 percent) is virtually the same as the percentages for Presidents Carter, Ford and Nixon.[26] But significantly more Reagan circuit court appointees have been rated Qualified rather than Well Qualified compared to previous Presidents. This is explained, however, by certain biases in the ABA rating system, recognized by Sheldon Goldman and others, which lead the ABA ratings to seriously understate the quality of Reagan's Circuit Court appointments.[27]

First, the ABA ratings are heavily weighted to favor those with experience in private practice, giving much less weight to high quality academic work. As a result, the top notch academics appointed by Reagan—such as Scalia, Posner, Easterbrook, and Winter—have generally only received ratings of Qualified. Yet, these appointees are recognized by all as judicial stars because of their outstanding legal minds and abilities. If the ABA ratings reflected the abilities of such appointees as actual jurists, the ratings of most of the 20 percent of Reagan's circuit court appointees who were academics would shift from Qualified to Well Qualified or Exceptionally Well Qualified. Greater emphasis on trial experience makes more sense for District Court appointees, who spend their time conducting trials, but the abilities of top scholars are probably more valuable for appellate judgeships, where the emphasis is on legal reasoning in applying the law and resolving conflicts.

Secondly, the ABA has traditionally disfavored younger appointees. A recent study concluded in fact that age was one of the factors most strongly correlated with higher ABA judicial ratings.[28] Reagan has named a number of unusually young circuit court judges, such as Alex Kozinski and Kenneth Starr, who are widely recognized as among the most brilliant circuit court jurists. If the ABA ratings had reflected the true abilities of these appointees, as appellate judges, then most would again have been rated at least Well Qualified.

If we combine all of Reagan's appointments to the district and circuit courts, we find that the percentage of Reagan's appointees rated Exceptionally Well Qualified or Well Qualified (53 percent) is in the middle of the range of such percentages for Carter (56 percent), Ford (50 percent), Nixon (51 percent) and Johnson (53 percent).[29] Moreover, three Carter appointees and four Johnson appointees were rated Not Qualified.[30] By contrast, not a single Reagan appointee was so rated. If we calculate a weighted average of ABA ratings, with 3 points for Exceptionally Well Qualified, 2 points for Well Qualified, 1 point for Qualified, and no points for Not Qualified, Reagan's and Carter's district and circuit appointees score an identical average of 1.6.[31] The average for Nixon's and Johnson's appointees would also each be 1.6, with Ford's at 1.5.[32]

Consequently, the ABA ratings for Reagan's appointees overall are remarkably similar to the ratings for the appointees of other recent Administrations. If Reagan's unusually large proportion of top scholars and young but brilliant circuit court appointees had received ratings reflecting their true abilities, Reagan would probably have a better overall record on ABA ratings than any recent President (even if similar ratings adjustments were made for the appointees of such Presidents).

It is noteworthy that, in contrast to the biases which led the ABA ratings to understate the quality of Reagan's appointees, members of the ABA judicial rating committee during the Carter years have effectively admitted that they relaxed their standards during that time to grant higher ratings than otherwise to Carter's numerous female, black and Hispanic appointees. The committee Chairman for 1978–1980, Robert Raven, has stated concerning the ABA ratings for Carter's judges,

> Judge Bell [Carter's Attorney General] made it clear that he and the President had an affirmative action program. We'd like to think that we apply the same standards consistently, but I think that we have stretched a little, giving the benefit of the doubt with regard to minorities and women. Not a lot, but a little . . . No points are given for race or sex . . . We'll look for trial equivalent a little harder in women, for example, than we would in white males.[33]

Brooksley Born, who served on the ABA committee during the Carter years and became chairman after Raven, also states concerning the rating of Carter's judges,

We were quite concerned about criteria not having been met by women and/or minorities because of the realities of professional discrimination . . . There were a number of women and minority candidates that we found 'qualified' despite the lack of 12 years at the bar. Less experience was sufficient in some women, but not in some white males.[34]

Born in fact relates that the Carter Administration lobbied the committee for favorable ratings for minority judicial nominees, through secret back door discussions. In some instances, the Carter Administration was able to get the committee to change an initially unfavorable rating to a qualified rating. Born states:

There have been instances, particularly on minority candidates and women, where there was much interaction with the attorney general and the White House. Much of the discussion focused on how standards should be applied, and we discussed standards in rather general terms. On one case, the attorney general asked for a reconsideration. We did a new investigation and got a new rating of 'qualified'.[35]

This relaxation of standards for Carter's appointees makes Reagan's record on ABA judicial appointment ratings look even better.

Some have suggested that a high number of Reagan's judges have been voted Not Qualified by a minority of the ABA judicial rating committee, even though a majority of the committee found the candidate qualified in each case. It clearly makes no sense to trumpet the view of a Committee minority which may be as small as one member when a majority has found otherwise, as the ABA itself points out regularly. In any event, the charge is not true. A minority of the ABA judicial committee voted 22 of Carter's appointees Not Qualified, and a majority voted three others Not Qualified.[36] During Reagan's initial six years, a 50 percent longer period, a minority of the Committee voted 23 Reagan appointees Not Qualified, with no Reagan appointee designated Not Qualified by a majority.[37]

Moreover, Goldman suggests that the ABA biases appear to be at work again in the Not Qualified votes for some Reagan appointees cast by a minority of the ABA committee.[38] He notes that in Reagan's second term, four out of the five circuit court appointees who were law professors when named were voted

161

Not Qualified by a committee minority.[39] He also notes that in Reagan's second term all five of the circuit court appointees under 40, and half the district court appointees below that age, were voted Not Qualified by a committee minority.[40]

The heavy reliance on ABA ratings by liberal critics of Reagan's judicial appointees is not only misplaced, because Reagan's appointees overall score well on such ratings, but also quite ironic. For during the Carter years, liberals blasted the ABA committee as a flawed source of judicial quality ratings.

For example, Charles Halpern of the liberal Judicial Selection Project testified before the Senate Judiciary Committee in January 1979 stating in regard to the ABA judicial committee and its ratings,

> We object . . . to the quasi-official status that is sometimes given to that committee and to its recommendations . . . We were troubled by the testimony of Attorney General Bell which seemed to think that the success of a judicial selection process could be measured by how many of the names submitted to the Senate have been [given a] very well qualified or exceptionally well qualified ABA imprimatur.[41]

Senator Patrick Leahy (D-Va.) echoed similar sentiments during the same hearing, stating:

> [W]ith all due respect to the American Bar Association, there have been some . . . who have suggested that their very significant role in determining the qualifications of judges has been on some occasions like Jack the Ripper determining the qualifications of surgeons in 18th century England.[42]

Liberals during the Carter years also applauded the head of the predominantly black National Bar Association when he said,

> Blacks have long suspected the ABA's rating of blacks has not been fair and is used primarily as a tool for maintaining segregated courts and for keeping strong black civil rights lawyers from becoming federal judges.[43]

In probably the most valid point of his political career, Senator Howard Metzenbaum (D-OH) harshly criticized the ABA practice of having one judicial committee member for each circuit with the sole responsibility for conducting investigations of all nominees from that circuit. In Metzenbaum's view, this left

too much of an opportunity for personal or ideological animosi-
ties or biases held by a single committee member to influence the
rating of a candidate. Metzenbaum stated during a Senate Judiciary Committee hearing:

> One person from each circuit. That one person really does all of this
> investigation . . . That one individual talks to everybody and then writes
> up the report. If that person has a preconceived idea, isn't there an ele-
> ment of subjectivity in that person, in that kind of an investigation?
> Don't we all hear what we want to hear and reject that which we don't
> want to hear? How do you assure yourself that the individual that has
> all the limitations that each of us has doesn't inject into the matter his
> own reaction as a practicing lawyer? . . . How do you protect yourself
> against that?
>
> I must tell you that I practiced law all the time until I came to this body .
> . . To this moment I haven't the slightest idea of who the individual is,
> nor did I ever know who the individual was that represented the Ameri-
> can Bar Association in the circuit in which I lived.[44]

With this climate of hostility towards the ABA and its ratings,
the Senate was willing to confirm relatively easily three Carter
nominees rated Not Qualified. The ABA judicial rating committee was consequently said to have fallen during the Carter administration to the lowest point of respect and influence in many
years.[45]

THE MANION CONTROVERSY

The Judges War has centered around particular Reagan judicial nominees who were challenged as unqualified. The bitterest
and most controversial was the nomination of Daniel A. Manion to the Seventh U.S. Circuit Court of Appeals.

In reviewing the facts, however, it is hard to fathom exactly
what the objection to Manion was. After serving in Vietnam,
Manion attended the University of Indiana Law School, graduating in 1973. Thereafter, he served as a Deputy Attorney General for the state of Indiana, where he dealt primarily with appeals of criminal cases. He was later elected to the Indiana state
Senate, where he served on the Judiciary Committee. After four
years, a bout with multiple sclerosis forced him to leave public
service, but he later recovered from the disease.

At the time Reagan nominated him to the Seventh Circuit, Manion was practicing law in a small law firm in South Bend, Indiana, with a total of 13 years litigation experience. He had personally tried 35 cases before a jury, a total matched by few of his critics. The ABA gave him a rating of Qualified. He was the first Vietnam veteran ever appointed to a federal appeals court.

Manion's critics were confounded by the broad base of support for his nomination by those who knew him in Indiana. The high profile liberal and former Chairman of the U.S. Civil Rights Commission, Father Theodore Hesburgh, President of the University of Notre Dame, had known Manion since childhood. Hesburgh wrote in a letter to Senator Quayle concerning Manion's nomination, "I strongly believe that he would serve this country and the Seventh Circuit extremely well if his nomination were approved."[46] Manion received similar endorsements from liberal Democratic state senators who served with him during his state senate terms, Democratic judges, activist liberal Democratic lawyers who had worked on cases with or against him, a Carter appointed U.S. Attorney, the Chairman of the Democratic party in his county, a former Democratic nominee for mayor of Indianapolis and leading attorney in the state, former liberal Democratic U.S. Senator Vance Hartke, and the Chief Justice of the Indiana Supreme Court, all of whom were personally familiar with him. Over 100 Democratic and Republican attorneys from his home county, more than one-fourth of all lawyers in the county, signed a petition supporting him as qualified for confirmation.

At the height of the Manion confirmation battle, the Los Angeles *Times* sent a reporter to Indiana to find out the real Manion story. The reporter found that Manion "receives surprisingly high marks from political foes and friends alike here in his home state for both his integrity and his legal talents."[47] He also reported that "Manion's defenders here—notably Democratic lawyers, judges, and former state Senate colleagues—insist that the amiable, soft-spoken South Bend attorney would be a credit to the Federal Appeals court."[48]

Manion's qualifications, in fact, seem analogous to those of Patricia Wald, appointed by Carter to the District of Columbia Circuit.[49] A graduate of Connecticut College and Yale Law School, Wald clerked for a D.C. Circuit judge for one year, was in private practice for one year, performed legal aid work for a D.C. Legal Service office for 3 years, and worked for 7 years in activities ranging from the Ford Foundation Project on Drug Abuse, the Center for Law and Social Policy and the Mental Health Law Project. At the time of her appointment to the D.C. Circuit, Wald was serving in her third year as the Assistant U.S. Attorney General for Legislative Affairs. She was rated Qualified by the ABA.

While Wald is as liberal as Manion is conservative, she was confirmed by the Senate without controversy. This comparison is not meant to disparage Wald's qualifications and background, which exhibit intelligence, talent and devotion to public service. Rather, it is intended to further illuminate the relative status of Manion's qualifications.

So what was the complaint against Manion? Believe it or not, critics complained that Manion had only received a rating of Qualified from the ABA, which they termed "the lowest passing grade." *But almost half the Federal judges appointed in the past two decades had received the same rating, including such acknowledged judicial stars as Scalia, Posner and Easterbrook.* The President asked, "At what point was it that an ABA rating of 'qualified' became an impediment to nomination to the Federal bench."[50] Or as the Washington *Times* put it, "a rating of Qualified would seem to have meant that he was qualified, not just the opposite."[51] Moreover, the Senate did not blanche at confirming Carter and Johnson appointees who were rated Not Qualified.

Some critics, such as the Chicago Council of Lawyers[52] (an unofficial, non-bar group of about 1,000 lawyers), argued that Manion had limited experience in the federal courts, had never been the lead counsel in a federal trial, and had never tried a case involving constitutional law issues. But Manion had worked as counsel or co-counsel in twenty federal cases, including several fairly large and complex cases involving federal securities laws. At the time of his nomination, he was the lead counsel in three cases in federal court. Moreover, his 35 jury trials is quite substantial, and whether they were tried in state or Federal courts makes little difference. Lawyers often bring cases in state rather than federal court if they believe that they will get a more favorable hearing there.

Manion also dealt with constitutional law issues during his days as Deputy Attorney General for Indiana, where he specialized in criminal law cases which routinely present such issues. In any event, only a small minority of lawyers have personally tried a constitutional law case in the federal courts. Lawyers specializing in corporate, tax, securities or regulatory advice, for example, never even go into court. Others, with a less commercial practice, generally deal with nonconstitutional issues in state courts, such as personal injury work. Even full time litigators in federal cases will tend to specialize in one of many areas not involving constitutional law. As the Justice Department argued, "It would be an insult to the qualifications of thousands of lawyers to suggest that only attorneys whose experience has been constitutional litigation in federal courts are fit to hold federal judgeships."[53] Indeed, most federal judges probably never personally tried a constitutional law case in federal court.

Some, incredibly, disparaged Manion's experience as involving a rural, small town practice. Manion's defenders argued properly that a judge from a primarily rural, state court background would bring balance and perspective to the circuit court, particularly in the Seventh Circuit which covers many rural areas. Judge Wilbur Pell, whom Manion replaced, had come from a rural practice similar to Manion's, and he was the only such judge on the Seventh Circuit. The other judges all had academic or urban corporate practice backgrounds. It would also be inappropriate to suggest, as Manion's critics seemed to do, that rural lawyers from small firms should be barred from serving on the federal courts.

Closer to the real reason for the controversy over Manion was the fact that his father, the Dean of the Notre Dame Law School and a senior official in the Eisenhower Administration, was a founding member of the John Birch Society. For a few years before completing law school, Dan Manion appeared frequently with his father on the elder Manion's nationally syndicated radio program. Many times, Dan Manion acted as a host or interrogator, while his father presented the substantive commentary. But the younger Manion never joined the John Birch Society, and while on a few occasions he generally praised some of his father's associates, he never endorsed or advocated any of the extremist views of the organization or its affiliates. He would never have received the endorsement of the ABA or the many liberal Democrats who knew him if he had.

Kenneth P. Feder, Chairman of the Democratic Committee in Manion's county, in fact told the Los Angles *Times* that he thought that "Manion is a victim of guilt by association: People figure that he is the strident ideologue his father was."[54] Frank L. O'Bannon, Democratic leader of the Indiana state Senate, also told the *Times* that "Manion pleasantly surprised him as 'not radical or strident, but very kind and quiet and almost gentle...a good listener, though very firm in his conservative convictions.'"[55]

Nevertheless, despite Manion's sound qualifications, the strong praise even from partisan opponents who knew him, and the lack of any serious charge against him, Illinois Senator Paul Simon said of him, "All I can say is, this kind of guy shouldn't be a judge in a rural county, much less on the second highest court in the land."[56] Delaware Senator Joe Biden was moved by the brutal force of the facts to say to Manion in a Senate Judiciary Committee hearing, "I think you are a decent and honorable man, but I do not think I can vote for you because of your political views."[57]

But as the President said in response to Biden, "I believe the Senate should consider only a nominee's qualifications and character, not his 'political views'."[58] Or as the *Washington Times* put it,

> If Mr. Manion is a decent and honorable man and has been examined and found suitable by the ABA and is the choice of the president, what's the objection to him? That he's not Cardozo or Holmes?
>
> Ideology is the objection—ideology and petty partisanship. He should be confirmed and the opposition ashamed.[59]

This was the real story behind the entire controversy. Manion's political views and judicial philosophy were conservative, vintage Reagan, and liberals in the Senate did not like it. They wanted to draw the line and send a message to the President that they wouldn't accept any further appointments of solidly conservative judges. Disgracefully, these opponents engaged in character assassination and phony demonization to achieve their objectives. In the end, 49 senators voted against

Manion on the basis of these flimsy charges.

Similar, though less extreme, abuse victimized other Reagan judicial nominees. Alex Kozinski was appointed to the Ninth Circuit Court of Appeals at the admittedly young age of 34. Kozinsky was widely acknowledged as a brilliant legal anayst, having finished first in his class at UCLA Law School. He had clerked for the Chief Justice of the U.S. Supreme Court, and when nominated already had served for two years as chief judge for the U.S. Court of Claims. Kozinski was rated Qualified by the ABA Committee, with some dissenters. The charge against him, incredibly, was that as special counsel to the Merit Systems Protection Board he was too strict in correcting and editing the writing of his subordinates, which supposedly exhibited a lack of judicial temperament. This was in sharp contrast to some of the complaints against Manion and his writing.

The confirmation process, as well as the character and qualifications of the nominees being considered, was radically different for a number of Carter judicial nominees who should have caused major controversies, but did not. As George Smith reports in Chapter 6, in 1978 Carter appointed Harry Claiborne as a District Court Judge in Nevada. He was confirmed with just 37 words in the *Congressional Record*. The clerk read his nomination, and he was approved without objection. In 1983, a federal grand jury indicted Clairborne on charges of bribery, obstruction of justice and mail fraud. In 1984, he was convicted of filing false income tax returns, thus becoming the first federal judge to be convicted of a felony while on the bench. Incredibly, Clairborne refused to resign, and continued to collect his judicial salary for almost three years while in jail, until Congress finally impeached and convicted him in late 1986.

Carter appointed Alcee Hastings as a U.S. District Judge for South Florida in 1979. The Senate Judiciary Committee asked him one question concerning recently enacted measures (which he opposed) for disciplining judicial misconduct. He was confirmed by unanimous consent. Within two years, Hastings had been indicted on charges of conspiracy, bribery, and obstruction of justice. The lawyer accused of bribing Hastings to influence a ruling was convicted. Hastings, however, was acquitted in a separate trial because the government did not have enough evidence to prove his guilt beyond a reasonable doubt. Two federal judges, unconvinced of his innocence, filed charges against him under the Federal Judicial Conduct Act. The Circuit Judicial Council and the Judicial Conference of the U.S. have now referred Hastings to Congress for impeachment.

Carter appointed U.W. Clemon as a District Judge for Alabama. Clemon was voted Not Qualified by the ABA Committee by a vote of 12–2. Clemon denied that any tax lien had ever been filed against him in answering a questionnaire for judicial nominees used by one of Carter's nominating commissions. But Federal and state tax liens had just recently been filed against him. After technically avoiding liability for speeding 97 mph because he was an Alabama state Senator on his way to a Senate session, he announced on the Senate floor he would do it again. Nevertheless, Clemon was confirmed.

As previously noted, two other Carter appointees with ratings of unqualified were similarly confirmed. Carter appointee Robert P. Aguilar was unanimously supported by the Senate Judiciary Committee after being asked just two friendly, irrelevant questions concerning his family and mutual acquaintances, even though he did not have a law degree.

Carter appointee Abner Mikva, a former U.S. Congressman, was also cited for judicial misconduct by a judicial conduct advisory panel, when he personally campaigned for contributions and membership for an ABA Committee committed to various liberal causes. When some opposed Mikva during his confirmation proceedings because of his sharply liberal views, Sen. Biden defended him. In sharp contrast to Biden's statement that he could not vote for Manion because of his political views, Biden said in support of Mikva,

> I frankly do not know how we could approve any member of the U.S. Senate, U.S. Congress, a member of any legislative body, or anyone who ever served in a policy decision, who has taken a position on any issue, if the rationale for disqualifying you is that you have taken strong positions. That is certainly not proof of your inability to be objective and avoid being a policymaker on the bench. If we take that attitude, we fundamentally change the basis in which we consider the appointment of persons to the bench.[60]

Similarly, Senator Kennedy, who voted against Manion, said in support of Mikva,

If strong political views were a disqualifying factor from serving on the Federal bench, then all of us here today—and every man and woman who has ever served in either House of Congress, or held a political office—would be disqualified . . . In my judgment, such a rule makes no sense at all.[61]

JUDICIAL SELECTION AND LITMUS TESTS

The Reagan Administration has a well organized, formal procedure for selecting judicial nominees. The Assistant Attorney General for the Office of Legal Policy has the lead responsibility, formerly working closely with the Special Counsel for Judicial Selection, who was on the Attorney General's personal staff. Now, these duties are performed by a Deputy Assistant Attorney General in the Office of Legal Policy. These officials collect recommendations for judicial openings from Senators, the White House staff, Justice Department officials, and other sources. Each prospective nominee is interviewed extensively by several Justice Department officials, sometimes totaling six hours of interviews altogether. The nominee's published works, judicial decisions, or public speeches are also scrutinized.

The Department of Justice Judicial Selection Working Group, composed of the Attorney General, Deputy Attorney General, and other leading judicial selection officials within the Department, then meets to choose a nominee for each judicial opening. This individual is then recommended by the Justice Department Working Group to the President's Committee on Federal Judicial Selection, which includes the White House Counsel, Assistant to the President for Personnel, Assistant to the President for Legislative Affairs, White House Chief of Staff, Attorney General, Deputy Attorney General, Associate Attorney General, and Assistant Attorney General for Legal Policy. After a further investigation of the prospective nominee by the White House personnel office, the Committee decides whether to recommend the candidate's nomination to the President. If the Committee decides to proceed with the candidate, his name is referred to the FBI for a background investigation and to the ABA for a qualification rating. If no problems develop, the candidate is recommended to the President for nomination.

Administration critics have criticized the extensive Justice Department interviews as a procedure that allows the Administration to employ a litmus test by drawing out a candidate's position on specific issues, such as abortion, school prayer or racial quotas, and selecting candidates on the basis of such positions. But the Administration has a formal policy of not asking judicial candidates for their positions on specific issues or cases. The Administration rejects the idea that a candidate might be disqualified from serving on the federal bench because of his position on a single issue.

In the personal interviews, the Administration is seeking to determine the candidate's overall judicial philosophy, as well as whether his or her temperament and character are suitable for a federal judge. The Administration seeks judges who adhere to the philosophy of judicial restraint, which means applying the law as specified by the legislature or the Constitution, rather than ruling according to the judge's own policy preferences. The President has explained this philosophy:

> . . . the function of America's courts, including the highest court, is not to make laws for the American people, but to interpret the law. Judges in a democratic society should not use their appointed offices to impose their social or political views upon society—in our system of government this is the province of elected officials.[62]

For judges who follow this philosophy, their positions or views on specific issues would not matter. Indeed, the Justice Department states, "Candidates who evidence a desire to impose the Administration's policies from the bench without a warrant in the law are *not* selected."[63]

The extensive interviews conducted by the Administration for lifetime judicial appointments should not be surprising. Similarly extensive interviews lasting several hours or even a whole day are conducted for a non-tenured faculty position at a university, or for an associate attorney position with a law firm, or even for summer associate positions with firms for students. Given the thousands of interviews conducted with hundreds of candidates, if improper questions about specific issues were being asked on a routine basis, hard evidence of this practice would have come to light by now, *but there is no such evidence.*

In his latest article on judicial selection, Sheldon Goldman recognizes that the Reagan Administration in fact does not ask questions on specific policy issues or employ litmus tests in its judicial selection process. He states regarding such claims:

> Justice officials deeply resent this charge and there is no credible evidence to support it. Justice officials correctly believe it to be improper to question candidates as to how they would decide cases raising these matters. Rather, they are concerned with an individual's overall judicial philosophy and concept of the judicial role . . . It is a candidate's general philosophy, not how he or she will decide a particular issue, that is of principal concern.[64]

Judicial selection in the Carter Administration was quite different. Carter set up a U.S. Circuit Judge Nominating Commission, with a separate panel of commissioners in each circuit to help select circuit court nominees. He also strongly encouraged Senators to set up commissions in each state to help select circuit court nominees. He also strongly encouraged Senators to set up commissions in each state to help choose District Court appointees, which many Senators did. The Circuit or District Court commissions sent lists of recommended candidates for each position to the Justice Department, which then made final recommendations to Carter after input from the White House staff.

Carter loaded the Circuit Court commission panels with Democratic party and liberal activists, with almost half the members not lawyers. The same was true to a lesser extent of a number of the District Court nominating commissions set up by Democratic Senators.[65] Because neither Carter nor these commissioners believed in judicial restraint, they in effect expected their judicial appointees to impose their own views on issues from the bench regardless of the law. Consequently, they considered the candidate's views on specific issues to be very important, and often asked about such views. Candidates who did not support abortion, the ERA, or racial and sexual quotas, or display a solicitous attitude towards criminal defendants, or oppose the death penalty, could forget about being recommended by these liberal activist commissioners, who considered a liberal position on these issues to be a defining characteristic of a "decent person" and, therefore, reflective of judicial sensitivity.

These commissioners in effect employed litmus tests concerning these issues in their judicial selection, the same litmus tests employed by Carter Administration officials themselves in their own final selection of judicial appointees.

The practice of Carter's commissioners asking for views on specific issues was confirmed by a thorough study of the Carter judicial appointment process by the American Judicature Society. The study reported:

> applicants had often been asked questions about nine contemporary social issues . . . The four areas which received most attention were the Equal Rights Amendment, affirmative action, first amendment freedoms and defendants' rights. Candidates were also asked about abortion, capital punishment, busing, economic regulation, and a number of pending United States Supreme Court cases.[66]

The study found that 62 percent of those surveyed on Carter's circuit court commission panels thought such questions were proper.[67]

Columnist Edwin Yoder described the experience of a friend who was a state judge questioned by one of Carter's commission panels for a circuit court position. Yoder wrote,

> The panel asked no questions about his attitudes toward the judicial process, or tending to reveal judicial temperament. He was, however, asked for *personal* views on substantive questions: abortion, women's rights, 'state sovereignty' and the Bakke case.[68]

One commissioner, Peter Fish, openly defended the use of such questions in an extensive magazine article.[69]

Phyllis Schlafly summarized the Carter judicial selection process this way:

> President Carter . . . made his judicial appointments on the basis of an ideological litmus test plus a race/sex quota . . . Carter required all his judicial appointments to be liberal, pro-abortion, pro-feminist Democrats.[70]

CONCLUSION

On the basis of all available evidence, including several exhaustive studies, Reagan's judicial appointments have been at least as qualified as Carter's and those of other recent Presidents, if not more so. Controversies over particular nominees, upon examination, turn out to be exercises in character assassination. The exacting scrutiny recently applied to Reagan's judicial appointments is in marked contrast to the usually easy going, perfunctory confirmation of Carter appointees, including a few who have turned out to lack character, integrity or judgment. The Carter Administration, not the Reagan Administration, asked judicial candidates for their personal positions on specific issues and employed litmus tests.

The loudly expressed concern over the qualifications of Reagan's judges is a hypocritical sham. The real concern of these critics is that they object to the appointment of judges who will adhere to the philosophy of judicial restraint, because under such a philosophy the courts will not make liberal rulings on racial quotas, busing, criminal cases, establishment of religion, abortion and other issues. The ultimate judicial work product on these issues are what the battle is all about in the Judges War.

REFERENCES

Qualifications and Confirmation of Reagan's Judges by Peter J. Ferrara

1. Sheldon Goldman, "Reagan's Second Term Judicial Appointments: The Battle at Midway," *Judicature*, April–May, 1987 (hereinafter referred to as "Goldman, Reagan's Second Term Judicial Appointments,") Table 1.
2. *Id.*
3. *Id.*, p. 328. The Administrations surveyed were Reagan, Carter, Ford, Nixon, and Johnson.
4. *Id.*, Table 1. A total of 46 percent of Reagan's district court appointees were in private practice when appointed, compared to 47 percent for Carter, 44 percent for Ford, 58 percent for Nixon and 48 percent for Johnson.
5. *Id.*, Table 3. Of Carter's Circuit Court appointees, 46 percent were judges at the time of appointment and 54 percent had judicial experience.
6. *Id.* The percentage includes three appointees who had briefly left their teaching positions for private practice or public service before appointment, but who had longstanding and first rate academic careers beforehand, including Robert Bork, Douglas Ginsburg and Jay Harvie Wilkinson.
7. *Id.*
8. *Id.*
9. *Id.*, p. 338.
10. "Federal law gets a Reagan-Meese stamp", *U.S. News & World Report*, June 30, 1986, p. 22.
11. Goldman, Reagan's Second Term Judicial Appointments, Table 1.
12. *Id.*, Table 3.

13. *Id.*, Table 1.
14. *Id.*, Table 3.
15. *Id.*, Table 1.
16. *Id.*, Table 1.
17. *Id.*, Table 3.
18. *Id.*, Tables 1 and 3.
19. *See, e.g.*, Address by Senator Paul Simon, "Judging Judges: The Senate's Role in Judicial Appointments," National Press Club, March 10, 1986; Tom Wicker, "Splendid for Starters," New York *Times*, May 5, 1986, p. A31.
20. American Bar Association Standing Committee on the Judiciary, *What it is and How it works*, p. 5, 1983. *See* Popeo and Kamenar, Chapter 8 in this book.
21. Goldman, Reagan's Second Term Judicial Appointments, Table 1.
22. *Id.*
23. *Id.*
24. *Id.*, p. 329.
25. *Id.*, Table 3.
26. *Id.*, Table 3.
27. *Id.*, pp. 329–334; Sheldon Goldman, "Reaganizing the Judiciary: The First Term Appointments," *Judicature*, April–May, 1986, pp. 326–327. *See also*, Popeo and Kamenar, herein.
28. Elliott E. Slotnick, "The ABA Standing Committee on Federal Judiciary: A Contemporary Assessment, Part 2," *Judicature*, April 1983, Vol. 66, No. 9, (hereinafter referred to as "Slotnick, The ABA Standing Committee, Part 2") pp. 387–388, 390, 392.
29. Calculated from Goldman, Reagan's Second Term Appointments, Tables 1 and 3.
30. *Id.* One Carter appointee did not even have a law degree. Imagine the outcry if Reagan tried to appoint as a federal judge a conservative who had not gone to law school.
31. *Id.*
32. *Id.*
33. As quoted in Elliot E. Slotnick, "The ABA Standing Committee on Federal Judiciary: A Contemporary Assessment–Part 1," *Judicature*, Vol. 66, No. 8, March 1983, (hereinafter referred to as "Slotnick, *The ABA Standing Committee*, Part 1") p. 355.
34. *Id.*, p. 355. The ABA follows a general rule of not granting a rating of qualified or better to any judicial nominee with less than 12 years of legal experience.
35. *Id.*, p. 360.
36. Goldman, Reagan's Second Term Judicial Appointments, p. 329.
37. *Id.*, pp. 329, 334.
38. *Id.*
39. *Id.*
40. *Id.*
41. Slotnick, *The ABA Standing Committee*, Part 1, p. 350.
42. *Id.*
43. *Id.*, p. 354.
44. *Id.*, p. 360.
45. *Id.*, p. 350. *See also* Slotnick, *The ABA Standing Committee*, Part 2.
46. Letter from Theodore M. Hesburgh to Senator Daniel Quayle, May 15, 1986. Another discussion of the Manion confirmation stuggle is in Pat McGuigan's essay, Chapter 1 in this book.
47. Paul Houston, "Political Foes also Support Manion Court Nomination" *Los Angeles Times*, July 13, 1986, p. 1 (hereinafter referred to as "Houston, Political Foes").
48. *Id.*
49. *Who's Who in America*, 44th Edition, 1986–1987, Vol. 2, p. 2881.
50. Letter from President Ronald Reagan to Senator Strom Thurmond, June 20, 1986.
51. "The Trouble with Manion," Washington *Times*, May 26, 1986, p. 9A.

52. [Editor's note: It was little noted during the confirmation battle that the Chicago Council itself is a liberal organization. Its members originally came together in support of the antiwar protests during the 1968 Democratic convention in Chicago and the defendants in the famed Chicago Seven conspiracy trial which resulted from those events. This organization even found Frank Easterbrook unqualified for his appointment to the Seventh Circuit, despite his broadly recognized first rate academic background and analytical skills, and his service as Deputy Solicitor General of the United States, where he argued constitutional law cases full time before the U.S. Supreme Court.]

53. U.S. Justice Department, Briefing Paper on Daniel A. Manion, p. 2.

54. Houston, "Political Foes."

55. *Id.*

56. *Id.*

57. United States Senate Transcript of Proceedings, Committee on the Judiciary, *Confirmation Hearings*, April 30, 1986, p. 129.

58. Radio Address of the President to the Nation, June 21, 1986, p. 2.

59. "The Trouble With Manion", Washington *Times.*

60. United States Senate Committee on the Judiciary, Hearings on the Confirmation of Abner Mikva, July 12, 1979.

61. *Cong. Rec.*, (Sept. 25, 1979), p. 26034 (bound volumes).

62. Letter from President Ronald Reagan to Senator Strom Thurmond, June 20, 1986.

63. Office of Legal Policy, U.S. Department of Justice, *Myths and Realities—Reagan Administration Judicial Selection*, February 27, 1987, p. 5.

64. Goldman, Reagan's Second Term Judicial Appointments, p. 326.

65. Larry Berkson, Susan Carbon and Alan Neff, "A Study of the U.S. Circuit Judge Nominating Commission: Findings, Conclusions and Recommendations," *Judicature*, Vol. 63, No. 3, Sept. 1979 (hereinafter referred to as "Berkson et. al., A Study of the U.S. Circuit Judge Nominating Commission"), pp. 106–108, 118–119; Elliot E. Slotnick, "What Panelists are Saying about the Circuit Judge Nominating Commissions", Vol. 62, No. 7, Feb. 1979, p. 321; Alan Neff, "Breaking with Tradition: A Study of the U.S. District Judge Nominating Commissions", *Judicature*, Vol. 64, No. 6, Dec.–Jan. 1981.

66. Larry Berkson and Susan Carbon, *The United States Circuit Judge Nominating Commission: Its Members, Procedures and Candidates*, (Chicago, Ill.: American Judicature Society, 1980) pp. 97–99.

67. Berkson et. al., A Study of the U.S. Circuit Judge Nominating Commission, p. 111.

68. Edwin M. Yoder, Jr. "Screening Judicial Candidates: New Politics in 'Merit Selection'," *Washington Star*, November 17, 1977 (emphasis added).

69. Peter G. Fish, "Questioning Judicial Candidates: What Can Merit Selectors Ask?," *Judicature*, Vol. 62, No. 1, June–July, 1978, pp. 8–17.

70. As quoted in Jon Gottschall, "Carter's Judicial Appointments: The Influence of Affirmative Action and Merit Selection on Voting in the U.S. Court of Appeals," *Judicature*, Vol. 62, No. 4, October 1983, P. 166.

8

THE QUESTIONABLE ROLE OF THE AMERICAN BAR ASSOCIATION IN THE JUDICIAL SELECTION PROCESS

by Daniel J. Popeo and Paul D. Kamenar

Article II of the Constitution vests the nomination and appointment of federal judges in the hands of the President, with the advice and consent of the Senate. Strictly speaking, Article II, sec. 2, cl. 2, provides only for the nomination and appointment of "Judges of the Supreme Court." The lower federal courts are creatures of Congress, and it has been suggested that appellate and district court judges may be considered "inferior officers" under Article II.[1] Consequently, Congress could vest the appointment of such officers or judges under Article II "in the President alone, in the Courts of Law, or in the Heads of Departments." However, the legislation creating the lower courts provides that those judges be appointed by the President, by and with the advice and consent of the Senate, just as Article II requires for Supreme Court justices.[2]

Nowhere, of course, is there any mention in the Constitution or any statute of the American Bar Association in the judicial selection process. Yet the ABA, an unincorporated trade association to which less than half of all of the American lawyers belong, has been allowed since 1952 by whatever Administration is in office, to screen or evaluate almost every judicial candidate long before the candidate's name reaches the President's desk, if it ever does.[3] Consequently, the power that the ABA has been allowed to wield through its Standing Committee on Federal Judiciary, is tantamount to providing this private special interest group with a virtual veto power exercised against those judicial candidates the ABA regards as unfit or unqualified for judicial office.

This chapter will review the ABA's quasi-official role in the judicial selection process and reveal certain aspects of the secretive process used by the ABA to thwart the nomination of conservative judicial candidates. In addition, this chapter will briefly discuss why the ABA's role in the judicial selection process is in violation of the Federal Advisory Committee Act.

While the ABA attempts for the most part to project an image of itself as an independent professional organization that objectively evaluates the qualifications of judicial candidates, the shocking reality is that the Committee and its members allow their liberal biases and the special interests of the ABA to affect the process, through activities ranging from working secretly with liberal public interest group to investigating the candidate's religious beliefs. The evidence demonstrates that the ABA has applied a subtle political litmus test to the detriment of conservative judicial candidates under consideration by the Reagan Administration. Before specific instances of ABA bias and conflicts of interest are described, it is helpful first to understand how the ABA evaluation process generally functions.

The ABA Standing Committee on Federal Judiciary consists of fourteen members—two members from the Ninth Circuit, one member from each of the other eleven federal judicial circuits and one member-at-large—all of whom are appointed by the President of the ABA rather than through any election procedure. The members serve for three years on staggered terms. On occasion, past Committee members may be called upon by the chairman and pressed into service to assist the current membership.

At best, the fate of a prospective judicial nominee lies in the hands of the fourteen voting members. During the crucial, initial (or investigatory) stage, the fate of the prospective nominee is actually in the hands of only two members—the member of the circuit in which the judicial vacancy occurs and the Committee chairman. At this so-called "informal" screening stage, the circuit member and the chairman receive the candidate's name and his comprehensive ABA-designed Personal Data Questionnaire from the Department of Justice. The circuit member then investigates what the ABA calls the candidate's "competence, integrity and temperament"[4] by conducting thirty to sixty confidential interviews in the legal community, including representatives of liberal public interest groups, individual attorneys and judges.

After the initial investigation, the circuit member prepares an informal written report for the Committee chairman. Based on this report, which may contain unsubstantiated allegations from the candidate's enemies, the chairman ventures a guess as to how the whole Committee would rate the prospective nominee. The four possible ratings are "not qualified", "qualified", "well qualified" and "extremely well qualified."[5] These ratings are ambiguously defined by the ABA, which produces arbitrary interpretation and application.[6] For example, during the confirmation hearings in 1984 of J. Harvie Wilkinson for the Fourth Circuit, Frederick G. Buesser, Jr., then Chairman of the ABA Committee, testified that he rated Professor Wilkinson merely "qualified" (the lowest of the three qualified ratings) "because, as I have said in my several letters, I believe that he has the capacity to become an outstanding appellate court judge. He was *remarkably well qualified* for that kind of work . . ."[7] Oddly, in ABA jargon, "remarkably well qualified" means something *less* than "well qualified." Perhaps this discrepancy is explained by a recent revelation by the Committee chairman that "well qualified" is reserved for those candidates whom the Committee would have chosen as *its* nominee for the position.[8]

The chairman's educated guess is then secretly forwarded to the Attorney General's office, but the details that underlie the basis of the guess are not always disclosed. In effect, an unidentified source can level unsupported allegations for personal or philosophical reasons against a prospective nominee and be fully protected against libel or slander, while denying the nation a qualified jurist. Indeed, the ABA proudly admits that it seeks input from the candidate's adversaries without indicating that the expected critical comments are in any way discounted considering the source.[9]

If the chairman anticipates (based on the informal report) that the candidate is "not qualified," this almost always is fatal to the formal nomination. If the prospective nominee is given an anticipatory rating of "qualified" with some reservations, he may have an opportunity to answer the charges or objections against him in a meeting with some Committee members before the full vote of the committee is taken to determine the final rating. However, the prospective nominee whom the chairman anticipates will be rated "not qualified" may never get a chance to respond to the Justice Department concerning adverse or vague allegations of misconduct. As Edward C. Schmults, former Deputy Attorney General, revealed in 1984 to the Senate Judiciary Committee: "At another meeting again on a Saturday morning, I met . . . with four members of the ABA committee and they outlined their concerns about a candidate the Department was considering. I agreed with them that their concerns were disqualifying and stated at the meeting that the administration would not proceed with the candidate. Another candidate was selected."[10] Thus, the ABA is able to derail a nomination even before the full Committee has an opportunity to formally vote and rate the candidate.

If the preliminary rating is "qualified" or better, the investigation is completed and a formal or final report is prepared by the circuit member in charge of the investigation.[11] The written formal report containing a summary of the interviews and investigation and the candidate's Personal Data Questionnaire, are then sent to each Committee member. After examining the report, each member transmits his vote to the chairman. If questions are raised, the Committee may discuss the prospective nominee by a telephone conference call or at a meeting before the vote is taken. The chairman secretly reports the Committee's final rating to the Office of the Attorney General. The actual vote count is so carefully guarded by the Committee that the Office of the Attorney General is not informed of the final tally unless it was unanimous. Otherwise, a divided evaluation of the candidate will be described in general terms, for example, as "Qualified with a minority report of Not Qualified."

The liberal bias of the Committee is especially manifested in the critical early stages of the evaluation process. For example, once the Justice Department gives the ABA Committee the candidate's name, the Committee claims that a representative sample of the profession is interviewed.[12] But the Committee unabashedly admits that it has consulted with such liberal groups as Common Cause, the ACLU, NAACP, Women's Legal Defense Fund, the National Organization for Women, and Center for Law and Social Policy.[13] Conservative organizations are conspicuously ignored by the ABA Committee. This preference for the liberal input is consistent with the ABA Committee's written policy that it consults with "legal services and public interest attorneys and attorneys who are members of various minority groups. Spokespersons of professional organizations including those representing women and minorities are also contacted."[14] Naturally, when these liberal groups are given the names of proposed Reagan nominees by the ABA Committee, they are apt to provide the ABA Committee with negative feedback, especially if the nominee expressed opposition to liberal court decisions in the civil rights area.

In late 1985, the Washington Legal Foundation ("WLF"), a conservative public interest group, requested that the ABA Committee give the names of the judicial candidates to WLF on the same basis as the liberal groups in order to provide some balance in the evaluation process. ABA Committee Chairman Robert Fiske, Jr. (a senior partner in the New York blue-chip firm of Davis, Polk and Wardwell and former Carter-appointed U.S. Attorney) flatly denied WLF's request.[15] Fiske, given the opportunity to have conservative input in the process, proclaimed that henceforth no private *groups* whatsoever would receive the candidates' names. Yet Fiske implicitly left the door open to the notion that *individuals* who represent these groups may still be contacted for their input on the nominees. The return to "business as usual" was confirmed in early 1987 when Mr. Fiske admitted that the ABA Committee relies on the views of women and minority groups in evaluating the judicial temperament of a candidate.[16]

In addition to relying on the views of liberal interest groups, the ABA Committee, apparently as part of its mission to evaluate "temperament," has indirectly admitted that it investigates the personal and ideological views of Reagan's judicial candidates. During the Carter Administration, the 1979 edition of the ABA's publication THE ABA'S STANDING COMMITTEE ON FEDERAL JUDICIARY: What It Is and How It Works, unambiguously stated: "The Committee does not attempt to investigate or report on political or ideological matters with respect to the prospective nominee." However, in the 1983 revision of the brochure, that sentence was significantly modified. It now reads: "The Committee does not investigate the prospective nominee's political or ideological philosophy *except to the extent that extreme views on such matters might bear upon judicial temperament or integrity*." This "exception" clause clearly swallows up the rule. How else will the Committee determine what views are "extreme" unless it undertakes—by itself or in cooperation with others—to investigate the political and ideological philosophy of the candidate? This "extreme views" clause has been used to disqualify or downgrade candidates because of their conservative and even religious beliefs. Thus, the subjective criterion of judical "temperament" is the pretext permitting the Committee's inquisition into the personal beliefs of the candidates, and allowing the biases of the ABA Committee to filter through the approval process.

It is clear that the ABA investigation of a candidate's personal beliefs has been used adversely against Reagan nominees. Because of the secret and confidential nature of the ABA's evaluation process, it is admittedly difficult to conduct a thorough review of the ABA's conduct to determine how widespread this practice is. However, the following case illustrations should give the reader a good idea of what may very well represent only the tip of the iceberg.

Case No. 1: James L. Graham. In 1986, James L. Graham was under consideration for a judgeship for the United States District Court for the Southern District of Ohio. His credentials were impeccable. A *summa cum laude* graduate of Ohio State University College of Law in 1962, he spent the next 24 years specializing in civil litigation with a substantial federal practice representing individuals and corporations. The founding partner of his highly reputable law firm, Graham devoted substantial time to serving as a lecturer and teacher in continuing legal education programs. He published articles, served as an instructor in trial advocacy, participated in numerous bar association seminars and workshops, and was a faculty member of the Ohio Judicial College, lecturing to Ohio trial, appellate, and supreme court judges.

He was also honored by being selected for a fellowship to the American College of Trial Lawyers, an exclusive association of trial specialists limited to only one percent of the practicing lawyers, based on a minimum of 15 years of trial practice and peer recognition as an outstanding advocate. He was also a 24-year member of the ABA and was a member of three ABA sections. The Supreme Court of Ohio appointed him a bar examiner for five years, the last of which he served as chairman. In addition to all of these legal and professional achievements, Graham is active in community service, is a solid family man, and enjoys a high reputation in the community. A screening panel of Ohio lawyers and others selected him as a top candidate for the judicial post.

With such an illustrious background, here was a Reagan candidate that many would regard as among the highest qualified. At least his experience and background merited an ABA "well qualified" rating. Yet the ABA Committee gave him their lowest rating of "Qualified" with a minority astoundingly finding him *not qualified*. This mixed rating was the subject of some inquiry by the Senate Judiciary Committee, but luckily, Graham was eventually confirmed.

How could the ABA Committee possibly have given Graham its lowest rating with even one or more members finding that he was unqualified? The answer may lie in the ABA's probe into Mr. Graham's religious beliefs and the totally subjective nature of determining "temperament." According to a published account of a letter from Graham to Chairman Fiske, the investigating Committee member, John C. Elam, probed Graham about his religious views because Elam had been told by anonymous sources that Graham was a conservative-orthodox (or "born again") Christian.[17] That Elam would even consider raising Graham's conventional religious preferences is disturbing. Even Fiske admitted that religion should not be a topic of inquiry in determining a candidate's qualification.[18] With so few people possessing the power to determine the fate of candidates, greater responsibility and accountability of the ABA must be demanded. This ABA inquisition into Mr. Graham's religious views was totally improper and should have been repudiated by anyone who regards himself as fair-minded. Yet the Graham incident was ignored (for the most part) by the media and totally ignored by the Senate. One can imagine the national uproar if a (hypothetically) conservative ABA had inquired of Carter's judicial nominees about their religious beliefs (or lack thereof).

The Chairman of the ABA Committee, when recently confronted with this blatant example of bias and improper line of inquiry, did not apologize or characterize the inquiry as an aberration.[19] Contrary to his earlier disavowal of the inquiry, he defended the probe of Graham's religious beliefs and expressed dismay as to why the judge had given a copy of his letter criticizing the Committee to the press in the first place.[20] (In fact, Judge Graham never gave his letter to the press; a copy was obtained from sources on Capitol Hill as indicated in the *Legal Times*.[21])

Graham's case not only illustrates the ABA's bias, but also demonstrates the inherent inability to make any meaningful comparison between the ABA ratings given to candidates from the Reagan and prior administrations. While other chapters in this book demonstrate that the ABA Committee ratings of Reagan nominees are, overall, as good or better as the ratings given to the Carter appointees, the Graham incident suggests that the ratings for the Reagan nominees are unfairly lower than they should be. Consequently, a more objective analysis would likely conclude that the Reagan nominees, as a whole, are better qualified than the Carter appointed judges.

Case No. 2: Professor William F. Harvey.   In 1985, Professor William F. Harvey of Indiana University Law School was under consideration for a judgeship on the United States Court of Appeals for the Seventh Circuit. A former dean of the law school, author of a treatise on federal practice, a man well regarded by attorneys and judges alike in Indiana, Professor Harvey was clearly a suitable, perhaps ideal, candidate for the position. Yet the ABA investigation of Professor Harvey's qualifications seemed tainted from the start because of the ABA's conflict of interest on account of Professor Harvey's past affiliation as President Reagan's controversial Chairman of the Board of the Legal Services Corporation ("LSC").

Professor Harvey, as head of LSC in the beginning years of the Reagan Administration, cut wasteful LSC grants to various grantees. The ABA has long been a staunch supporter of LSC and is critical of anyone who dares suggest that the agency be abolished or reformed. Only recently at the 1987 ABA midwinter convention, ABA President Eugene Thomas publicly called for the resignation of LSC President Clark Durant for suggesting that the LSC may need to be replaced. Thomas was also indignant that Durant proposed that non-lawyers be allowed to provide routine counseling to the indigent.[22] If Reagan were to nominate Durant for a judgeship, could the ABA be anything but biased against him? The Harvey situation is similar in that respect, but the conflict of interest is much worse.

Before President Reagan could gain control of the LSC board in 1981, approximately $485,000 of taxpayers' money was given directly to the well-funded ABA by LSC. During part of that pre-Harvey period, the then-Chairman of LSC was simultaneously serving as Secretary of the ABA. The conflict is much worse than mere ABA self-dealing. The fact is that the taxpayers' funds were deposited in an ABA account called the "Fund for Public Education." A chief spokesman and fundraiser for this Fund was none other than Steven E. Keane. Keane, also a member of the ABA's Committee on Federal Judiciary, became the chief investigator of Professor Harvey's qualifications. The conflict of interest is obvious: neither the ABA nor Keane is particularly fond of Professor Harvey, who cut off the federal funding spigot to the ABA and other ABA-favored grantees. Again, the major media continues to ignore this obvious scandal.

Despite this glaring conflict, neither Mr. Keane nor the ABA Committee recused themselves from the investigation of Harvey. The ABA inordinately delayed its investigation of Professor Harvey so that he felt it necessary as the new academic year approached to honor his commitment to teaching that year. Harvey still expressed his interest and availability to be a judge, but no further action has been taken on the Harvey nomination even though a seat remains open on the Seventh Circuit. Although the Department of Justice and the White House expressed serious concerns in mid-1986 about the ABA's conflict of interest,[23] no alternative action by the Administration, such as establishing an independent panel to review Professor Harvey's qualifications, was taken.

Questioned about this matter, Fiske publicly stated that he saw no conflict of interest in the Harvey investigation and stated that Harvey's charge that Keane was affiliated with an ABA committee affected by LSC decisions was false.[24] Yet the ABA's own publication in 1985 describes in detail Keane's active role with the ABA's Fund for Public Education, the past recipient of LSC largesse.[25]

Case No. 3: Miriam Cedarbaum. Even the ABA Committee members, while generally blind to conflict of interest considerations, recognized they had a problem when the Administration nominated Miriam Cedarbaum for a district judgeship in New York. Cedarbaum, a Democrat, was suggested for nomination in 1985 by Senator Daniel Moyniham (D-NY) through an arrangement with Senator Alfonse D'Amato (R-NY). Cedarbaum was a senior associate at Davis, Polk and Wardwell, Fiske's law firm. After public questioning about the conflict of interest, Fiske admitted that while he disassociated himself from Cedarbaum's consideration, the rest of his Committee did not.[26] Fiske apparently believes that there is not even an appearance of favoritism in having his Committee members investigate his colleague.

Case No. 4: Professor Lino Graglia. In 1985, Professor Lino Graglia of the University of Texas at Austin was under consideration for a circuit judgeship on the Fifth Circuit. Professor Graglia is a nationally noted constitutional law professor who has written widely on the jurisprudence of original intent.[27] He is easily qualified to be a circuit judge and his jurisprudential views are certainly consistent with the President's.

The ABA, however, strongly disapproved of the professor's learned criticism of certain court decisions, especially those mandating forced busing. It seems that anyone who dares challenge the ABA's sacred cows in the civil rights area must have something wrong with his temperament. Professor Graglia stuck to his principles and did not recant for the benefit of the ABA, thus earning him a negative rating. The Administration sought ABA reconsideration of the ruling, and even briefly considered circumventing the Committee, but to no avail.

Members of the ABA Committee make it no secret that they are ideologically opposed to the Reagan Administration's civil rights position, and, presumably, any judicial candidate who shares that view. For example, Committee members Joan Hall and Jerome J. Shestack, who are also on the Board of Trustees of the liberal Lawyers' Committee for Civil Rights Under Law, submitted joint testamony with other trustees of the civil rights group before the Senate Judiciary Committee in June 1985, viciously attacking the nomination of William Bradford Reynolds to become Associate Attorney General because of his civil rights policies. Hall and Shestack characterized Reynold's record as one that "reflects an abdication of responsibility for the enforcement of civil rights and, even more disturbing, a disregard for the rule of law as it governs those rights." Reynolds, of course, was vigorous in carrying out the Reagan Administration's "color blind" policy in enforcing the civil rights laws. Consequently, the objections by Hall and Shestack are more properly seen as an objection to the Administration for not accepting the agenda of the liberal civil rights establishment. Could *any* Reagan nominee who agrees with Brad Reynolds' position hope for a fair evaluation from the ABA Committee? Obviously not.

FEDERAL ADVISORY COMMITTEE ACT

In addition to these doubts about the ABA's liberal bias and conflicts of interest, there is a serious question whether the Committee's Star Chamber-like proceedings are in violation of the Federal Advisory Committee Act of 1972 ("FACA") which requires private advisory panels to be officially chartered and to hold proceedings open to the public. That issue may soon be resolved by courts due to lawsuits brought in 1985 and 1986 by the Washington Legal Foundation against the ABA and the Department of Justice.[28]

That the ABA Committee is an advisory committee subject to FACA is obvious. The Committee has freely admitted to its "advisory relationship" with the President, but continues to operate in violation of FACA. Section 3 of FACA defines the term "advisory committee" as "[a]ny committee, board, commission, council, conference, panel, task force, or other similar group, or any subcommittee or other subgroup thereof which is . . . established or utilized by the President, or established or utilized by one or more agencies, in the interest of obtaining advice or recommendations for the President or one or more agencies or officers of the Federal Government . . ." The express language of FACA covers the Committee because it is utilized by the President and the Justice Department for the purpose of obtaining advice on the qualifications of a prospective nominee for the federal judiciary.

Moreover, courts have interpreted FACA broadly, eliminating all doubt whether groups such as the ABA would be covered. In *Food Chemical News, Inc. v. Davis* (1974)[29] for example, it was held that two separate "informal" agency meetings with consumer groups and distilled spirits industry representatives were meetings of "advisory committees" within the meaning of FACA, when the purpose was to give advice to the Bureau of Alcohol, Tobacco and Firearms on the drafting of proposed regulations. Judge Henry Friendly for the United States Court of Appeals for the Second Circuit held in *National Nutritional Foods Association v. Califano* (1979)[30] that a group of five physicians who were in town for a conference and met with Food and Drug Administration officials only *once* during an afternoon, for the purpose of advising them on proposed regulations, was a federal advisory committee. Judge Friendly reasoned that the group, like the group of industry representatives in *Food Chemical News,* was relied upon so heavily by government officials that FACA applied. "If the straitjacket [of FACA] is too tight," he observed, "Congress is free to loosen it."[31] Thus, if FACA is applicable to loosely organized, ad hoc groups, it certainly applies to formal committees such as the ABA Committee.

The President and the Justice Department rely significantly, in some cases almost exclusively, on the ABA Committee for advice on qualifications of federal judicial nominees. Though not sanctioned by law, this reliance has been publicly acknowledged, regular, and longstanding. The inescapable conclusion is that the Committee is subject to FACA.[32]

The ABA and the Justice Department respond to these charges by weakly claiming that despite the broad language of FACA, Congress did not intend to cover the ABA because the ABA was not specifically mentioned in the legislative history of FACA. In the alternative, they make the novel argument that FACA violates the separation of powers if it were to apply to the ABA because the advice the ABA gives relates to the President's appointment powers under Article II. WLF counters by arguing that the express language of a statute overrides congressional silence on a subject, which is the preferred method of determining legislative intent. As for the constitutional argument, WLF argued that FACA simply does not usurp any substantive power of the President. Furthermore, if FACA is unconstitutional just because it tangentially relates to a Presidential power, then the Freedom of Information Act, the Sunshine in the Government Act, and similar laws would all be unconstitutional as it applies to the entire Executive Branch because those laws relate to the President's exclusive power under Article II that he take care that the laws be faithfully executed.

If the court rules in WLF's favor, the Committee must open its meetings and records to the public. The Freedom of Information Act and the Sunshine Act are both incorporated in FACA. Thus, the Committee must publish notices of its meetings in the Federal Register and holds its meetings with a designated federal official present and with the approval of such federal official.

The ABA Committee is also subject to Section 5 of FACA, which requires that advisory committees be "fairly balanced in terms of points of view represented and the functions to be performed . . ." The Committee clearly violates this provision. For one thing, only practicing lawyers are members of the Committee. Moreover, these practicing lawyers are mostly from corporate law firms in large metropolitan areas. The Committee membership is also unbalanced philosophically, because it openly exhibits a liberal bias. Not surprisingly, some of the Committee members were part of the Carter Administration or are openly supportive of the liberal agenda.

FINAL THOUGHTS

The foregoing suggests that there are indeed serious flaws with the ABA screening process, which allows the liberal biases of the ABA and the members of its Standing Committee to work against conservative nominees. Unfortunately, the Department of Justice and the White House have permitted this special interest group to continue to produce such skewed advice. No other private group wields such power over the judicial selection process, and there is nothing analogous in the rest of government. The American Medical Association, for example, does not screen or pass judgment on the qualifications of proposed nominees for the Surgeon General. Why should the ABA be given such a preferred status?

The only real hope of reform is a successful outcome of our current litigation against the ABA. The application of FACA to the ABA, requiring an open and balanced forum, would go a long way toward correcting the abuses of the screening process.

REFERENCES

The Questionable Role of the American Bar Association in the Judicial Selection Process by Daniel J. Popeo and Paul D. Kamenar.

1. *Clark v. United States*, 72 F. Supp. 594 (Cl. Ct. 1947), *cert. denied*, 333 U.S. 833 (1948).
2. *See* 28 U.S.C. §§44(a), 133.
3. For an excellent historical review of the ABA's influence in the judicial selection process, *see* Joel B. Grossman, *Lawyers and Judges* (New York: John Wiley and Sons, 1965).
4. American Bar Association, "American Bar Association Standing Committee on Federal Judiciary: What It Is And How It Works" (1983), p. 3 (hereinafter *"ABA Committee Brochure"*).
5. If the rating is unanimous, the final rating so states. Otherwise, a mixed rating may be given, e.g., "qualified/not qualified," but the exact tally of the majority and minority votes is not revealed.
6. The *ABA Committee Brochure*, pp. 4–5 defines the ratings as follows:
   "To be rated *Exceptionally Well Qualified*, the prospective nominee must stand at the top of the legal profession in the community involved and have outstanding legal ability, wide experience and the highest reputation for integrity and temperament. In addition to preeminence in the law, the prospective nominee should have a reputation as an outstanding citizen, having made important community and professional contributions in order to merit the sparingly awarded 'Exceptionally Well Qualified' evaluation.
   To be *Well Qualified*, the prospective nominee must have the Committee's strong affirmative endorsement and be regarded as one of the best available for the vacancy from the standpoint of competence, integrity and temperament. The evaluation of *Qualified* indicates that it appears the prospective nominee would be able to perform satisfactorily as a federal judge with respect to competence, integrity and temperament.
   When a prospective nominee is found *Not Qualified*, it means that the Committee's investigation indicates that the prospective nominee is not adequate from the standpoint of competence, integrity or temperament."
7. Confirmation Hearings On Federal Appointments: Hearings Before the Senate Comm. on the Judiciary, 98th Cong., 2d Sess. 330 (1984) (statement of Mr. Buesser) (emphasis added).
8. Speech by Robert B. Fiske, Jr. before a meeting of the Washington, D.C. Chapter of the Federalist Society, on March 20, 1987.
9. *Id.*
10. Confirmation Hearings on Federal Appointments: Hearings Before the Senate Comm. on the Judiciary, 98th Cong., 2d Sess. 274 (1984) (testimony of Edward C. Schmults).
11. Only in very rare occasions will the Administration continue to press for a formal report if the preliminary rating indicates a "not qualified rating." This happened once in the Reagan Administration when Sherman Unger was nominated despite a "not qualified" ABA rating. During his confirmation hearings, Unger was highly critical of the ABA evaluation process and the lack of fundamental fairness in the manner in which he was accused of improper activities by anonymous sources. He even suggested that the ABA's advisory role was violative of the Federal Advisory Committee Act. The ABA nevertheless boasts that only in rare instances—less than one percent—has a President gone ahead and nominated an individual who received a "not qualified" rating. *ABA Committee Brochure*, p. 6.
12. *ABA Committee Brochure*, p. 5.

13. Selection and Confirmation of Federal Judges: Hearings before the Senate Comm. on Judiciary, 96th Cong., 1st Sess. (Jan. 25, 1979) (testimony of ABA Committee Chairman Brooksley Born).

14. *ABA Committee Brochure*, p. 6.

15. *See* Letter of Robert B. Fiske, Jr. to Paul D. Kamenar dated November 26, 1985.

16. Fiske speech, *supra* n. 8.

17. *Legal Times*, Dec. 15, 1986, p. 7.

18. *Id.*

19. Fiske speech, *supra* n. 8.

20. *Id.*

21. *Legal Times, supra* n. 17.

22. *See* Washington *Post*, March 1987.

23. *See* Indianapolis *Star*, June 18, 1986, p. 18.

24. Fiske speech, *supra* n. 8.

25. ABA, "Ways and Means of Investing the ABA Fund for Public Education," Spring 1985, p. 1.

26. Fiske speech, *supra* n. 8.

27. Graglia is a profound legal scholar whose work product belies the small-minded criticisms of his enemies. He is the author of the definitive examination of Supreme Court precedent on forced busing, *Disaster by Decree: The Supreme Court Decisions on Race and the Schools* (Cornell University Press, 1976). Other Graglia works include "How the Constitution Disappeared," *Commentary*, February 1986; "Constitutional Mysticism: The Aspirational Defense of Judicial Review," 98 *Harvard Law Review* 1331 (1985); "Racially Discriminatory Admission to Public Institutions of Higher Education," in R. Collings, ed., *Constitutional Government in America* (Carolina Academic Press, 1979); and "How the Constitution Came to Require Busing for School Racial Balance," forthcoming in 85 *Michigan Law Review* (1987).

28. *Washington Legal Foundation v. ABA*, Civil Action No. 85-3918 (D.D.C.); *Washington Legal Foundation v. Department of Justice*, Civil Action No. 86-2883 (D.D.C.)

29. *Food Chemical News, Inc. v. Davis*, 378 F. Supp. 1048 (D.D.C. 1974).

30. *National Nutritional Foods Association v. Califano*, 603 F. 2d 327 (2d Cir. 1979).

31. *Id.*, at p. 336.

32. 5 U.S.C. App. I, §§10(a), (e), (f).

9

BIAS: THE LAW SCHOOL DILEMMA

by Jeffery D. Troutt

Law students and some professors are increasingly concerned about ideological bias and intolerance in the law schools. At some of the nation's most prominent law schools, internecine faculty battles over ideology have disrupted the primary mission of schools: transmitting a body of knowledge to the lawyers and leaders of tomorrow. As a result, some tenured faculty have sought greener pastures.

It is no secret that the ideological bent of most law schools is to the left. Three elements combine to produce this bias: the type of persons who are attracted to teaching, prevailing philosophies of jurisprudence, and the abuse of the case law method.

Although teaching, even in a prestigious law school, may not appeal to many, there is a natural attractiveness to teaching, cultivated while they are students, in those individuals who can "creatively" manipulate the law. The top students who possess that creativity are attracted to such positions. It is frequently said, and with some merit, that C students become lawyers, B students become judges, and A students become law professors.

There is a second element producing bias in the prevailing theories of jurisprudence—the theory of law. The prevailing theories of jurisprudence contribute to bias because jurisprudence has become a platform for many to argue that the law lacks certainty, and, indeed, is capable of manipulation. Jurisprudence becomes the driving engine for leftist reform—not because it properly indicates the need for reform, but because the law becomes pliable with the explanations that many find in jurisprudence.

The third element is the abuse of the case law method—the principal method of education in law schools today. The case method, valuable in instilling sharp analytical skills, can be rendered a tool of reconstruction of the legal system absent a healthy balance in the cases and materials reviewed.

These factors encourage both the faculty and the students to a view fundamental to liberal activism in this country: that the judiciary is a super-legislature—the only branch of government which can be trusted to protect citizens from their elected representatives. But this view only underscores the fact that the judicial branch of government is the branch most easily influenced by law school advocacy.

The liberal character of law schools is part of a problem to be found in nearly all institutions of higher learning. The case of Wayne Dick was an ominous example of the extent to which academia has become intolerant of persons who dare to defy the liberal establishment. Dick, a sophomore at Yale, satirized the university's Gay/Lesbian Awareness Days (GLAD) by posting notices proclaiming Bestiality Awareness Days (BAD). Dick was hauled before the school's disciplinary committee and placed on probation. In the "Retrial" called by Yale president Benno Schmidt, Guido Calabresi, dean of Yale Law School, represented Dick. In a victory for free speech, Dick was acquitted.[1]

Justice was done in the Wayne Dick case, but only with the assistance of a noted law school dean. Unfortunately, not all professors are as principled as Dean Calabresi. The Dick case is an example of the extent to which academia has been politicized by the left. Along with that politicization has come intolerance for anyone who expresses ideas that vary from the liberal dogma. This intolerance has had a chilling effect upon free speech in law schools.

When I was in law school[2], several colleagues encouraged my advocacy of conservative positions. Yet they were unwilling to vocalize their own views for fear of persecution from faculty and students alike. These students did not doubt their principles. They hesitated because they feared that they would be ridiculed and ostracized.

This is not a sign of a healthy academic system. In an atmosphere of true academic freedom, students need not fear expressing their views. Rather, they are encouraged to do so. But in the present system, such experiences—and countless other incidents all over academia—have given students the message that not all opinions may be freely expressed. Academic freedom is under attack, and all students are the worse for it.

The politicization of academia has been noted by Thomas Sowell, who cited the example of a Texas professor who devoted most of his American History course to a diatribe against President Reagan's Strategic Defense Initiative. Sowell stated, "[t]he professor's opinions are his own business, but turning his course into an indoctrination center . . . is a betrayal of trust."[3]

JURISPRUDENCE

Some non-lawyers think that jurisprudence is a hard and fast understanding of the application and basis of the law, but this is far from the truth. Rather, it is merely a collection of competing ideas about the nature and purpose of the law.

Law schools are at the forefront of jurisprudential innovation. Because of their scholastic pursuits, law professors are concerned about, and influenced by, jurisprudence.

Our nation's history is founded upon a clear understanding of the rule of law in our society. But the concept of the rule of law necessarily requires an objective view of the law.[4] Otherwise, men, not law, rule. This same understanding of the rule of law also prescribes the responsibility and correlative limitations of the government and each of its branches. *An understanding of the law as objective is necessary to ensure that unbounded personal discretion does not become the dominant rule.* However, jurisprudence in American legal thought has moved steadily from an objective to a subjective view of the law.

This slide into subjectivism in American jurisprudence follows a piecemeal, though identifiable, movement. One of the first American steps came from Christopher Columbus Langdell, dean of the Harvard Law School in the late Nineteenth Century. Langdell is known not so much for any theoretical contribution to jurisprudence, but for pioneering the study of law.

Langdell provided a method of analysis, one logically derived from the English scholar John Austin's earlier legal concept of analytical positivism—that law can be understood by comparing, classifying and analyzing theories, rather than upon principles of rights and equity. As Jeffrey P. O'Connell writes:

With the theory of Austin, there was a need to be able to implement the theory. The implementation here came not in the government but in the classroom and through the enthusiasm for the comparison of case law. Austin told of the value of the comparison of positive law. But aside from the pre-existing comparative law concept, he presented no effective system of comparison.[5]

Langdell provided that method, along with an understanding of the scientific nature of law. The concept of Langdell, although it satisfied the need to compare the law, never fit well into the legal positivist understanding of the law because it offered a certainty that most were not willing to concede. Langdell wrote of the simplicity of the law:

> [T]he number of fundamental legal doctrines is much less than is commonly supposed; the many different guises in which the same doctrine is constantly making its appearance, and the great extent to which legal treatises are a repetition of each other, being the cause of much apprehension. If these doctrines could be so classified and arranged that each should be found in its proper place, and nowhere else, they would cease to be formidable from their number.[6]

Langdell studied both contracts and torts to observe and apply unifying rules to all legal actions. O'Connell observes, "Langdell's contribution, then, was to advance a method for examining law, which others could adapt for their purposes. The effect of the method was to move from a consideration of principle to a consideration of the commonality of cases."[7]

Austin's theory had removed the certainty of law and substituted the control of the sovereign. As a result, he separated law and morals, principle and pragmatism. More consistent with this view of law was Arthur Corbin, noted contracts professor at Harvard Law School in the early part of this century. As O'Connell notes:

> Perhaps one of the unique attributes of Corbin was his passion for avoiding principles in explaining the law, preferring instead a rigorous transactional examination. In some ways, he represented the opposite of Langdell's scientific approach. Indeed, Langdell spent time reducing the rules to as few theories as possible, while Corbin seemed intent to show the pre-Langdell complexities. Corbin saw a complexity in the law which the rules did not properly account for. This conscious movement

from doctrine to a practical dealing with the individual components was another step in losing sight of an underlying base [of the law]. Corbin, because of his extensive involvement in the commercial area proved a major impact on law in this century.

Corbin's analysis of the law is that there could not be universal rules of law. The growth of the common law was simply the result of the accretion of centuries of cases. Case law may have a pattern and that pattern may be discernable if properly analyzed, but such pattern had nothing to do with any invariable, general body of principles.[8]

Anyone familiar with Corbin's treatises knows of the wealth of cases that he found necessary to explore to discern such patterns.

This logical analysis of Corbin, however, sowed the seeds for future theories that adopted Corbin's view of the law. This was the beginning of the slide into subjectivism which opened the floodgates for the too frequent dissension found in law schools today.

John Chipman Gray's jurisprudence stressed the role of the courts in defining the law. Gray modified Austin's concept of the sovereign, by positing that true power resided in the courts. Gray effectively attacked the notion that courts follow neutral principles in deciding cases. He taught that courts were constantly innovating, "constantly making *ex post facto* law."[9] O'Connell observes, "Case law was not seen as an expression of preexisting law, but the law itself. Even statutes were not law, merely sources of law which could find expression in their construction by the court."[10]

LEGAL REALISM

Legal realism was the next step on the road to subjectivism, emerging as a reaction to the notion that judges apply neutral rules to resolve cases. Legal realists believe that court decisions could be explained outside of traditional logical analysis. According to one explanation of Legal Realism, "Legal decision-making does not involve application of neutral principles but subjective choice."[11] A given judge's socioeconomic class or his mood were more likely to affect his decision-making than a series of neutral principles.[12] Yale professor Grant Gilmore aptly explained the basis of Legal Realism:

Generally stated rules of law do not so much explain as conceal the bases of judicial decision. A judge's holding in a case is an *ad hoc* response to a unique state of facts, rationalized, after the event, with a dissimulation more or less conscious, and fitted willy-nilly into the Procrustean bed of approved doctrine.[13]

Foremost among Legal Realists was Karl Llewellyn, professor at Columbia Law School. Llewellyn argued that substantive rules of law were not the basis upon which judges decided cases. Llewellyn wrote, "The theory that rules decide cases seems for a century to have fooled, not only library-ridden recluses, but judges."[14] To Llewellyn, the law was not black-letter law, but what judges do. And what a judge may do is dependent upon a variety of factors, most of which are subjective. Llewellyn said:

> I think it . . . clear that after study of a group of cases and estimates of just how far courts do follow what prior courts have done, one can set about constructing generalized statements, generalized predictions of their action. I have no hesitancy in calling these predictions rules; they are, however, thus far only rules *of* the court's action; they are statements of the practices of the court. Thanks to the doctrine of precedent the courts themselves regard them also and simultaneously as rules *for* the court's action, *precepts* for the court . . . Yet the moment that you forsake the relatively solid rock of attempted prediction, you run into difficulty, and for this reason: that when you are told by anyone that a given rule is *the proper rule* (not "an accurate prediction") you are dealing with his value judgment, based on no man knows what.[15]

Legal Realism's contribution to contemporary legal thought was the concept that social, political, and personal factors were elements in judicial decision-making. All too often, it was an accurate description of how many jurists functioned. Legal Realism's failing was that it effectively justified what judge's did, i.e., judicial activism. Additionally, Legal Realists erred in defining the law solely as the decisions of judges, to the exclusion of other actors, especially the other two branches of government.

CRITICAL LEGAL STUDIES

Critical Legal Studies ("CLS") took this a step further, combining elements of neo-Marxism and nihilism into a broadly-defined legal movement. CLS is a broadly-based concept, embracing disciplines other than the law such as philosophy, economics, and political science. It is more of a movement than a philosophy, and as such it is difficult to define. The basic premise of the movement is that the law cannot be understood as a set of neutral principles, or the predilections of individual judges, but as politics. In the words of a leading proponent of CLS, Joseph William Singer:

> Those of us associated with Critical Legal Studies believe that law is not apolitical and objective: Lawyers, judges, and scholars make highly controversial political choices, but use the ideology of legal reasoning to make our institutions appear natural and our rules appear neutral. This view of the legal system raises the possibility that there are no rational, objective criteria that can govern how we describe that system, or how we choose governmental institutions, or how we make legal decisions.[16]

Historically, CLS proponents contend, law in America has been a tool of capitalists to uphold class divisions. One CLS adherent has written that:

> An abstraction called The Law is seen as an instrument through which another abstraction called The State exercises power on behalf of the bourgeoisie. The Law, while pretending to be a benign, neutral force dispensing justice, equality, and due process, actually is but a fraudulent cover-up for the force through which The State rules.[17]

CLS advocates attack the very basis of legal reasoning. According to a major CLS proponent, Harvard's Duncan Kennedy, when law professors attempt to teach black letter law, they teach nothing, because legal rules do not exist. Kennedy has written, "There are no overall unifying principles of law which make legal reasoning different from other kinds of reasoning and give the subject an internal necessity."[18]

CLS champions abound in the nation's most prominent law schools, including Harvard, Stanford, and Georgetown. Disputes between the proponents of Critical Legal Studies and more traditional professors at Harvard have been widely publicized. Paul Bator, a tenured Harvard Law School professor (and one of the rare conservatives in legal education) recently resigned, opting instead to teach at the University of Chicago. Bator explained his move, noting, "It is my sad opinion that CLS has had an absolutely disastrous effect on the intellectual and institutional life of Harvard Law School."[19]

CLS and the legal nihilism that often underpins it led Dean Paul D. Carrington of Duke University School of Law to suggest that the CLS professor has no place in the law school:

> The professionalism and intellectual courage of lawyers does not require rejection of Legal Realism and its lesson that who decides also matters. What it cannot abide is the embrace of nihilism and its lesson that who decides is everything, and principle nothing but cosmetic. Persons espousing the latter view, however honestly held, have a substantial ethical problem as teachers of professional law students . . . [T]he nihilist who must profess that legal principle does not matter has an ethical duty to depart the law school, perhaps to seek a place elsewhere in the academy.[20]

If law stands for nothing other than upholding social values, it stands on shifting sand. This leaves both lawyers and law professors in an ethical quagmire. What should prevent a practicing attorney from offering or accepting a bribe, especially if it is offered in order to achieve the lofty goal of equality and justice (as defined by the lawyer)?

Addressing the threat to legal ethics that CLS represents, Carrington stated:

> The nihilist teacher threatens to rob his or her students of the courage to act on such professional judgement as they may have acquired. Teaching cynicism may, and perhaps probably does, result in the learning of the skills of corruption: bribery and intimidation. In honest effort to proclaim a need for revolution, nihilist teachers are more likely to train crooks than radicals . . . A lawyer who succumbs to legal nihilism faces a far greater danger than mere professional incompetence. He must contemplate the dreadful reality of government by cunning and a society in which the only right is might.[21]

The preservation of academic freedom at law schools remains a vital concern to the legal profession. However, CLS advocates have been accused of intolerance toward differing viewpoints. In fact, many stories have been published about attempts by CLS advocates to intimidate students with differing viewpoints, or heckle and harass lecturers who appear at their law schools' functions.[22] Hal Scott has stated:

[W]e must come to grips with the attempted politicization of law schools and law students by the critical legal studies movement, which wants a leftist nonhierarchical law school and society, and which is totally against the existing open and pluralistic system. The movement's teachers seek to bring about leftist institutions by indoctrinating students to the "correct" perspective through advocacy in whatever course they happen to be teaching—to the exclusion of other points of view.[23]

Because of this intolerance, many CLS adherents pose a threat to academic freedom, and to the rule of law itself. CLS, in contrast to Legal Realism, abandons both honesty and neutrality to formulate an instrumentalist jurisprudence.

The openness with which CLS proponents proclaim their agenda at least leaves no question of their motives. One of the greatest dangers CLS poses is not that judges and lawyers will overtly adopt their arguments, but that they will adopt their solutions[24] to the perceived problem of class division and, in the process, attempt to explain their results under conventional legal thought.[25]

This is an alarming possibility. Given the enormous amount of power judges have accrued to themselves in recent decades, the spectre of judges who are not motivated by principle—but rather by the raw application of power—is frightening, indeed. Such a judiciary could conceivably move to redistribute wealth on the basis that a "constitutional right" to "economic equality" exists within "penumbras" of the Constitution. Further, if, as CLS advocates posit, law is merely politics by other means, there is nothing to law-making other than the application of brute strength. A lawyer with this world-view could have no qualms about lying to the court, or bribing judges, because in his view law rests on no other foundation than naked political power.

Essentially, such a view destroys the traditional underpinnings for the validity of the judicial process. The integrity of an unelected judiciary depends on its being limited to certain functions appropriate for it. Lawmaking must be by representatives controlled through the normal democratic process.

While these theories of jurisprudence are part of the law school problem, they are not the only problem. Another aspect of that problem is the abuse of the primary tool of legal education—the case method.

THE CASE LAW METHOD

Much contemporary liberal bias in law schools results from the abuse of the case method, the process of examining cases, gleaning rules of law from them, and synthesizing the holdings of several cases in order to discover a principle of law.

The case method was first implemented at Harvard Law School by Dean Langdell in 1870.[26] Prior to the late 1800s, few lawyers received a formal legal education. Most entered the profession either by reading or serving an apprenticeship under a practicing attorney.[27]

Langdell's reasons for implementing the case method were varied. Chief among them was that he believed that the case method was the "scientific" method of teaching the law. According to Langdell, the justifications for the case law method were:

> First, that law is a science: secondly, that all the available materials of that science are contained in printed books. If law be not a science, a university will best consult its own dignity in declining to teach it.[28]

The case method, under Langdell's reasoning, is analogous to the natural sciences, with the appellate cases being to the scientific study of law what rock and fossils are to the study of geology. As the geologist discerns the Earth's history from rock and mineral samples, the law student and law professor discover what the law is through case synthesis, examining the holdings from several cases and unearthing a legal principle underlying the decisions.

The case method was not an immediate success in the academic world. For ten or twenty years, its main proponents taught at Harvard, Columbia, and Iowa. Others continued to use a mixture of lecture, text, recitation, and case analysis.[29] One-by-one, however, law schools adopted the case law method. The University of Virginia remained a bastion of the non-case law method, refusing to adopt it until the 1930s, when a faculty member earned a J.S.D. at Harvard.[30] By the end of World War II, however, virtually all American law schools had adopted the case law method.[31]

There are several justifications posited for continuing to use the case method. First, cases represent a primary source of the law, rather than a secondary source such as treatises (in fact, professors generally discourage students from using secondary sources, at least in the first year of law school). Second, proponents of the case law approach believe that it motivates students through a problem-solving approach, as opposed to simple lectures. Third, the case method trains students to be advocates—they must develop and defend a position in a highly pressured situation, preparing them for later court room encounters. Fourth, the case method, if it approaches cases in an historical context, gives the student an idea of how the law has progressed (or regressed) over the years.

Yet, the case law method has several serious shortcomings which create the potential for abuse. First, by its very nature, the case law method gives the student the impression that the law is a relative, constantly evolving entity, which has no absolutes, only temporary rules. Second, the case law method ignores historical documents and literature which have impacted upon the formation and evolution of the law. Third, the case law method also ignores the legislative process. Finally, the case law method leads to an implicit sanction of judicial activism.

The case method, combined with the socratic method, creates a relativistic attitude toward the law. The student is exposed to a plethora of cases which often have contradictory holdings. In today's law school, the professor usually supplies little or no guidance as to what the law actually is. Whenever a student begins to speak of absolutes, he is met with sneers and challenges—from both faculty and students.

The term "case law method" implies exclusive attention to judicial cases. Actually, few casebooks are exclusively devoted to cases and case commentaries. Most contain excerpts from treatises and law review articles. Casebooks on administrative law or criminal law may contain statutory excerpts. The legislative history behind statutes and the cases which challenge them is virtually ignored. The history behind the passage of legislation—or behind major legal and constitutional reform—is also ignored.

By ignoring the legislative process, the case law method overemphasizes the role of the judiciary in our system of government. In this view, legislatures are seen as usurpers of constitutional rights, courts as noble guardians of liberty. Students come to believe that courts should legitimately seize power from majoritarian institutions, which cannot be trusted in the same way courts can.

Further, professors with an ideological axe to grind can easily abuse the case law method. The student is usually presented only with recent cases which reflect the views of the professor. The rest of legal history is brushed aside. The student is forced to look at the law through blinders which dramatically narrow his field of vision. Because he looks only at cases from the last twenty-five years or so, the student has no understanding of why the law has changed, or what were the reasons for doctrines which courts have rejected in those years. The professor can easily abuse this method of teaching in order to indoctrinate students.

THE CASE LAW METHOD AND CONSTITUTIONAL LAW

The abuses of the case law method are most apparent, and harmful, in the area of constitutional law. As Professor Charles Rice of Notre Dame has noted, "A major constitutional problem today is the acceptance by Congress, the Executive and the legal profession of the notion of judicial supremacy, through which the Constitution is . . . whatever the judges say it is."[32] In many classes, the students are not required to read the Constitution, let alone the historical documents which underpinned its adoption such as the *Federalist*.

What students are required to read, however, is a multitude of cases, starting with *Marbury v. Madison* (1803)[33], continuing through *Brown v. Board of Education* (1954)[34], and ending with whatever Supreme Court cases happen to be new. Professor Rice ably noted the deficiencies of the case law method, as used to teach constitutional law, stating:

The student looks at a case and asks whether the rule of that case follows from the rule of an earlier case which serves as a precedent or from a statute . . . In the case-oriented study of constitutional law, the intent of the framers becomes less important in the light of the presumed responsibility of judges to adapt the Constitution to modern conditions.[35]

During law school, students read little, if any, of the text of the Constitution. Many professors do assign the Constitution, but usually as background, and even then it is not required reading. History, and the documents which accompanied the ratification of the Constitution, are often unmentioned. (As an undergraduate political science major, I was required to read portioins of the *Federalist*. As a law student, I was not.)

Concentrating exclusively upon case law, law schools implicitly sanction judicial activism. Law professors cite with approval cases which represent what the professor considers to be a good policy result. The fact that the Court may be usurping the authority of other branches of government, or of the states, is irrelevant.[36] William Bradford Reynolds noted this, stating, "At the core of the problem is the failure of law schools today to inculcate in their students an appreciation of the role of the judiciary as the Framers of our Constitution saw it."[37] Case-by-case, professors legitimate the manner in which courts have vivisected the Constitution: twisting and contorting it to such a point that its contemporary meaning bears little resemblance to that intended by the Framers. As a result, the Constitution, which was written to limit the powers of the federal government and preserve the liberties of the people, is reshaped into a tool for the expansion of federal powers, and enhancement of libertine values, at the expense of public safety—with the approval and assistance of the current generation of law professors.

Professor Rice has stated:

> The uncritical reliance on Supreme Court decisions as if they were the only authoritative factor in constitutional interpretations reinforces the notion of judicial supremacy. One obvious remedy is a greater exposure of law students to the legislative history of the Constitution and to the impact of Supreme Court decisions on the other branches and on the lower courts. The constitutional system is complex and to understand it requries more than a simplistic overemphasis on Supreme Court opinions.[38]

An attorney once told me that when he took constitutional law at the University of Pennsylvania School of Law, the students asked if they could bring a copy of the Constitution to the exam. "Yes," replied the seasoned professor, who added tongue-in-cheek, "but don't let it confuse you." That cogently demonstrates the problem: the student is not expected to know what the Constitution says, but what the Supreme Court says it means.[39]

Most practicing attorneys and judges will never question the propriety of judicial activism. In fact, the question of whether judicial activism is proper was probably never raised by their law school professors.[40] This represents the failure of the law schools adequately to teach a legal doctrine which was commonly accepted until just a generation or two ago, and which is currently undergoing a renaissance among conservative and libertarian legal scholars.

Students leave law school lacking a knowledge of the history of, and historical documents relating to, the adoption of the Constitution. They therefore are inadequately prepared to grapple with the complex issues they may face as practicing attorneys and judges. These professionals assume that government by judicial fiat is the legitimate way of doing business, and argue and decide cases accordingly. The result is arbitrary justice.

The legal profession accepts without question the authority of courts to second-guess the legislatures and subvert the law. Victory or defeat for a client depends, in large part, upon what judge fate has picked for him. King Solomon recognized the dangers inherent in the rule of man, rather than the rule of law, "When the righteous are in authority, the people rejoice; but when the wicked beareth rule, the people mourn."[41]

CONCLUSION AND RECOMMENDATIONS FOR REFORM

Alexis de Tocqueville noted the potential power of American judges, stating, "Whenever a law that the judge holds to be unconstitutional is invoked in the United States, he may refuse to admit it as a rule; this power is the only one peculiar to the American magistrate, but it gives rise to immense political influence."[42]

The political influence exercised by contemporary judges is clearly outside of that intended by the Framers of the Constitution, and has usurped powers belonging to other branches of government, or to the states.

Law schools have been the primary instrument of legal education for over one hundred years. They have contributed to judicial usurpation of power by teaching students that judicial activism is both acceptable and necessary. This has flowed from the jurisprudence taught at the law schools and the abuse of the case law method. The result is highly politicized institutions, often intolerant of differing points of view.

Two changes should be made in the structure of the law schools in order to rectify, at least partially, the liberal bias inherent in the system.

• The case law method, while it should not be abandoned, should be taught in such a way that it is not abused. Recent cases should be supplemented with cases and materials which teach the history of current legal doctrines. The case method teaches an essential element of legal analysis—case synthesis—and concomitantly sharpens the student's verbal skills. However, it also gives students a myopic view of how law is made and interpreted. Concentration on legal history, as well as arguments against legal doctrines which are currently in vogue, would do much to rectify the abuses of the case method.

Constitutional law courses, especially, should include the history of the founding of the Constitution, and an analysis of the documents which were involved in its adoption. This would give law students a thorough perspective of the Constitution, and would bring the doctrine of Original Intent—the doctrine that the words of the Constitution and its Amendments should be interpreted in the light of the meaning the Framers attached to them—to their attention.

• Law schools should have no more room for ideological intolerance. Professors who demonstrate intolerance for views which differ from their own, and especially those who disrupt or encourage students to disrupt speakers with whom they disagree, should not be allowed to continue teaching. In other words, law schools should be intolerant toward intolerance.

One of the professors at my law school was renowned for telling his class, "This is not fairness school; this is law school!" That was a good reminder that the practice of law is not always about being fair. But the concept of fairness should still be important in legal education. Simple fairness necessitates that law schools take action to correct the institutional factors which create and sustain the liberal bias in legal education.

REFERENCES

Bias: The Law School Dilemma by Jeffery D. Troutt

1. "Yale Wins," *National Review*, November 7, 1986, p. 19.
2. 1983-1986.
3. Washington *Times*, April 6, 1987, p. 1D.
4. Supreme Court Justice Joseph Story noted the importance of a strict adherence to the meaning of the words of the Constitution in his *Commentaries on the Constitution*. Story wrote that "The Constitution of the United States is to receive a reasonable interpretation of its language, and its powers, keeping in view the objects and purposes, for which these powers are conferred. By a reasonable interpretation, we mean, that in case the words are susceptible of two different senses, the one strict, the other more enlarged, that one should be adopted, which is most consonant with the apparent objects and intent of the Constitution." *Commentaries on the Constitution*, I, Section 419, as quoted in James McClellan, *Joseph Story and the American Constitution: A Study in Political and Legal Thought* (Norman: University of Oklahoma Press, 1971), p. 115.
5. Jeffrey P. O'Connell, "Law and Competing Jurisdictions: Diversity of Citizenship Clause and the Application of State Law" (unpublished manuscript March 1986) (hereinafter referred to as, O'Connell, "Law and Competing Jurisdictions"), p. 65.
6. Grant Gilmore, *The Ages of American Law*, (New Haven: Yale University Press, 1977), p. 43, quoting from Christopher Langdell, *Cases on Contracts*, (Birmingham: Legal Classics Library 1871).
7. O'Connell, "Law and Competing Jurisdictions", p. 66.
8. O'Connell, "Law and Competing Jurisdictions", p. 68.
9. John Chipman Gray, *The Nature and Sources of Law*, (New York: MacMillan, 1924), p. 100.
10. O'Connell, "Law and Competing Jurisdictions", p. 67
11. George H. Taylor, "Deconstructing the Law", 1 *Yale Law and Policy Review* 158 (1982).
12. "Philosophies at War in Law Schools," *Insight*, September 29, 1986, p. 52.
13. Grant Gilmore, "Legal Realism: its Cause and Cure", 70 *Yale Law Journal* 1037, 1038 (1961).
14. Karl Llewellyn, *The Bramble Bush*, (New York: 1960), p. 3.
15. *Id.* pp. 77-78 (emphasis in text).
16. Joseph William Singer, "The Player and the Cards: Nihilism and Legal Theory," 94 *Yale Law Journal* 3, 5 (1984).
17. David Kairys, ed. *The Politics of Law: a Progressive Critique*, (New York: Pantheon Books, 1982), Rabinowitz, "The Radical Tradition in the Law", at 312. George H. Taylor contrasts the views of Legal Realists and CLS adherents, stating, "The legal realists have argued that legal decision-making involves not formal, deductive logic but subjective choice; any legal choice made is never logically compelled. In the Marxian tradition the objection has been not so much that the law is imbued with values, but that the distribution of legal outcomes is skewed to particular values, particular interests; the law reflects dominant economic interests." George H. Taylor, "Deconstructing the Law", 1 *Yale Law & Policy Review* 158 (1982).
18. Duncan Kennedy, "The Political Significance of the Structure of the Law School Curriculum," 14 *Seton Hall Law Review* 1, 16 (1983).
19. Clark, "Philosophies at War in Law Schools", *Insight*, September 29, 1986, p. 52.
20. Paul Carrington, "Of Law and the River", 34 *Journal of Legal Education* 222, 227 (1984).

21. *Id.* at 227.

22. For example, Harvard Law Professor Randall Kennedy recently advocated in a speech entitled, "In Defense of Disrupting Speech by South African Government Officials" the heckling of officials of South Africa who spoke at the University. Kennedy's speech was advertised by a pamphlet entitled, "Hey, Hey . . Ho, Ho, . . Free Speech Has Got to Go." In a question and answer session, Kennedy remarked that he would accord the same treatment to Nicaraguan Contras and the Secretary of Defense. When asked what would be his response to an incident in which a lecturer was beaten or killed, Kennedy responded, "It's a close call, something I'd have to think deeply about." Don Feder, "Noose-knotting," Washington *Times,* May 15, 1987.

23. Hal Scott, "Proposals for Change," 8 *Harvard Journal of Law and Public Policy* 317, 320 (1985).

24. For example, Chester maintains that property crime could be significantly reduced by a system of wealth expropriation aimed mainly at inheritance. He suggest periodic across-the-board grants to all American citizens funded, at least in part, through a limitation on wealth transfers between generations. C. Ronald Chester, "The Effects of a Redistribution of Wealth on Property Crime," *Crime and Deliquency,* July 1977, p. 274.

25. William Kristol, "On the Utility of Critical Legal Studies," 8 *Harvard Journal of Law and Public Policy* 327, 328 (1985). [Editor's Note: The increasing tensions caused by the presence of CLSers at Harvard led to a divisive confrontation over the denial of tenure to two CLS professors in June 1987. However, at least one press account— with no apparent sense of irony—referred to the conflict between Neo-Marxists and liberals as "A long battle between left-wing and conservative faculty members..." *See* Ruth Marcus, "Ideologies Collide at Harvard Law," Washington *Post,* June 12, 1987, p. A4.]

26. Grant Gilmore, "Legal Realism: its Cause and Cure", 70 *Yale Law Journal* 1037, 1038 (1961); and Edwin W. Patterson, "The Case Method in American Legal Education: its Origins and Objectives," 4 *Journal of Legal Education* 1, 2 (1951).

27. E. Gordon Gee & Donald W. Jackson, "Bridging the Gap," 1977 *Brigham Young University Law Review,* 695, 722-723 (1977).

28. Charles Warren, "History of the Harvard Law School," 3 *Law Quarterly Review* 123, 124 (1887), quoted in Patterson, "The Case Method in American Legal Education: its Origins and Objectives," 1 *Journal of Legal Education* 1, 3 (1951).

29. Alfred S. Korefsky & John Henry Schlegel, "Mirror, Mirror on the Wall: Histories of American Law Schools," 95 *Harvard Law Review* 833, 834 (1982) (hereinafter cited as "Korefsky & Schlegel, 'Mirror, Mirror on the Wall' ").

30. Korefsky & Schlegel, "Mirror, Mirror on the Wall" pp. 836-7.

31. Korefsky & Schlegel, "Mirror, Mirror on the Wall", p. 837.

32. Charles Rice, "The Role of Legal Education in Judicial Reform," McGuigan & Rader, eds., *A Blueprint for Judicial Reform* (Washington: Free Congress Foundation, 1981), p. 273 (hereinafter cited as "Rice, 'The Role of Legal Education in Judicial Reform' "). See also, Patrick B. McGuigan, "An interview with Judge Bork," *Judicial Notice,* June 1986 (reprinted June 1987).

33. *Marbury v. Madison* 5 U.S. (1 Cranch) 137 (1803).

34. *Brown v. Board of Education of Topeka,* 347 U.S. 483 (1954), supplemented 349 U.S. 294 (1955).

35. Rice, "The Role of Legal Education in Judicial Reform," p. 273.

36. *See, e.g.,* George Tushnet, "Following the Rules Laid Down: A Critique of Interpretivism and Neutral Principles," 96 *Harvard Law Review* 781 (1983).

37. William Bradford Reynolds, "Renewing the American Constitutional Heritage," 8 *Harvard Journal of Law and Public Policy* 225 (Spring 1985).

38. Rice, "The Role of Legal Education in Judicial Reform" p. 275.

39. Professor Grotin has argued that the intent of the Framers is meaningless to contemporary constitutional analysis because of changes in mores, values, and world views. *See*, "Historicism in Legal Scholarship," 90 *Yale Law Journal* 1017 (1981). The problem with Grotin's view is that it separates our legal system from its roots. Without the foundation of precedent and the intent of the framers, the bramble bush will go in whichever way the judicial winds happen to be blowing. In that case, none of our liberties are secure.

40. However, many of their professors will be quick to raise the question of whether or not the capitalist system is moral, and what the courts can do to bring about social and economic "reform." *See, e.g.*, "Reassessing Law Schooling: the Sterling Forest Group," 53 *New York University Law Review* 561 (1978). As long as the arguments against judicial activism are raised alongside the justifications for it, I have no objection. The problem is that in many law schools, the interpretivist position is either not mentioned at all, or ridiculed where it is mentioned.

41. Proverbs 29:2.

42. Alexis de Tocqueville, *Democracy in America* (New York: Random House, 1981), p. 73.

10

WHY LAWYERS LIKE JUDICIAL ACTIVISM: UNDERSTANDING THE LEGAL ESTABLISHMENT

by Dan Peterson

When the lawyers are through
What is there left, Bob?
Can a mouse nibble at it
And find enough to fasten a tooth in?

Why is there always a secret singing
When a lawyer cashes in?
Why does a hearse horse snicker
Hauling a lawyer away?

—From "The Lawyers Know Too Much,"
by Carl Sandburg

Let's lay the cards on the table. I am a lawyer, as was my father before me. I have practiced law, clerked for an appellate judge, and even engaged in full time public interest litigation. To make full disclosure, I should confess that some of my best friends are lawyers. Why, then, it is reasonable to ask, do I now propose to denounce the legal profession as a menace to Western Civilization, an enemy to republican government, and a threat to the people's freedom, prosperity, safety, and virtue?

Certainly, it is not due to lack of respect for the law itself, or a want of esteem for individual lawyers. I cherish the law, and have been known to find the after-hours lies of trial lawyers not only amusing, but plausible and instructive, when assisted by two or three bourbons. Thus my quarrel is not with the essence of the lawyerly vocation, or even with what the legal profession historically has been and done. But I do take exception—vociferous, even unruly exception—to what the legal profession has recently become under the reign of judicial activism. To retell an

211

old tale, judges and lawyers have been tempted by unfettered power and have joyfully succumbed. Since this usurpation puts their interests at odds with the common weal, they must be hauled back into line.

Why have lawyers as a class become so enamored of judicial activism? Before any very searching inquiry into this question can be made, we must describe definitely what we mean by "judicial activism."

At bottom, judicial activism consists of two related tendencies. The first is an increasing willingness by judges, either overtly or covertly, to ignore the plain meaning of text (whether of a statute, a constitution, or a precedent) and to substitute instead their own views of desirable policy or outcome. The second is a trend on the part of the judiciary to expand continuously the types of cases the courts will decide, and the varieties of persons and institutions that can be compelled to come under their sway.

These two tendencies, of course, reinforce each other. Fidelity to text implies limits on the scope of judicial authority. Slipping this textual harness not only allows judges to disregard the substantive rules of law that govern the outcome of cases, but also permits them to expand or ignore the limits on their own decision-making power. In turn, as the courts assume greater and greater power in society, and come to be viewed as omnicompetent arbiters of virtually any kind of dispute, a growing institutional arrogance diminishes further the felt need for the courts to respect the letter of statutes, precedents, and the Constitution.

So to return to our original question: Why do lawyers preserve, protect, and defend judicial activism? What's in it for them? The answer is brief: *money* and *power*. The subject of power is the more complex of the two, shading, as such subjects tend to do, into the realm of ideology. Let's look at the money issue first, then, before turning to the implications that the increased power of courts and lawyers has for the polity as a whole.

Judicial activism, quite simply, expands business opportunities for lawyers by increasing the number of occasions on which they can ply their trade. As judges drag more and more types of societal decisions into the courtroom, lawyers have that many more occasions to advise, to negotiate, and, often, to litigate.

212

Questions that formerly were committed to political institutions, to the family, to business, to the church, or to other bodies are transformed into legal questions, and effective "demand" for lawyers is stimulated.

In any market, an increase in demand calls forth an increase in supply, or else the market price goes up. In the case of lawyers, the profession as a whole benefits no matter which occurs. Either fees go up, or the profession is increased in numbers and influence. Law schools prosper when demand for a legal education rises or at least remains steady. Bar associations flourish when membership is continually augmented by new admissions to practice. Partners in law firms (who are in the business of buying legal services wholesale, and selling them retail) see their compensation and status rise when they sit atop a steadily expanding pyramid.

The singular beauty of the law, for lawyers anyway, is that the demand for legal services is almost infinitely expansible, and is to a considerable extent under the control of the legal profession itself. Judges, after all, are recruited from the ranks of lawyers, and there is no logical limit to the circumstances under which a court can say that one person has wronged another, and must pay him money. Once the judges have invented a new theory of liability, there is rarely a shortage of willing plaintiffs ready to try their luck at obtaining a big award of damages. And once a defendant has been sued, he has no choice but to hire a lawyer to defend his interests and his bank account. We can identify at least three main methods that courts have used to expand the scope of their own decision-making power, while simultaneously enlarging the volume of legal business for lawyers.

First is the simple creation of a new claim or cause of action at common law. Perhaps the most notorious judicial invention has been products liability law, particularly that theory of liability known as "strict liability in tort." Prior to the rise of this theory, a manufacturer or distributor of a product could, generally speaking, be held liable for an injury caused by a product only if he had been negligent in manufacturing or handling it. Reasonably enough, liability was not imposed unless there was some degree of *fault* on the part of the manufacturer or seller. But, beginning in California with the case of *Greenman v. Yuba*

Power Products, Inc. (1963)[1] virtually all American jurisdictions have now abandoned the notion of fault, and imposed liability for harm caused by products even when "the seller has exercised all possible care in the preparation and sale of his product. . . ."[2] The predictable result has been a torrent of lawsuits that has drastically raised the price of many products, sent insurance premiums through the roof, and driven manufacturers and others out of business. The bankruptcies of two major corporations (A. H. Robins because of the Dalkon Shield cases, and the Manville Corporation because of asbestos-related litigation) are only the most spectacular and visible instances of the harm caused to American business and the public by the judge-made products liability rules.

In the case of A. H. Robins, the company had paid out $530 million in product liability damages relating to Dalkon Shield claims before it finally sought protection in bankruptcy.[3] More than 320,000 claims are still pending against it.[4] No one can know what the total legal fees generated out of this mess will be, but undoubtedly they run into hundreds of millions of dollars already, and will climb much higher before the curtain is rung down. (To put the matter in perspective, Robins realized net profits of about $500,000 from marketing the Dalkon Shield.[5])

There are plenty of examples of new types of lawsuits recently created or expanded beyond recognition by the judiciary—too many, in fact, to list. But a few will illustrate. The "medical malpractice crisis" (which, among other things, has caused insurance premiums for some doctors to soar into six figures, forced some obstetricians simply to stop delivering babies because of the threat of liability, and seriously contributed to inflated medical costs) is almost wholly a judge-made phenomenon. Or reflect for a moment on such nebulous theories as "intentional infliction of emotional distress" and "tortious interference with business relationships." These are open-ended judicial invitations to bring almost any dispute involving personal unpleasantness, or any contest between business competitors, into the courtroom. In the past decade or so, courts in many states have been busy fundamentally rewriting the law of employment by giving employees a legal right to their jobs, regardless of the bargain struck between the employer and employee. In the process, they are undermining one of the most fundamental principles of free enterprise, the "employment at will" contract, which allows the employer or employee to terminate the employment relationship for any reason satisfactory to either of them. Not surprisingly, suits by employees against their employers shot up fifteen-fold between 1975 and 1983.[6] The subject matter of these rules may differ, but they all have one thing in common: they annex further territory to the judicial empire, and at the same time augment the gross income of lawyers.

A second method used by activist judges to accomplish these goals is expansive interpretation of statutes and constitutional provisions. When straightforward language, that was meant to cover only certain delimited circumstances, can be transmuted into something arcane, mysterious, elastic, and fanciful, and can be stretched to cover thousands of circumstances never dreamed of by those who drafted it, business opportunities for lawyers bloom abundantly. Nowhere has this hocus-pocus achieved more splendid successes than in the Supreme Court's interpretation of the United States Constitution.

Consider the four little words "due process of law." The Fourteenth Amendment, ratified by the states in 1868, provided that no state shall "deprive any person of life, liberty, or property, without due process of law". The principal purpose of this language, most serious historians of the period would agree, was to help secure for the newly emancipated blacks the regular administration of justice, particularly criminal justice, in the state courts. The Supreme Court of the United States, however, thinks that this language prohibits schoolchildren from reciting a prayer in school,[7] grants young women the constitutional right to dance topless in public places,[8] and bestows upon all of us the valuable right to threaten to kill a police officer performing his duties.[9] Employing a doctrine of "selective incorporation," the Court has held (contrary to the historical evidence)[10] that most of the provisions of the federal Bill of Rights apply to the states by being "incorporated" into the Due Process Clause. It has then imposed its own distorted construction of those rights to reach results like those just described. Cases based on the Court's imaginative interpretations of the Fourteenth Amendment account for the bulk of the constitutional litigation that comes before it, and before the lower federal courts as well. Were these decisions to be reversed at a stroke, and the activity of the courts returned to constitutional bounds, there would be a lot of idle courtrooms and unemployed lawyers.

A third way in which judicial activism increases demand for lawyers is perhaps less obvious, but is equally potent. I refer here to the revolution in *remedies* that has taken place over the past few decades. Many types of cases that now are staples of litigation never could have been brought previously because the courts had not fashioned the procedural mechanisms to hear those kinds of cases, or to enforce the decisions arising from them. For example, the sweeping use of mandatory injunctions, commanding a party to perform some act or series of acts, is a relatively recent development. Without this weapon in his arsenal, it is doubtful that a judicial activist such as Judge William Wayne Justice of Texas could have administered the state prison system from his courtroom,[11] or uprooted families in the name of equality, ordering twenty-five black residents of public housing to trade apartments with twenty-five whites in another complex (thereby requiring both of these groups to move across town).[12] Class actions, which allow the aggregation of thousands of claims together in a single suit, permit multi-million dollar suits to be brought against businesses (usually) that formerly would never have been asserted at all. Expansions of the scope of declaratory judgments have facilitated the bringing of ideological or political lawsuits that until recently would have been considered incapable of adjudication. And no discussion of remedies would be complete without mentioning 42 U.S.C. Sections 1983 and 1985. These statutes, enacted in 1877 and long considered a relic of Reconstruction, were judicially resuscitated in the early 1960s to provide a remedy for swarms of claimed deprivations of constitutional rights, and have enabled constitutional litigation to become one of the premier growth industries for lawyers.

Without question, all of these three methods for increasing the number and scope of lawsuits have created a harvest of riches for the legal profession. But perhaps an even juicier benefit for the profession is the changing character of those suits. In particular, activist jurisprudence is heavily pro-plaintiff, both in skewing the outcome of the case toward victory by the plaintiff and in multiplying the size of the damage awards the plaintiff can recover.

While this was being written, Texaco, the fifth largest corporation in the United States, declared bankruptcy because it had lost a lawsuit.[13] The judgment that Pennzoil obtained against Texaco was for more than $11 *billion*, or about a quarter of one percent of the gross national product of the United States.[14] Consider for a moment: what is a lawyer who can obtain such a judgment worth to Pennzoil? He's worth more to the company than all of its employees combined, who together could not produce such an income stream even over a period of several years. More starkly, what should Texaco (or any corporation that finds itself the target of high dollar suits) pay a law firm that might prevent such a colossal judgment from being entered against it? The answer, clearly, is: anything. Whatever it takes. Lawyers that can prevent the business from being destroyed by a courtroom raid on its treasury are more valuable than the corporation's employees, patents, plants, customers, or any asset it might possess. When courts put property up for grabs, lawyers become the brokers, and legal fees can zoom along with the ascending value of the property at stake.

Activist courts have rewritten the law in countless ways to make it easier for plaintiffs to win, and to increase the size of damage awards. Looking once again at tort law, one sees that most of the traditional defenses to negligence suits have either been eliminated or substantially weakened. The defense of contributory negligence—which prevented a plaintiff from winning a tort suit if he also was at fault—has been superseded in most jurisdictions by the comparative negligence rule, which allows such suits to be brought and won much more easily. Other defenses of long standing such as assumption of risk, last clear chance, and interspousal immunity from tort are also rapidly being abandoned. Some courts have even abandoned the fundamental concept that the defendant must have *caused* the plaintiff's injury, and have imposed liability simply because the defendant's products were on the market and *might* have been used by the plaintiff.[15]

Meanwhile, judgments have ballooned in size. A variety of changes in legal doctrine and other factors have led to swollen verdicts and judgments, but let's look for now at just one: punitive damages. I have in front of me a report of a case recently decided in Texas, called *Sammie Joe Skeen, et al. v. Monsanto*

Co.[16] The jury awarded $7.75 million in actual damages to the survivors of a chemical worker who died of leukemia, allegedly as the result of exposure to the chemical benzene. Let us not even consider whether $7.75 million is a rational measure of damages for the future earnings of a chemical worker, or whether the worker's disease was actually caused by benzene exposure (the scientific evidence on this point is, in fact, vigorously disputed). Multi-million dollar awards have become common enough in such cases. But in this instance the six-member federal jury went on to award to the plaintiffs an additional *$100 million* in punitive damages. Punitive damages, we should note, are designed to punish defendants, not to compensate plaintiffs, although the plaintiffs (and their attorneys) receive the money. Consequently, judges and juries have almost *carte blanche* authority to determine the amount of punitive damages, and their determination may be completely divorced from any measure of the magnitude of the harm. In effect, open season can be declared on the property of defendants. It certainly wouldn't take too many more cases like *Skeen* for Monsanto to join the ranks of major corporations like A.H. Robins, Manville, and Texaco, all bankrupted by an activist judiciary and legal profession.

There is a method to this madness. Most personal injury plaintiffs' lawyers receive their compensation on a "contingent fee" basis; that is, they take as their fee a percentage of the judgment recovered by the plaintiff. These fees usually range between 25 percent and 50 percent of the amount awarded to the plaintiff. If the plaintiff loses, his lawyer gets nothing. Defendants' attorneys, on the other hand, typically bill on an hourly basis. They get paid regardless of whether their client wins or loses. Thus, the plaintiffs' bar is highly motivated, out of a direct financial interest, to work tirelessly for legal rules permitting expanded liability, fewer defenses, and larger damage awards. The defense bar—many of whom are philosophically opposed to such trends—must rely upon a more detached idealism to counter these efforts since, after all, more suits and greater risk of liability also work to their financial advantage, though less palpably. Unsurprisingly, the forces favoring expanded liability have been triumphing with a consistency that approaches inexorability.

All of these factors, I have argued, promote a diversion of economic resources to the legal profession, increasing its wealth and size. But do the figures bear these arguments out? They do, in spades. Although the beginnings of activist jurisprudence can be traced to the 1930s, it was not until the advent of the Warren Court in the 1950s that the dikes began to crumble, and not until the 1960s that the flood waters came pouring through. Let's look at the size of the legal profession historically and see how it has fared.

Admissions to the Bar (00)		U.S. Population (000,000)
1948	11,300[1]	146,730[2]
1951	13,141	154,878
1954	9,928	163,026
1957	9,592	171,984
1960	10,505	180,671
1963	10,788	189,242
1966	14,637	196,560
1969	19,123	204,878
1972	25,086	205,052
1975	34,930	215,973
1978	41,662	222,580
1981	44,679	230,019
1984	42,630	236,413
1985	42,450	238,648

[1]Source for 1948–1972 is American Bar Foundation, The 1971 Lawyer Statistical Report 20 (1972). Data for 1975–1985 is taken from Bar Examiner, volumes 45, 48, 51, 54, 55 respectively.

[2]Source used for 1951–1969 is U.S. Bureau of the Census, Statistical Abstract of the United States: 1975, 5 (96th ed. 1975). Statistics for 1948 and 1978 received per phone conversation with Bureau of Statistics. Statistics for 1972–1985 taken from Statistical Abstract of the United States: 1985, 26 (105th ed. 1985).

In 1850, there were 23,939 lawyers in the United States, out of a total population of 23,192,000.[17] Thus, one out of every 969 Americans was a lawyer. Over the next century, during which the United States was transformed from an essentially rural society to a highly urbanized, industrial economy, this lawyer to population ratio increased to about 1 in 700.[18] Between 1951 and 1960, with large-scale judicial activism just getting underway, the growth in the size of the profession began to speed up. The total number of lawyers went from 221,605 to 285,933, an increase of 29 percent.[19] By 1970, the number of lawyers had risen to 355,242, and one out of every 577 Americans was a lawyer.[20] By 1980, there were 542,205 lawyers (one lawyer for every 420 people).[21] Just between 1960 and 1985, the number of lawyers multiplied nearly two and one-half times. The American Bar Foundation predicts that by 1995 there will be about 930,000 lawyers, or one out of every 279 Americans.[22] All of this occurred, of course, at a time when the total population of the country was increasing only gradually.[23]

By counting only the total number of lawyers, these figures actually understate the rate of increase in attorneys during the past twenty or thirty years. The chart on the preceding page compares the increase in the total United States population to the number of new admissions to the bar for the period between 1948 and 1985.

Not only has the legal profession flourished in terms of numbers, it has prospered financially as well. Between 1980 and 1985, at a time when inflation was low by recent standards, the annual receipts for legal services doubled, from $25.7 billion to $51.2 billion.[24] In absolute terms, this national legal bill of over $50 billion a year is a gross underestimate, because it does not include attorneys employed as in-house counsel to corporations, as government lawyers, and by tax-exempt organizations.[25] It may be that the rise in the wealth and numbers of the legal profession, concurrently with the explosion of judicial activism, is just a coincidence. When ants show up at a picnic, well, that might be just a coincidence, too.

Although the affection that the legal profession nurtures for judicial activism is in good part traceable to these economic benefactions, money is certainly not the sole animating motive. It may not even be the principal stimulus for this durable love affair. Earlier, I adverted to power as a potent explanatory factor and, while money is a form of power, it is to power in its more direct and political forms that I would now like to turn.

It is a matter of fact that, over a few short decades, judges and courts have appropriated final authority over a wide range of societal and political decisions that previously were not considered to be legal questions at all. Courts now routinely decide minute (and major) issues about religious observances in public life, and lately have concerned themselves with questions of religious doctrine in churches themselves and in church-run schools. They have asserted a broad jurisdiction over just about every aspect of public education, from selection of textbooks, to hiring and firing of teachers, to disciplining of students, to participation in athletics, even to the election of the homecoming queen. They have arrogated authority to proscribe or permit practices relating to conception, childbearing, and sexual conduct, in their decisions on subjects such as contraception, abortion, and homosexuality. They have assumed a supervisory role over the prison systems. Operating, in part, under a web of regulatory statutes, every day they prescribe or overrule the decisions of businesses in marketing, product design, pensions, employment and personnel matters, finance, plant safety and operations—there is hardly any aspect of running an enterprise over which the courts will not take jurisdiction. The criminal laws of states and municipalities are habitually rewritten or thrown out by the federal courts. Decisions of the executive branch are routinely reviewed and often second-guessed by judges. It is becoming difficult, in fact, to name any major aspect of societal decision-making that will not be considered (and usually decided) by the courts.

Throughout history, every court has had its courtiers, sharing in the sovereign's power and basking in reflected glory. In present day America, the court is a court of law, not a royal court, and the courtiers are called lawyers. When the principal business of the judicial branch was to settle disputes over land, interpret contracts, construe codicils to wills, and perform similarly unexciting tasks, the opportunities for power and glory in the law were few. But as all types of political decision-making and societal dispute resolution gravitate into the hands of judges, the courts become a combination of court, legislature, and executive, of parent and school board, of city council and church, of business manager and policeman, all rolled into one. Lawyers, as the class that is professionally expert at manipulating the decisions of judges, are the power brokers for this new concentration of authority. But in playing this role, they also act a part in a much larger drama.

In this connection, it is instructive to recall the composition and outlook of what Irving Kristol has called "the new class." According to Kristol:

> This "new class" is not easily defined but may be vaguely described. It
> consists of a goodly proportion of those college-educated people whose

skills and vocations proliferate in a "post-industrial society" (to use Daniel Bell's convenient term). We are talking about scientists, teachers and educational administrators, journalists and others in the communication industries, psychologists, social workers, those lawyers and doctors who make their careers in the expanding public sector, city planners, the staffs of the larger foundations, the upper levels of the government bureaucracy, and so on. It is, by now, a quite numerous class; it is an indispensable class for our kind of society; it is a disproportionately powerful class; it is also an ambitious and frustrated class.[26]

These are the people who run the government, shape public opinion, and provide other support functions for the liberal welfare state. Although Kristol specifically mentions only public sector lawyers, it is becoming increasingly clear that most lawyers—even those with a purely private practice—are, because of judicial activism, coming to share the functions (and thus the values and interests) of the "new class." Kristol describes the members of this class as:

keenly interested in power. Power for what? Well, the power to shape our civilization—a power which, in a capitalist system, is supposed to reside in the free market. The "new class" wants to see much of this power redistributed to government, where *they* will then have a major say in how it is exercised.[27]

Here Kristol begins to touch upon the major political division of our times: the line between those who want to see even more power snapped up by an already swollen centralized government, and those who want to preserve or restore autonomy for private institutions. It is, to be quite candid, a watershed between Left and Right. For example, in defining the term "conservative" Robert Nisbet has stated that "The essence of this body of ideas is the protection of the social order—family, neighborhood, local community, and region foremost—from the ravishments of the centralized political state."[28] At the opposite end of the spectrum, the proclivity of the political Left for statist intervention at the expense of local and private institutions is equally well-known.

The short-term professional interests of lawyers place them squarely on the side of centralized state power in this conflict. When disputes are settled privately, and final decisions are made by non-governmental institutions, lawyers have no opportunity to perform their professional functions. It is only when the state intervenes—usually through the judicial system, but also through executive or legislative action—that the lawyers are called in. But wait a minute. Lawyers? On the Left? How can that be, when everyone knows that the lawyers' professional organization, the American Bar Association, is nothing but a bunch of crusty, arch-conservative, corporate establishment attorneys? It may have been—sixty years ago. But that image—still carefully perpetuated in the popular press—has not been accurate for a long time now.

Every two years, the ABA publishes its formal positions on legislation pending before the Congress. Although many of the bills the ABA supports or opposes are relatively technical or deal with obscure areas, it also takes positions on major legislation. The bills of deepest concern to the ABA are identified as "priorities." A look at the ABA's priorities for the 99th Congress (1985–86) reveals an unmistakable ideological slant.[29] A few of the priorities would simply provide direct benefits or exemptions from liability for lawyers and judges.[30] But most of the legislative priorities of the ABA are directly supportive of judicial activism and of the agenda of the political Left. What follows is not exhaustive, but should show the general orientation of the ABA.

In these two years, the ABA has: supported permanent reauthorization of the Equal Access to Justice Act (which allows many parties who sue the government to recover attorneys' fees if they win, thereby having the taxpayers pay for their lawyers); opposed a bill that would have limited the award of attorney's fee in litigation against the government; opposed bills that would have removed jurisdiction from the federal courts to decide cases involving busing, abortion, and school prayer; opposed measures to limit or abolish the "diversity jurisdiction" of federal courts (which permits suits between residents of different states to be brought in federal court); supported judicial salary increases; opposed the "good faith" exception to the exclusionary rule for warrantless searches and seizures; supported handgun control and opposed repealing federal restrictions on firearms; opposed legislation to limit monetary damages and attorneys' fees in medical malpractice lawsuits; opposed reform of the product liability laws; supported the Genocide Treaty; and supported funding for the Legal Services Corporation, with "minimal restrictions" on the often political (and usually left-liberal) activities of the Corporation's grantees.[31]

The ABA's staunch support for the Legal Services Corporation is illustrative of the causes and effects of the legal profession's love affair with radical activism. The ostensible mission of LSC is to provide legal representation to the poor for divorces, landlord-tenant disputes, credit problems, and the like. The naive observer might think that the legal profession might actually oppose such a government-financed program since, at the margins at least, it might divert potentially paying clients from the private bar to these legal services attorneys. Not at all. The legal profession has at least three powerful reasons for supporting the Corporation, or more specifically, for supporting the more than 300 local "recipient" organizations to which LSC distributes funds, and which actually take the cases to court.

First, the existence of LSC and the local recipients helps relieve the private bar of its historical obligation to provide aid to poor people on a voluntary basis, whether through individual lawyers' waiving or reducing their fees, or through more organized programs of volunteer assistance at the local level. Second, this annual infusion of government cash—more than $300 million from the federal government each year, plus additional support from state and local governments—supports a lot of lawyers (over 6,000 attorneys and paralegals).[32] But third, and perhaps most significantly, many of these LSC lawyers are left-wing activists of the first magnitude, busily filing lawsuits aimed more at "reform" and "structural changes" than at helping real poor people with their very real and immediate legal problems.[33] Thus, the LSC lawyers are some of the advance scouts for the expanding judicial empire, pushing the frontiers of activism farther forward at the expense of traditional values and private institutions. And each time they do so, they marginally increase the power of the State, of judges, and of the legal profession as a whole.

Once the ABA's commitment to judicial activism is grasped, and the reasons why its members have a powerful stake in defending activism are understood, the ABA's behavior in screening President Reagan's judicial nominees makes perfect sense.

The last thing the organized bar wants to see is a bench populated by judges committed to judicial restraint. Thus, the ABA's torpedoing of men such as Prof. Lino Graglia and Dean William Harvey—eminently qualified, except that they oppose judicial activism—is not an aberration, but is exactly in line with the ABA's interests.

When it is seen that the bar has a professional interest in consolidating and expanding the power of the centralized state, new light is also shed on many of the legal theories implemented by activist judges. While it is true that products liability laws and other theories promoting recoveries by plaintiffs generate business and fees for the legal profession, they also help tip the balance of public and private power in favor of the government. By placing the disposition of the assets of business increasingly under the control of the judicial branch of the state, these rules weaken the institution of private enterprise and undermine the very conception of property rights. Because secure rights of property and a free enterprise system are indispensable conditions for liberty, the assault on these things by activist judges and their supporters in the legal profession is just one part of the continued siege by government against the private domain and the freedom that it supports.

The Founders of our nation were well aware of the profound connection between the preservation of private property and the existence of a free society. The constitutional and legal system that they bequeathed us contained safeguards for property as well as carefully limiting the powers of the national government, so that encroachments on the private domain and on local institutions could be prevented. Security of property and the inviolability of contract together were a *sine qua non* for the rise of a modern, industrial economy. Huge aggregations of capital were necessary to enable large-scale production, to provide a surplus for research and development, to finance the building of a national infrastructure, and to support the other prerequisites of the explosive economic development that occurred in the latter part of the Nineteenth Century and much of the Twentieth Century. Capital on this scale simply could not have been accumulated without legal guarantees of its secure possession. Not coincidentally, the great figures of the law in this period of growth were predominantly corporate lawyers, those who excelled at building and defending the business enterprises that were the engine for creating an unprecedented degree of economic prosperity and growth. Elihu Root is perhaps paradigmatic of this type of lawyer.

But who are the new paradigms for the legal profession? Lawyers of the type represented by Joe Jamail, Melvin Belli, Philip Corboy; the plaintiffs' lawyers whose mission is stripping assets out of corporations, even to the point of bankrupting them. Their specialty is an economic one: unsettling property rights, breaking up productive enterprises, giving the state a power of appointment over private wealth. Their only competitors for this mantle are the ideological activists: the Naderites, the ACLU lawyers, the Legal Services lawyers, and their kin. While these ideological activists frequently concern themselves with economic issues, too, their specialties tend to be more social and political: rooting out religion, extending court power over schools, weakening local law enforcement, promoting state intervention in family matters, and the like. Together, they assist the state in extending its domination, and are usually well-rewarded in terms of money or power.

Need I point out that this consolidation of power in the hands of courts and lawyers is subversive of republican self-government, and contrary to the most essential principles on which this country was founded? The Founders were careful to circumscribe the power of the federal government within narrow and specific bounds; activist judges have burst those bounds. Those who framed the Constitution recognized that all political power had its source in the people, and could be legitimately exercised only by the representatives of the people; unelected activist judges have usurped the power of representative bodies and officials. The founding generation realized that property was an indispensable bedrock of liberty; activist judges are undermining it. The Framers knew that freedom depends on the rule of law, not men; activist judges are substituting their own views and policies for established laws and precedents.

This latter point, particularly, is crucial. We have described previously how activist judges have worked a revolution in the common law and in constitutional interpretation by changing the rules. But some things are even worse than simply changing the rules. Though outwardly maintaining the forms of law, much of what judges do these days is not properly speaking "law" at all, but only an elaborate subterfuge for unbridled judicial discretion.

The essence of a rule of law is that it is indeed a *rule*; it is something that can be stated in advance and to which conduct can be conformed. The rule may have exceptions, but these exceptions should also be able to be formulated and understood. Lately, however, the courts have become fond of what they call "balancing tests," in which various factors allegedly governing the decision are listed, and then "weighed" by the court to determine how the case is to be decided. The metaphor of "balancing" and "weighing" sounds just and judicious, but in practice this balancing simply reserves the matter to the judge's discretion. The factors to be balanced cannot be quantified, so the "weighing" of them is illusory. Because such factors are subjective and frequently involve choices of values, no two persons will ever "weigh" them in exactly the same fashion.

An example will show how this device works. The case of *In re Spring*,[34] decided by the Supreme Judicial Court of Massachusetts in 1980, considered whether hemodialysis treatment should be given to a mentally incompetent, elderly man with endstage kidney disease. Such a case involves questions of life and death, and opinion in society is strongly divided not only as to when such treatment should be given or withheld, but who should decide such cases. Historically, questions regarding such medical treatment have been resolved by the patient's family in consultation with the physicians involved. But in the late 1970s, courts began to intrude themselves into these decisions. What circumstances, if any, should trigger involvement by the courts thus became a crucial problem.

Here is how the highest court in Massachusetts resolved the issue. It noted first that "our opinions should not be taken to establish any requirement of prior judicial approval that would not otherwise exist."[35] This in itself was a rather Delphic statement, since the state's statutes were silent on the subject, and the court was preparing to specify those instances in which prior judicial approval *was* indeed needed. The court then set forth the factors that would need to be "taken into account in deciding whether there should be an application for a prior court order with respect to medical treatment of an incompetent patient."[36]

The court stated that among these factors "are at least the following":

> the extent of impairment of the patient's mental faculties, whether the patient is in the custody of a State institution, the prognosis without the proposed treatment, the prognosis with the proposed treatment, the complexity, risk and novelty of the proposed treatment, its possible side effects, the patient's level of understanding and probable reaction, the urgency of decision, the consent of the patient, spouse or guardian, the good faith of those who participate in the decision, the clarity of professional opinion as to what is good medical practice, the interests of third persons, and the administrative requirements of any institutions involved.[37]

Clear as tobacco juice? I suggest that that is exactly how clear the court *intended* to make this "rule" of law. Because no two persons can be expected to arrive at comparable conclusions regarding the treatment of a particular patient by "weighing" the balance of the factors listed by the court, it becomes impossible for the family and physicians to make any decision without a severe risk of being judicially second-guessed. To make doubly sure that confusion would reign, and that cases could not be decided without judicial intervention, the court volunteered that "We are not called upon to decide what combination of circumstances makes prior court approval necessary or desirable, even on the facts of the case before us."[38] And if some blockhead failed to get the message, the court blandly noted two sentences later than "Action taken without judicial approval might be the subject of either criminal or civil liability."[39]

This "balancing" technique has become a favorite of the Supreme Court in deciding constitutional cases. By shattering the very notion of a "rule of law," this technique vastly enlarges judicial discretion, makes well-established rights insecure, and allows the court to extend favored "rights" (and duties corresponding to those "rights") into areas wholly unanticipated by the Founders.

The "balancing test" is just one example of a variety of contrivances that the courts have used to depart from the rule of law and to increase their own power. Whether the indefinite continuation of these subterfuges will be permitted is what the current controversy about "original intention" or "original meaning" of the Constitution is all about. Attorney General Meese has performed a public service beyond measure by bringing this issue to the forefront of national debate.[40] If we cannot return to a principled, disciplined interpretation of our fundamental national charter, we as a nation will no longer proceed under the rule of law, but under the rule of lawyers.

This prospect I note with sorrow, because the legal profession, by and large, has placed itself squarely on the wrong side of this debate. Lawyers are not educated in constitutional history; they barely are trained in the text of the Constitution itself. Instead they are taught to look only to the pronouncements (preferably the latest pronouncements) of the Supreme Court, as if the Court's decisions, and not the Constitution, were the supreme law of the land. Understanding the Constitution, and adhering to it, would be inconvenient, since it would result in drastically cutting back the jurisdiction assumed by the courts, and throwing half the lawyers in the country out of work. And nobody wants that, right?

Well, anyway, the lawyers don't. Lawyers don't just tolerate judicial activism; they don't just like it. Because the size, wealth, and power of their profession have come to depend on activism, now they're addicted to it; they *need* it. Which is why we won't see an end to it, as long as the scope of judicial authority remains the exclusive province of judges and lawyers themselves.

REFERENCES

Why Lawyers Like Judicial Activism: Understanding the Legal Establishment by Dan Peterson.

1. 59 Cal. 2d 57, 377 P.2d 897, 27 Cal. Rptr. 697 (1963).
2. RESTATEMENT (SECOND) OF TORTS, Sec. 402A (1966).
3. Telephone interview with Mr. Roger Wilson, General Counsel, A.H. Robins Corporation (April 15, 1987).
4. *Id.*
5. *Id.*
6. Comment, "Erosion of the Employment-At-Will Doctrine: Choosing a Legal Theory for Wrongful Discharge", 14 *Cap. U.L. Rev.* 461, 462 (1985).
7. *Wallace v. Jaffree*, 472 U.S. 38 (1985); *School District v. Schempp*, 374 U.S. 203 (1963).
8. *Doran v. Salem Inn, Inc.*, 422 U.S. 922, 932–34 (1975).
9. *Gooding v. Wilson*, 405 U.S. 518, 519–20 (1972).
10. Fairman, "Does the Fourteenth Amendment Incorporate the Bill of Rights?", 2 *Stan. L. Rev.* 5 (1949).
11. *Ruiz v. Estelle*, 503 F. Supp. 1265 (S.D. Tex. 1980).

12. *Young v. Whiteman*, No. P-82-37-CA (E.D. Tex. 1983) (see Orders and Mandatory Tenant Transfer Plan filed Oct. 11, Oct. 19, Nov. 29, and Nov. 30, 1983).

13. Washington *Times*, April 13, 1987, p. 1, Col. 7.

14. According to the Office of Economic Analysis of the Department of Commerce, the Gross National Product of the United States for 1986 in current dollars was $4.206 trillion.

15. *Sindell v. Abbott Laboratories*, 26 Cal. 3d 358, 607 P. 2d 924, 163 Cal. Rptr. 132 (1980).

16. *The Texas Lawyer*, March 30, 1987, pp. 1, 10–11.

17. The source for the number of lawyers in 1850 is A. Andrews, *Lawyers and Population: United States and Alabama*, unpaginated supplementary table (1943). The total 1850 population figure is taken from U.S. Bureau of the Census, *Statistical Abstract of the United States: 1975*, 5 (96th ed. 1975).

18. The data are for 1951. The number of lawyers was 221,605 and the total population was 154,878,000, for an actual ratio of 1 in 699. The population figure is from U.S. Bureau of the Census, *supra* n.17. The figure for the number of lawyers is from American Bar Foundation, *The 1971 Lawyer Statistical Report* p. 6 (1972).

19. American Bar Foundation, *The 1971 Lawyer Statistical Report* 6 (1972), p.6.

20. *Id.* The population in 1970 was 204,878,000, which figure is taken from U.S. Bureau of the Census, *supra* n.17.

21. The 1980 and 1985 lawyer figures are taken from American Bar Foundation, *The Lawyer Statistical Report: A Statistical Profile of the U.S. Legal Profession in the 1980s*, p. 4 (1980). The 1985 figure is an estimate. The population figures are from U.S. Bureau of the Census, *Statistical Abstract of the United States: 1985*, 26 (105th ed. 1985).

22. American Bar Foundation, *supra* n.21.

23. Between 1960 and 1985, the population increased from 180,671,000 to 238,648,000, a percentage rise of 32%. The 1960 figure is from U.S. Bureau of the Census, *supra* n.17. The 1985 is from American Bar Foundation, *supra* n.21.

24. Figure for 1980 was taken from U.S. Bureau of the Census, *Current Business Reports: Annual Survey*, 9 (August 1985, Doc. 763–7662). Figure for 1985 was obtained by telephone from the same Bureau.

25. The figures are "derived from a sample of taxable employers only and, therefore, do not include nonemployer receipts or receipts from tax-exempt organizations." *Id.*

26. I. Kristol, *Two Cheers for Capitalism*, p. 25 (1978).

27. *Id.* p. 26.

28. R. Nisbet, *Prejudices: A Philosophical Dictionary*, p. 55 (1982).

29. American Bar Association, *Washington Letter*, January 1, 1987, pp. 3–15.

30. For example, the ABA opposed a bill to repeal an exemption in the Fair Debt Collection Practices Act for attorneys who regularly collect consumer debts; supported a bill to improve financial benefits to the survivors of federal judges; supported a bill to make senior status judges retroactively and permanently exempt from Social Security taxes; opposed any legislation that would have brought the legal profession under the regulatory jurisdiction of the Federal Trade Commission; and opposed the concept that money derived from drug dealing (and later paid to defense lawyers as fees) could be seized under forfeiture statutes like other assets derived from criminal activity. *Id.*

31. *Id.*

32. Telephone interview with Legal Services Corporation.

33. *Legal Services Corporation: The Robber Barons of the Poor?* (Washington Legal Foundation, 1985).

34. *In re Spring*, 405 N.E.2d 115 (Mass. 1980).

35. *Id.* at 120.

36. *Id.* at 121.

37. *Id.*

38. *Id.*

39. *Id.*
40. *See, e.g.,* E. Meese, "Toward A Jurisprudence of Original Intention", *Benchmark,* Jan.–Feb. 1986, p. 1.

11

THE WORK-PRODUCT OF CARTER'S JUDICIARY: ADJUDICATION AS POLICYMAKING

by George C. Smith

As seen in Chapter 6, the judicial selection policies of President Carter were designed to pack the federal judiciary with activist judges who would be receptive to the concerns of the constituencies from which they sprang. With highly ideological groups such as the Federation of Women Lawyers playing an ubiquitous role in the select and confirmation process,[1] the vast majority of Carter's appointees were either overtly supportive of liberal judicial policy or suitably submissive to its orthodox canons. Those rare Carter nominees who showed signs to the contrary—such as Judge Cornelia Kennedy and Judge Edward C. Reed of Nevada[2]—were so harshly criticized at their confirmation hearings that they could not help but be wary of appearing "insensitive" to the concerns of the Left in their future decisions.

Given this background, it was inevitable that the 262 federal judges appointed by Jimmy Carter would infuse federal jurisprudence with an unprecedented degree of liberal-activist predispositions and tendencies. While a comprehensive survey of the collective output of Carter-appointed judges is beyond the scope of this chapter, significant empirical evidence exists to substantiate this conclusion.

The evidence is especially striking in the criminal law area. Empirical studies conducted by a team of political scientists from three universities in 1985-86 demonstrated that Carter-appointed district court judges are roughly twice as likely to issue rulings favorable to criminal defendants than district judges appointed by Reagan or Nixon.[3] At the appellate level, the increased tendency of Carter appointees to rule in favor of criminal defendants is even more striking. In non-unanimous decisions at the appellate level, the Carter appointees are almost *five times* more likely than Reagan appointees to support the criminal defendant's position.[4] Further, Carter appointee support for criminal defendants was also well above the level of such support reflected in the decisions of the Johnson Administration's largely liberal appointees.[5]

The disparity at the appellate level is especially significant because appellate reversal of criminal convictions represents the most sensitive—and the most dangerous—area for the exercise of discretionary judicial activism. To the extent that the Carter judges' extremely high rate of criminal reversals reflects the ideological roots of their selection, the consequences for the safety of society could be quite severe. The release of large numbers of violent recidivists to the streets is a high price to pay for the abstract virtues of a liberalized judiciary.

The consequences of Carter's appointment policies are by no means confined to the criminal area. A 1983 study published in *Judicature* surveyed the effects of Carter's appointments on the outcome of sex and race discrimination cases and produced some highly significant findings.[6]

In non-unanimous appellate rulings on claims of sex discrimination, Carter appointees cast votes supporting the claimants 67 percent of the time. The corresponding rate of support for claimants among the appointees of preceding Presidents Ford and Nixon was 23 percent. In race discrimination cases, Carter appointees voted with the claimants in 56 percent of the non-unanimous cases, compared to 30 percent for Ford appointees and 23 percent for Nixon appointees.[7]

This radical difference in outcomes cannot be dismissed on the theory that Ford and Nixon were especially conservative in their judicial appointments. Ford's moderate-to-liberal approach on judicial/legal issues was typified by his appointments of the very liberal John Paul Stevens to the Supreme Court and the equally liberal (and former National Lawyer's Guild member) Edward Levi as Attorney General. Mr. Levi, like other Attorneys General, played an important role in overseeing the selection of judicial nominees during President Ford's tenure. The futility of Nixon's efforts to appoint a conservative judiciary is underscored by the doctrinaire liberalism of Justice Harry Blackmun (author of the notorious *Roe v. Wade* decision) and the pivotal role of Justice Lewis Powell in establishing the legality of reverse discrimination in the form of employment preferences and quotas.[8]

Mere cold numbers, however, do not begin to capture the true impact of Carter's judges on the legal system which increasingly pervades every area of American life. To appreciate fully how these judges are shaping policy at every level of government, it is necessary to consider concrete examples of their judicial handiwork.

The exemplary cases discussed below give some flavor of how the breed of judges appointed by President Carter are expanding the outer limits of judicial policymaking. A common theme of their judicial approach is to invoke the broadest "principles" underlying a statute or constitutional provision as a justification for disregarding the limitations of its actual text. Such expansive interpretations are invoked in turn to justify the exercise of vastly expanded jurisdiction and the most sweeping forms of remedies. The result is to consign the traditional elements of sound judicial restraint—which are critical to maintaining proper equilibrium between the judiciary and the other two branches—to the status of ineffectual relics.

Consequently, we find Carter's judges imposing their personal policy predilections in settings ranging from the election of high school homecoming queens[9] to the formulation of an entire state's employee compensation policy.[10] They have used their jurisdiction over civil rights complaints as a toehold for completely supplanting the authority of local governments over housing and educational policy, to the point of directly ordering city council members how to vote on particular measures.[11] In purporting to vindicate the First Amendment rights of critics of government, they have sought to censor the United States Congress in its choice of legislative terms and phrases.[12] Significantly, their disdain for the prerogatives of other government authorities extends even to the authority of the Supreme Court to have the last word in declaring the supreme law of the land. When the High Court announced a more restrictive constitutional standard for judicial intervention in prison conditions disputes, Carter's judges simply repudiated or ignored it.[13]

Although space limitations foreclose discussion of many equally disturbing examples of the excesses of Carter's judges,[14] the following cases are offered as representative illustrations of how that judicial legacy is affecting the functioning of our democracy.

REPUDIATING THE SUPREME COURT: THE PRISON CASES

Perhaps no area of law has seen more violence done to the principles of constitutional fidelity and judicial restraint than that of prison conditions litigation.

While the persistent problem of overcrowded and substandard prisons unquestionably demands the concern and commitment of government, it remains essentially a legislative problem which must be addressed in the context of other equally pressing demands on limited state resources.[15]

The primary cause of today's prison problems is simply too much violent crime, creating the inescapable necessity of incarcerating large populations of violent felons who present a "clear and present danger" to society. If state and local government fall short of the standards of the ACLU and other prisoners' lobbies in providing commodious prison lodgings, it is largely a function of too many diverse demands on overextended government budgets. It has little or nothing to do with official "cruelty," and it is hardly an "unusual" condition.[16] Nonetheless, the past 20 years have seen the federal courts all but dismantle state and local authority over prison management. In a constitutional encroachment of extraordinary dimensions, courts have invoked an elastic interpretation of the Eighth Amendment's cruel-and-unusual punishment clause to justify comprehensive judicial supervision over prison conditions throughout the nation.[17] Whereas the Eighth Amendment was originally intended to proscribe barbarous and torturous punishments exemplified by the rack and the thumbscrew,[18] is is now routinely deployed by the courts to micro-manage the calorie-count of prison menus and the temperature of prison showers.[19]

In 1981, however, the Supreme Court firmly admonished the lower courts against excessive intervention in prison cases. In *Rhodes v. Chapman* (1981)[20] a nearly unanimous Court (Justice Marshall alone dissenting) held that the practice of "double-celling"—housing two prisoners in a cell originally designed for one—did not constitute cruel and unusual punishment. In rejecting the Sixth Circuit's condemnation of what it considered to be sub-standard prison conditions, Justice Powell's opinion stressed that:

> [C]onditions that cannot be said to be cruel and unusual under contemporary standards are not unconstitutional. To the extent that such conditions are restrictive and even harsh, they are part of the penalty that criminal offenders pay for their offense against society.[21]

The High Court then set forth an unmistakable directive for the lower courts to refrain from the kind of interventions typified by the lower court's ruling in *Rhodes:*

> Perhaps they reflect an aspiration toward an ideal for long-term confinement. But the Constitution does not mandate comfortable prisons, and prisons . . . which house persons convicted of serious crimes cannot be free of discomfort. Thus, these considerations are properly weighed by the legislature and prison administration rather than a court. There being no constitutional violation, the District Court had no authority to consider whether double-celling . . . was the best response to the increase in Ohio's statewide prison population.[22]

The Supreme Court having spoken with such clarity, it might have been expected that the lower courts would obey and withdraw from the business of supervising state and local prisons. But such an assumption would have failed to account for the audacious activism of the lower federal courts—and particularly the policy-prone district judges appointed by Jimmy Carter.

In the 1981 case of *Smith v. Fairman,*[23] Judge Harold Baker of the Central District of Illinois (appointed by Carter in 1978) held that double-celling in an Illinois prison *was* unconstitutional on the very grounds held insufficient in *Rhodes.* So determined was Judge Baker to impose his views of enlightened penal policy on the state system that he disregarded evidence which refuted his assessment of conditions as well as directly-controlling Supreme Court precedent.[24]

The Seventh Circuit's emphatic reversal of Baker's decision exposed its profound errors. First, the appeals court demonstrated that the measures which Baker had condemned as unconstitutional had actually *improved* prisoner safety and well-being. As the Seventh Circuit observed:

> It is true that several experts were against double celling and perceived it as harmful, but the stark reality is that physical violence in the institution has declined markedly in the last few years. Thus, the facts fail to support the experts' dire projections. Moreover, the experts' opinions as to what constitutes contemporary standards of decency are merely helpful, not binding.[25]

The appeals court further explained that to follow the course charted by Judge Baker "... would be nothing more than a substitution of our judicial values for those of prison administrators as to what is good for prisoners. The Supreme Court forbade such subjective adjudication in *Rhodes*."[26]

But even while the Seventh Circuit was reversing Judge Baker's ruling in *Fairman*, another Carter appointee was openly repudiating the *Rhodes* holding in another prison conditions case. Judge Stewart Newblatt of the U.S. District Court in Michigan did not even conceal disdain for the High Court's judgement on the prison conditions issue. In overruling a variety of restrictive measures taken by Michigan prison authorities in response to an outbreak of major prison riots, Newblatt stated that, "This Court disagrees with much of the content of the *Rhodes* statement."[27] When inferior federal judges so openly voice their opposition to nearly-unanimous Supreme Court rulings, it is not surprising that inmates feel justified in rejecting the legitimacy of their confinement.

In his decision in *Walker v. Johnson*, Judge Newblatt engaged in precisely the kind of prison micro-management that the Supreme Court had admonished against in *Rhodes*. Among the more noteworthy aspects of his ruling was a determination that the Constitution requires at least 4.5 hours per week of "law library time," plus liberalized access to "jailhouse lawyers."[28] Although prison administrators were coping with perilous conditions in a riot-torn system, Newblatt further overruled them in requiring a minimum of two hours of "yard-time" per day. He also construed the Eighth Amendment as authority for imposing regulations governing the frequency and quality of showers, and imposed extensive due process requirements upon the prison's system of administrative segregation for major misconduct.[29]

Judge Newblatt justified his intervention in prison policy with a statement that is remarkable in its unconcealed disdain for judicial restraint:

> The Court would also note that the federal judiciary should not be restrained from acting in a prison case merely because the letter of the Eighth Amendment does not apply to specified modern prison practices. It is enough that the Courts can point to the cruel and unusual punishment principles embodied in the Eighth Amendment. From this principle, courts can infer whether a modern prison practice is unconstitutional.[30]

If it is "enough" for the courts merely to "point" to these unspecified "principles," one must wonder what role, if any, is left for the plain language of the constitutional text. The jurisprudence of Judge Newblatt and like-minded activists of the Carter era reduces constitutional and statutory language to the status of mere launching pads for flights of judicial fancy.

That Judge Newblatt would use the federal bench in this manner should have surprised no one, however. To his genuine credit, he was candid and forthright on this point during his 1979 confirmation hearing.[31] Newblatt was one of those rare nominees who openly acknowledged that he would be a judicial activist. He stated that he believed "a federal judge *must* be an activist" in order to render "efficient justice."[32] He further told the Judiciary Committee that, in his opinion, stiff criminal sentences only have a deterrent effect on white collar crime, but do not deter violent street crime or drug-related crime.[33]

Whatever the validity Judge Newblatt's observation on sentencing deterrence when he made it in 1979, the penal philosophy which he and fellow Carter appointees are imposing from the bench may well validate it in the long run. The knowledge that such judges are waiting to review the habeas corpus petition to be composed during "law library time," with the ready assistance of jailhouse lawyers and ACLU activists, undoubtedly tends to dilute the sense of certain and sustained punishment which is the engine of deterrence. This tendency remains an enduring component of the Carter judicial legacy.

239

JUDICIAL RECEIVERSHIP IN YONKERS

Amid the remnants of school systems devastated by court-ordered busing and other divisive desegregation remedies, some modest but encouraging signs of reason have begun to surface in the jurisprudence of school desegregation. The termination of decades-old judicial receiverships over various public school systems, typified by the Fourth Circuit's decision approving the restoration of local control over the Norfolk public school system,[34] offers some hope that the federal judiciary will at last withdraw its meddlesome hand from the management of our nation's public schools.

But even while this encouraging phenomenom develops, the advocates of judicial supremacy in public education continue their search for new theories, new scapegoats, and new champions of their cause. They have found one such new champion in the person of Judge Leonard B. Sand, a millionaire corporate lawyer appointed by President Carter in 1978 to the U.S. District Court for the Southern District of New York.

Judge Sand's controversial decision in the combined housing/school desegregation case of *United States v. Yonkers Board of Education* (1985)[35] has given great comfort to those who pine for the halcyon days of Judge Arthur Garrity's imperious decimation of the Boston public school system. But Sand's divisive and heavy-handed ruling should set off loud alarms for those who still believe in the fundamental principles of federalism, local and rational public school systems.

Judge Sand's original opinion in this far-reaching case—now on appeal to the Second Circuit—was over 600 pages in length. Those unfortunate lawyers compelled by professional necessity to wade through this tome may have been tempted to paraphrase Shakespeare's classic barb on the employment of verbosity to obscure simple truth: "Methinks the judge doth protest too much!" In this instance, Judge Sand's lengthy opinion serves primarily to compensate for the lack of a clearly principled basis to justify an unprecedented and Draconian ruling.

In the first part of his opinion, Sand held that the City of Yonkers was liable for massive housing discrimination violations because it had failed to force the dispersal of publicly-as-

240

sisted, low-income housing projects throughout the residential neighborhoods of Yonkers. Recognizing the paucity of evidence showing actual discriminatory intent on the City's part—a mandatory element for liability in such cases—Sand equated the expression of legitimate citizen concerns for neighborhood quality with actionable racism. Perfectly valid considerations, such as density and safety issues, were skeptically belittled and ascribed to racial motivation. Sand then held that the City was guilty of racial discrimination in housing because it had taken such citizen concerns into account in its decisions as to the authorization and placement of the subsidized housing projects. In short, the decision treated the responsive and effective nature of local democracy in Yonkers as fatal evidence of the City's "discriminatory" intent.

Sand's ruling on the Yonkers housing issue reveals some of the most disturbing and dangerous elements of contemporary liberal jurisprudence. In the case of *City of Memphis v. Greene*, (1981), the Supreme Court has ruled that the kinds of neighborhood concerns (safety, tranquility, aesthetics) which motivated citizen opposition to inappropriate public housing placements in Yonkers are "unquestionably legitimate."[36] But despite the fact that these concerns were shared by black Yonkers citizens as well as white, Sand reflexively equated such genuine misgivings with illegal racism. He then displayed his disdain for the workings of democracy by condemning the Mayor and the City Council for giving due consideration to these issues in their resolution of complex housing decisions which would seriously affect the quality of life in Yonkers.

In essence, Sand ruled that objectively valid reasons for declining to place subsidized housing in given neighborhoods simply lose their legitimacy if the result is to impede the progress of maximum racial dispersal. Such an approach constitutes an insupportable expansion of federal housing discrimination law and a distortion of the very concept of discrimination.

Worse was yet to come, however, for the school desegregation portion of Sand's decision proved even more disturbing in its implications. Sand held that the City's failure to disperse public housing projects throughout its neighborhoods (which presumably would have increased their racial diversity) somehow made the *School Board* liable for intentional *school* segregation.

Sand himself acknowledged the unprecedented nature of this aspect of his ruling. Both the Supreme Court and the lower federal courts have unmistakably rejected the invitation to link a city's housing policies with a school board's liability for school segregation.[37] But Judge Sand determined that the need to achieve greater racial balance in the Yonkers schools was sufficient to justify a sharp departure from established precedent. He therefore proceeded to sow the seeds of enormous complication and confusion in the law by linking local governments' compliance with school desegregation requirements to their willingness to embrace the inescapable safety and environmental problems associated with subsidized low-income housing projects. Under Judge Sand's "Yonkers Doctrine," a municipality's refusal to embrace public housing projects can be directly equated with a policy of illegal school segregation.

Not content with his drastic reformation of substantive law, Judge Sand proceeded to devise a "remedy" which effectively supplanted local democracy in Yonkers with *ad hoc* judicial dictatorship. Aside from imposing a multi-million dollar school reorganization plan which devastated neighborhood school patterns and drained the city's treasury, he ordered the City Council to ignore its accountability to the voters and adopt *specific resolutions* implementing Sand's policy directive with respect to housing, site selection, city finance, and administration.

Rarely have the powers of a federal judge been so indiscriminately applied to deprive a city of its governing authority. Judge Sand's disposition of the *Yonkers* case flouted both longstanding judicial precedent and the most fundamental precepts of federalism and democratic government. His ruling represents the epitome of the anti-democratic tendency which pervades the Carter-appointed faction in the federal judiciary.

HOMOSEXUAL ADVOCACY AS RELIGION

The courts' approach to religious issues over the past two decades has reflected a strange and ironic dichotomy. On the one hand, efforts to preserve even the most circumscribed expressions of traditional religion in the public schools have been consistently and emphatically quashed by the courts. An especially telling example was the 1985 ruling in *Wallace v. Jaffree,*[38] where an Alabama law which merely authorized a one-minute period of silence to allow school children to meditate or pray, if they wished, was condemned by the Supreme Court as a violation of the First Amendment ban on the establishment of religion.

Meanwhile, however, the rituals of bizarre cults and the essentially political activities of social reform movements have evoked the courts' solicitous protection when portrayed in terms of religious expression.[39]

An equally curious phenomenom can be seen in the courts' divergent approaches to religious issues depending upon the setting in which they arise and the character of the litigants who invoke them. Thus, in the Michigan prison case of *Walker v. Johnson,* Carter appointee Judge Stewart Newblatt vigorously intervened to assure that imprisoned felons would be allowed to participate in group Muslin religious meetings at least twice a week.[40] Judge Newblatt's concern for prisoners' religious freedom was so great that he would not countenance the prison authorities' proposals to limit these meetings even as a prudent response to recurrent riots.

Meanwhile, children compelled by law to attend school are prohibited by court rulings from participating in group prayer during *their* compulsory confinement. Why the school children's right to organized prayer is less compelling than that of the imprisoned felons has never been satisfactorily explained. These anomalies of contemporary jurisprudence in the religious area are so confounding that they readily invite acerbic humor. But it is doubtful that the Founding Fathers would be amused.

Whether or not they would be amused, the Framers would certainly be bewildered by recent decisions of President Carter's judicial appointees giving strange new meaning to the concept of religious freedom.

In one case, Judge Richard L. Williams of the U.S. District Court for the District of Virginia held that the practice of "White Witchcraft" by prison inmates was entitled to constitutional protection on freedom of religion grounds.[41] The case arose when a convict asserted the right to pursue the bizarre rituals of this cult while serving his sentence, and demanded that the prison supply the peculiar paraphernalia he required to do so.

Judge Williams could see no apparent basis for distinguishing White Witchcraft from the concept of religion which the Framers protected under the First Amendment. Perhaps the prevailing judicial disdain for the concept of "original intent" prevented him from ascertaining that the "free exercise" of witchcraft would have been tolerated nowhere, let alone protected, during the Era of the Framers.

Another Carter appointee produced an even more remarkable interpretation of religious freedom principles in the 1986 case of *Dorr v. First Kentucky National Corporation* (1986).[42] Judge Nathaniel Jones of the Sixth Circuit, formerly General Counsel of the NAACP, held that the religious discrimination provisions of Title VII of the Civil Rights Act of 1964 protected a homosexual activist from employer sanctions resulting from his public advocacy of homosexual rights. In brief, Judge Jones equated homosexual advocacy with religion in the eyes of the law.

The plaintiff in the *Dorr* case was a bank executive. He had informed his superiors that he was homosexual and planned to engage in public advocacy of homosexual rights in his capacity as president of a homosexual group (called "Integrity") affiliated with the Episcopal Church.

The bank's official policy prohibited employees from engaging in outside activities that might undermine public confidence in the bank. Understandably, the bank decided that this policy applied to Mr. Dorr's activities and he was told that he would have to resign as president of the Integrity group if he wished to retain his position with the bank.

But Mr. Dorr claimed that his homosexual rights advocacy was a religious "calling" and an "area of ministry" which he was committed to pursue. When the bank would not relent, Dorr resigned. In his ensuing lawsuit, Dorr claimed that the bank's actions constituted illegal religious discrimination under Title VII. The district court rejected this claim, finding that Dorr's homosexual rights activities could not be equated with genuine religious belief.

On appeal, Judge Jones held to the contrary and reversed the lower court's decision. He concluded that Dorr's commitment to homosexual advocacy must be equated with protected religious activity as long as Dorr sincerely *felt* that it was. As Judge Jones stated:

The concept of religion embraced by Title VII is not one of an external set of forces and rules compelling an individual to act one way or another. The question is not one of compulsion, but of motivation.[43]

Under Judge Jones' analysis, the scope of legally protected religious activity is as broad and flexible as the motives of the person invoking it. If a person "sincerely believes" that homosexual advocacy is a religious calling, then the law must treat is as such. The mind reels at what other forms of deviant or antisocial behavior would be encompassed and protected under this extraordinary doctrine.

In severing the legal (and, presumably, the constitutional) concept of religion from the constraints of "external" rules and precepts, Judge Jones' approach renders the concept so elastic and amorphous as to lose its genuine meaning. If religion is viewed as nothing more than a "sincerely held" motivation or principle, there will be no limit to the variety of "religious" accommodations that employees can demand of employers under Title VII. Not surprisingly, the expansive legal theory employed by Judge Jones in the *Dorr* case paves the way for even more adventurous judicial policymaking by likeminded judicial activists.

NEW FRONTIERS FOR COURT INTERVENTION: THE HIGH SCHOOL HOMECOMING QUEEN CASE

Few cases better illustrate the interventionist tendencies of Carter's judges than a 1983 dispute over the election of a high school homecoming queen in a small Arkansas town which soon became a constitutional confrontation in federal court. That such purely intramural squabbles must now be conducted under the meddlesome scrutiny of federal judges is a sad commentary on just how far we have succumbed to judicial activism.

The author of this remarkable decision was Judge George Howard, Jr., who was appointed to the U.S. District Court for Eastern Arkansas in 1980. Judge Howard, one of the many former civil rights lawyers appointed by Carter, had previously stirred major controversy when he imprisoned the County Sheriff in connection with a dispute over Howard's appointment of a special monitor for County jail operations.[44] One year later, Howard shifted his attentions from prison management to intervention in high school extra-curricular programs in the case of *Boyd v. McGehee High School District No. 17.*[45]

The homecoming queen election in question was traditionally an informal vote by members of the high school varsity football team. Although McGehee High School District has a fully-integrated high school and football team, a black girl had never been elected homecoming queen by the players.

During the 1983 season, the black players had hoped to elect the first black homecoming queen, since 26 of the 54 voting members of the varsity team were black. According to the plaintiffs' allegations, the black candidate received the most votes in the informal "show-of-hands" vote first taken on the four nominees (the other three nominees were white). However, when the team's coach called for a "run-off" election by secret ballot on the two highest vote-getters, the white candidate prevailed according to the coach's tally. Upset by the result, the black players complained that the coach had manipulated the election on racial grounds, and all but one of them protested by walking out on a pre-game pep rally. Twenty-four of the black players then refused to play in the game that evening, leaving the team at half-strength only a few hours before game time. The coach then suspended the players who had refused to play for the duration of the season. It is fair to say that most high school coaches would have done the same if they hoped to maintain any degree of discipline and integrity in their program.

Represented by taxpayer-funded lawyers of the Arkansas Legal Services Corporation, the black homecoming queen candidate and one of the suspended players took their complaints to federal court, where this parochial dispute soon escalated to the level of a major constitutional confrontation.

Initially, Judge Howard issued a preliminary injunction against the white girl's investiture and ordered a new election. Not content with that, the judge required that the players' vote had to be recorded on an official voting machine to be acquired from county election officials. He also ordered immediate and unrestricted reinstatement of the plaintiff-player pending full trial on the merits.

The court-ordered election machine vote confirmed the election of the white homecoming queen by a vote of 30 to 24. Although the initial allegations against the coach may have raised a plausible inference of discriminatory motive on his part (based on past use of tasteless epithets unrelated to the election), the indisputable final tally should have laid the matter to rest. Instead, Judge Howard forged ahead to further excesses of judicial intervention.

Treating the player's refusal to play for his team as protected "speech," and the coach's decision to suspend him as a violation of property rights under the Fourteenth Amendment due process clause, the court awarded $2,500 in compensatory and punitive damages against the embattled coach,[46] as well as indeterminate attorney's fees. Although such an award might seem modest in other contexts, it is clearly a major financial setback for an impecunious high school coach in rural Arkansas. Due to the exorbitant costs of the litigation and the ensuing death of the coach, MeGehee High School District abstained from any appeal. Hence, this decision still stands as an ominous warning to Arkansas teachers and coaches that routine intrascholastic disciplinary measures entail the risk of harsh judicial redress and punitive damage assessments.

REWRITING TITLE VII: COMPARABLE WORTH, JUDGE TANNER, AND THE AFSCME CASE

The leading goal on the political agenda of feminist and civil rights activists in the 1980s has been government-mandated leveling of wages and salaries across gender lines under the doctrine of "comparable worth" (now sometimes referred to as "pay equity" for obvious tactical reasons).[47] This doctrine holds that disparities in the average wages of males versus females are attributable to sex discrimination rather than to such factors as career preferences, traditional family roles, workforce continuity, and the inescapable differences between the sexes in physical attributes, psychological tendencies, and personal priorities. Working from this premise, comparable worth doctrine holds that the anti-discrimination provisions of Title VII of the Civil Rights Act require that female-dominated jobs deemed comparable in value to male-dominated jobs be paid the same wages—even if the jobs compared are totally unrelated in nature and content. The truly radical nature of this doctrine is demonstrated in the fact that it requires abandonment of a market-based wage system responsive to supply and demand factors.

It should surprise no one that the comparable worth doctrine would receive judicial endorsement from a Carter-appointed federal judge whose credentials were established in large part as a plaintiffs' civil rights lawyer. The judge was Jack E. Tanner of the Western District of Washington State. The case was *American Federation of State, County, and Municipal Employees (AFSCME) v. Washington* (1985).[48]

The dimensions of Judge Tanner's errors in this decision—which was subsequently overturned by the Ninth Circuit—are difficult to exaggerate. Not only did he apply a profoundly distorted interpretation of Title VII, but he compounded the error with a wildly disproportionate remedy which (but for the Ninth Circuit's timely intervention) could have cost the taxpayers of Washington State up to *one billion* dollars.

In essence, Judge Tanner ruled that the state was obligated by Title VII to adopt a comprehensive wage revision plan that would raise the wages of all female-dominated jobs to the same levels as male-dominated jobs determined to be of equal value by a group of hired consultants. Neither the consultants nor Judge Tanner were able to explain how such radically different jobs as secretaries and truck drivers could be fairly and rationally compared using a single set of evaluation criteria.

Tanner's decision also rejected the state's defense that the cross-gender wage disparities simply reflected a pay system tied to prevailing market rates in the relevant regional job market, as required by state law. Further, Tanner erroneously held that the state's pay system could be judged under the "disparate impact" theory of employment discrimination, which imposes liability regardless of any discriminatory intent if a "facially neutral" employment practice has a disparate impact on protected classes. That this legal theory is confined to cases challenging such screening devices as standardized tests for hiring and promotion, and is *not* applicable to compensation policy, was of small concern to Judge Tanner.

Inasmuch as all other federal appeals courts faced with the issue had rejected the legal validity of comparable worth doctrine, the Ninth Circuit's sharp reversal of Tanner's ruling was not surprising.[49] The clarity and scope of Tanner's multiple errors were so great that the appeals court did not even consider it necessary to remand the case for any further proceedings.

The Ninth Circuit's decision pointedly rebuffed Tanner's position on the "prevailing rates" defense, stating that "Neither law nor logic deems the free market system a suspect enterprise."[50] The appeals court summed-up the essence of Tanner's billion-dollar error with the following admonition:

> While the Washington legislature may have the discretion to enact a comparable worth plan if it chooses to do so, Title VII does not obligate it to eliminate an economic equality that it did not create.[51]

The Ninth Circuit had thus put its finger on the policy initiative which was the true object of the *AFSCME* decision: economic redistribution in the name of civil rights.

The *AFSCME* decision was not an isolated instance of major error produced by Judge Tanner's unfrettered judicial adventurism. Tanner was also the originator of the highly-publicized high school speech case that was ultimately reversed by the Supreme Court in *Fraser v. Bethel School District* (1986).[52] There, Tanner had ruled that the First Amendment prohibits school officials from taking disciplinary action against lewd or ribald speeches by students at school assemblies. Other Carter appointees, such as Judge Howard of the Arkansas homecoming queen case, might well agree. But a seven-justice majority of the Supreme Court—including even preeminent liberal Justice William Brennan—has made it clear that no plausible reading of the First Amendment requires such a result. It remains to be seen whether repeated reversals of his decisions will moderate Judge Tanner's tendency towards adventurous and sometimes disastrous judicial experimentation.

INVERTING THE FIRST AMENDMENT: CENSORING OFFICIAL EXPRESSION

In the post-Warren era, federal courts have shown boundless creativity in stretching the contours of the First Amendment to accommodate the ideological agenda of the left. Activities ranging from nude dancing to walking out on high school football games[53] have been brought within the ever-expanding circle of protected speech to the point that the original constitutional object has been all but totally obscured by judicial gloss. But at least it can be said that these cases have followed a consistent line of reasoning, however inadvisedly, in persistently expanding the boundaries of unfrettered free expression for all "speakers."

More recently, however, self-styled civil libertarians have advanced a more novel twist to First Amendment activism which aims to *limit* the "robust and wide-open debate" which they purport to cherish.

This new approach posits that *official* expression which tends to denigrate or discredit any form of non-official expression creates an intolerable "chilling effect" on free speech and, therefore, should be suppressed in the name of the First Amendment. This doctrine is especially convenient for those who seek to limit the terms of debate on government policy, since it sanctions the most extreme forms of attack on government actions while depriving the government of the freedom to respond.

Federal judges appointed by President Carter have been especially receptive to these efforts to suppress government expression in the name of the First Amendment. In one recent case, *Playboy* magazine claimed that the Attorney General's Commission on Pornography violated its First Amendment rights when the Commission sent letters to certain magazine distributors regarding their policies on carrying magazines with pornographic content, as identified in testimony before the Commission. Although the Commission had done nothing to interfere with *Playboy's* right to publish as it pleased, and had no power to interfere with the distributors' right to sell its magazines, *Playboy* contended that it was unconstitutional for the Commission (a toothless advisory commission) even to communicate with the distributors regarding their policy on selling pornography.

Judge John Garrett Penn, a 1979 Carter appointee to the U.S. District Court for the District of Columbia, accepted the curious argument that *Playboy's* "right" to be protected against even indirect criticism of its magazine justified an injunction against the Commission's right to communicate in letters such as those it had sent to the distributors.[54] The First Amendment was thus utilized as an instrument to *suppress* legitimate discussion and exchange of views on an issue of critical public importance.

A further example of this distorted approach to First Amendment jurisprudence occurred in the case of *Keene v. Meese*,[55] where another Carter-appointed judge took his turn rewriting the Constitution.

A Democratic California legislator challenged the constitutionality of the Foreign Agents' Registration Act ("FARA") requirement that propaganda materials disseminated by foreign agents be filed with the Justice Department and marked with a legend disclosing the identities of the foreign agent and its foreign principal.[56] The well-established purpose of this legislation—which in no way limits the right to disseminate the propaganda materials—is to prevent foreign governments from concealing the source and motives of their propaganda campaigns in the United States. The constitutionality of the basic filing and disclosure requirements has long been confirmed by federal court decisions and was not at issue in *Keene v. Meese*. What *was* challenged wa the statute's use of the term "foreign propaganda" in describing the materials subject to the Act's requirements. In brief, the plaintiffs alleged that the use of this term by Congress "denigrates" or disparages the materials regulated by the Act and thereby impedes their optimal dissemination, in violation of the First Amendment.

The logical and necessary implication of this theory is that *any* "official" denigration of any form of protected speech or expression would raise similar First Amendment concerns. A presidential denunciation of a libelous newspaper column at a press conference, or a congressional resolution criticizing a child pornography magazine, would also become unconstitutional under this novel doctrine. But none of these implications prevented Judge Raul Ramirez (appointed by Carter to the U.S. District Court for Eastern California in 1980) from ruling that Congress is barred by the First Amendment from using "an inflammatory phrase" to describe foreign propaganda or any other form of protected speech.[57] Ramirez held that the purveyors of the propaganda would be "chilled" and "stigmatized" if their materials were adversely characterized by official voices, and that this effect was constitutionally intolerable.

A more perceptive federal judge was soon confronted with the exact same issue, but produced a markedly different result. In *Block v. Meese* (1986), the D.C. Circuit Court of Appeals rejected an identical challenge to the FARA's "foreign propaganda" classification in an opinion written by Judge (now Supreme Court Justice) Antonin Scalia. As Judge Scalia observed, "We know of no case in which the First Amendment has been held to be implicated by government action consisting of no more than government criticism of the speech's content."[58]

The Supreme Court had the final say when it reversed Judge Ramirez' decision in the *Keene* case (Justice Scalia recused himself, presumably on the basis of his participation in *Block*). Describing Ramirez' analysis as "unpersuasive" and "untenable," the Court stressed that "Congress' use of the term 'political propaganda' does not lead us to suspend the respect we normally owe to the Legislature's power to define the terms that it uses in legislation."[59]

But such constraints had presented no obstacle to the free-wheeling constitutional improvisations of Judge Ramirez. Nor was Ramirez deterred by the fact that the reasoning of his decision in the "foreign propaganda" case would necessarily apply to the countless provisions in the federal and state codes which use similarly "denigrating" terms to describe various forms of regulated communications and expression.[60] It was sufficient for him that the propaganda disseminators had invoked the standard talismans of First Amendment advocacy and the necessity of judicial intervention. It is a formula which does not often fail to work in the courtrooms of the Carter-appointed activists.

CONCLUSION

Whatever else may be said about his administration, Jimmy Carter had a profound and lasting impact on national legal policy through his appointment of hundreds of liberal federal judges. These judges have performed to the fullest expectations of the ideological constituency groups which were so instrumental in their selection and confirmation. In fields ranging from prison reform to civil rights law to criminal procedure, they have used the swollen powers of the federal bench to impose liberal policy initiatives which could never have been sustained by the accountable branches of government.

The extent of Carter's impact in shifting federal jurisprudence to the left provides the critical context for President Reagan's own judicial appointment philosophy. In no other area of policy were Ronald Reagan and his successive presidential campaign rivals more diametrically opposed. The American electorate's emphatic demands for a more conservative judiciary in 1980 and 1984—demands which were powerfully re-echoed in the 1986 rejection of Chief Justice Rose Bird and her liberal brethren in the California Supreme Court election—have yet to be fully satisfied. It remains for President Reagan to fulfill that mandate through the important judicial appointments he will have the opportunity to make during the balance of his term.

REFERENCES

The Work-Product of Carter's Judiciary: Adjudication As Policymaking by George C. Smith

1. Senate Judiciary Committee Hearings, 96th Cong., 1st Sess., Serial No. 96-21, Part 3, pp. 1, 3-4 (July 13, 1979). [Editor's note: The views expressed in Mr. Smith's article are solely those of the author, and do not reflect the views of any member of the Senate Judiciary Committee.]
2. Id., pp. 43-132 (July 18, 1979) (Judge Kennedy) and pp. 324-405 (July 30, 1979) (Judge Reed).
3. C. K. Rowland, Robert A. Carp, and Donald Songer, "The Effect of Presidential Appointment, Group Identification and Fact-Law Ambiguity on Lower Federal Judges' Policy Judgments: The Case of Reagan and Carter Appointees," p. 15 (unpublished empirical study prepared for delivery at the 1985 meeting of the American Political Science Association, New Orleans, La., Aug. 29-Sep. 1, 1985). The political science professors who prepared this study are from the University of Kansas, the University of Houston, and the University of South Carolina, respectively.
4. Rowland, Songer, and Carp, "Presidential Effects on Criminal Justice Policy in the Lower Federal Courts: the Carter and Reagan Judges," p. 20 (unpublished empirical study, Fall 1986). This 1986 study refines and expands upon the study cited supra n.3.
5. Id., p. 28 n. 8.
6. J. Gottschall, "Carter's Judicial Appointments: The Influence of Affirmative Action and Merit Selection on Voting on the U.S. Courts of Appeals," 67 Judicature 164 (Oct. 1983).
7. Id., pp. 170-71, Tables 2 and 3.
8. See Local 28, Sheet Metal Workers v. EEOC, 106 S.Ct. 3019 (1986); United States v. Paradise, 107 S.Ct. 1053 (1987); and Johnson v. Transportation Agency of Santa Clara County, 55 U.S.L.W. 4379 (March 25, 1987). In each of these cases, Justice Powell's vote was critical to decisions upholding quotas or preferences based on race or sex.
9. Boyd v. Bd. of Directors of McGehee High School District No. 17, 612 F. Supp. 86 (E.D. Ark. 1985).
10. AFSCME v. State of Washington, 578 F. Supp. 846 (W.D. Wash. 1983), rev'd, 770 F.2d 1401 (9th Cir. 1985).

11. *United States v. Yonkers Board of Education*, 624 F. Supp. 1276 (S.D.N.Y. 1985), *appeal pending*, No. 86-6136 (2nd Cir).

12. *Keene v. Meese*, 619 F. Supp. 1111 (E. D. Col. 1986), *rev'd*, 55 U.S.L.W. 4586 (April 28, 1987).

13. *Walker v. Johnson*, 544 F. Supp. 345, 361 (E.D. Mich. 1982); *Smith v. Fairman*, 528 F. Supp. 186 (C.D. Ill. 1981), *rev'd*, 690 F.2d 122 (7th Cir. 1982), *cert denied*, 103 S.Ct. 2125 (1983).

14. *E.g., Baker v. Wade*, 553 F. Supp. 1121 (N.D. Tex. 1982), *rev'd*, 769 F.2d 289 (5th Cir. 1985), *cert denied*, 54 U.S.L.W. 3867 (U.S. 1986) (decision holding Texas antisodomy statute unconstitutional, reversed by Fifth Circuit); *Liddell v. Bd. of Educ.*, 567 F.Supp. 1037 (E.D. Mo. 1983), *aff'd in part and remanded in part*, 731 F.2d 1294 (8th Cir. 1984), *cert. denied*, 83 L.Ed. 30 (1984) (massive school desegregation/busing remedy, enforced by confiscatory court-ordered finance plan usurping local government budget power); *NAACP Legal Defense Fund v. Devine*, 727 F.2d 1247 (D.C. Cir. 1984), *rev'd*, 105 S. Ct. 3439 (1985) (holding that 1st Amendment barred federal government from excluding political advocacy groups from Combined Federal Campaign, reversed by Supreme Court).

15. For a comprehensive analysis of the prison problem from a variety of original perspectives, *see Crime and Punishment in Modern America* (Patrick McGuigan and Jon Pascale, Ed.) (Institute for Government and Politics, Free Congress Research and Education Foundation, 1986).

16. See *Id.*, ch. 21, Daniel Popeo and George Smith, "Prisons, Priorities, and Judicial Fiat: The Need for Constitutional Perspective," pp. 349-364.

17. *Id.*

18. R. Berger, *Death Penalties*, (Harvard Univ. Press, 1982) pp. 44-58.

19. *See, e.g., Walker v. Johnson, supra* n.13, 544 F. Supp. at 364 (three showers per week, plus guarantee of hot water, held constitutionally required for prison inmates).

20. *Rhodes v. Chapman*, 452 U.S. 337, 101 S.Ct. 2392 (1981).

21. *Id.*, 101 S.Ct. at 2399.

22. *Id.*, p. 2400.

23. *Smith v. Fairman*, 528 F. Supp. 186 (C.D. Ill. 1981), *rev'd*, 690 F.2d 122 (7th Cir. 1982), *cert. denied*, 103 S.Ct. 2125 (1983).

24. *Id.*, 690 F.2d at 124-25.

25. *Id.*, at 125.

26. *Id.*

27. *Walker v. Johnson, supra* n. 13, 544 F. Supp. at 361.

28. *Id.* at 364-65.

29. *Id.* at 352, 364.

30. *Id.* at 359 n. 52.

31. Senate Judiciary Committee Hearings, 96th Cong., 1st Sess., Serial No. 96-21, Part 3, p. 294 (July 27, 1979).

32. *Id.*, p. 295. (emphasis added).

33. *Id.*, pp. 295-97.

34. *Riddick v. City of Norfolk*, 784 F.2nd 521 (4th Cir. 1985), *cert. denied*, 55 U.S.L.W. 3316 (U.S. Nov. 3, 1986).

35. 624 F. Supp. 1276 (S.D.N.Y. 1985), *appeal pending*, No. 86-6136 (2nd Cir.).

36. 451 U.S. 100, 127 (1981).

37. *E.g., Austin School Dist. v. United States*, 429 U.S. 990, 994 (1976); *Bell v. Akron Bd. of Educ.*, 683 F.2d 963, 968 (6th Cir. 1982); *Deal v. Cincinnati Bd. of Educ.*, 369 F.2d 55, 60 n.4 (6th Cir. 1966).

38. *Wallace v. Jaffree*, 472 U.S. 38 (1985).

39. *See, e.g. Dettmer v. Landon*, 617 F.Supp. 592 (E.D. Va. 1985), *rev'd in part, aff'd in part*, 799 F.2d 929 (4th Cir. 1986); *Dorr v. First Kentucky National Corp.*, 55 U.S.L.W. 2071 (6th Cir., July 17, 1986); *Toledo v. Nobel Sysco, Inc.*, 41 FEP Cases 282 (D.N. Mex. 1986) (religious accommodation of peyote smoking).

40. 544 F. Supp. at 352-362.

41. *Dettmer v. Landon, supra*, n. 39.
42. *Dorr v. First Kentucky National Corporation*, 55 U.S.L.W. 2071 (6th Cir., July 17, 1986).
43. *Id.*, at 2071.
44. *Almanac of the Federal Judiciary*, 8th Circuit Section, p.2 (Winter 1984).
45. 612 F. Supp. 86 (E.D. Ark. 1985).
46. *Id.*, at 94.
47. For a thorough and effective analysis of the comparable worth doctrine representing a broad range of views, see U.S. Civil Rights Commission, *Comparable Worth: Issue for the 80's*, record of the Commission's Consultation on Comparable Worth, June 6-7, 1984.
48. 578 F.Supp. 846 (W.D. Wash. 1983), *rev'd*, 770 F.2d 1401 (9th Cir. 1985).
49. Other federal court decisions rejecting the comparable worth doctrine's viability under Title VII include *Spaulding v. Univ. of Washington*, 740 F.2d 686 (9th Cir. 1984), *cert denied*, 105 S.Ct. 511 (1984); *Christiansen v. State of Iowa*, 563 F.2d 353 (8th Cir. 1977); *Lemons v. City of Denver*, 620 F.2d 228 (10th Cir.), *cert. denied*, 449 U.S. 888 (1980); and *Gerlach v. Michigan Bell Telephone Co.*, 501 F.Supp. 1300 (E.D. Mich. 1980).
50. 770 F.2d at 1407.
51. *Id.*
52. *Fraser v. Bethel School District*, 755 F.2d 1356 (9th Cir. 1985), *rev'd*, 54 U.S.L.W. 5054 (July 7, 1986).
53. *See e.g., Boyd v. McGehee School District, supra* n.9.
54. *Playboy Enterprises, Inc., v. Meese*, 639 F.Supp. 581 (D.D.C. 1986).
55. 619 F. Supp. 1111 (E.D. Cal. 1986), *rev'd*, 55 U.S.L.W. 4586 (Apr. 28, 1987).
56. 22 U.S.C. §611, *et seq.*
57. 619 F.Supp. at 1120-1126.
58. *Block v. Meese*, 793 F.2d 1303 (D.C. Cir. 1986), Slip Op. No. 84-5318 at 16, *cert. denied*, 106 S.Ct. 3335 (1986).
59. 55 U.S.L.W. 4586 (Apr. 28, 1987).
60. *E.g.*, 39 U.S.C. §3008 (prohibition of "pandering advertising" in U.S. mails); 18 U.S.C. §1464 ("broadcasting profane language"); 15 U.S.C. §1692d (categories of commercial speech/communication labeled as "harassment and abuse"); 39 U.S.C. §3006 ("Filthy or vile things" sold through U.S. mails); 50 U.S.C. §782(3)-(5) ("communist front organization," "control of subversive activities").

12

CONTEXT IN THE JUDGES WAR: WORK PRODUCT FROM REAGAN'S JUDGES

by Peter J. Ferrara

The real concern of most critics of Ronald Reagan's judicial appointments is revealed by examination of the judicial work product flowing from those appointments—the decisions actually made by the appointed Reagan judges, especially in contrast to the decisions of Carter judges.

An examination of those decisions shows that Reagan's appointees have complied strictly with the limitations on their judicial authority, meeting the obligations and responsibilities of fair, sound judicial decisionmaking, while avoiding abuses of their power. Within these constraints, Reagan's appointees have taken a strongly conservative direction where the law allows, though not radically more conservative than the appointees of previous Republican Presidents. Moreover, when the issues are examined closely, the positions taken by Reagan judicial appointees on the controversial issues generally seem to be supported by broad majorities of the American people.

LIMITATIONS ON REAGAN'S JUDGES

The impact of Reagan judicial appointments on the substantive decisions of the federal courts is limited by two factors. The first is the legally binding authority of precedent. Judges on the circuit courts and district courts are bound by applicable precedents decided by the Supreme Court. Judges on the district courts are bound by the applicable precedents of their circuit court as well. Even if the applicable precedent in these cases is a liberal activist decision which the Reagan appointee thinks is wrong, Reagan's judges still have no legal authority to do anything but follow such binding precedent.

Judges have some leeway to avoid such precedents if they can legitimately find distinguishing facts in the case before them which can provide the basis for a different ruling. Particularly at the district court level, within certain bounds a conservative judge may also legitimately see the facts differently than a liberal judge (or vice versa), which may provide the basis for avoiding a precedent on the grounds that the facts legitimately present a different situation. In some areas of the law, decisions may be so heavily based on the differing facts of each case that precedents may effectively provide little constraint.

Moreover, in many instances precedents may not be binding. Reagan circuit court judges can override precedents from their own circuits and rule contrary to those of other circuits. Reagan district court judges can rule contrary to precedents from other circuits as well. The Supreme Court can overrule any of its own precedents or those of any lower court.

But, in many areas, precedents still effectively bind the lower court Reagan judges and prevent them from rendering the more conservatively oriented rulings they might like. And Reagan judges do not have a majority on the Supreme Court.

The second factor is the doctrine of judicial restraint—the key element in the judicial philosophy of Reagan judges. Under this doctrine, a judge must apply the law as specified by the Constitution, Congress or other binding authority, rather than ruling according to his or her own policy preferences.

This means Reagan judges can only strike down laws as unconstitutional if the Constitution requires them to do so, and otherwise cannot overturn laws which are objectionable to their personal conservative philosophies. They must also strike down laws they favor, if the Constitution requires it. They must rule thoroughly in accordance with the requirements of constitutionally valid statutes passed by the Congress or state legislatures, even if such statutes require liberal policies. They must, similarly, rule in accordance with the requirements of constitutionally valid regulations issued by proper authority, even if such regulations involve liberal policies. They must, of course, follow binding precedents, but judicial restraint means as well that they should respect even non-binding precedents and not rule contrary to them or overrule them unnecessarily. But when a precedent itself is contrary to the doctrine of judicial restraint or otherwise erroneous, Reagan judges will properly rule contrary to it or overrule it *when they have the authority to do so.*

Much of the controversy over Reagan's judicial appointees is due to a failure to recognize completely these limitations on Reagan's judges. This failure occurs because liberal activist judges and their allies do not recognize these limitations on themselves to the same degree, particularly the doctrine of judicial restraint. Consequently, liberal critics of Reagan's judges fear these judges may be able to use the courts to impose their personal political philosophies, as liberal activist judges do. This fear is clearly unfounded.

THE MAJOR ISSUES IN CONTROVERSY

The judicial philosophy of Reagan's judges leads them to disagree strongly with liberal activist judges on a number of specific, highly controversial areas of the law.

One hotly contested area is criminal law and procedure. Reagan judges are far more strict with criminal defendants and far less likely to create unnecessary obstacles for criminal prosecutors than liberal judges. They also tend to hand down harsher sentences for criminal defendants. They believe that some crimes are so heinous that the death penalty is warranted (as well as clearly constitutional) and are willing to impose it under the proper procedures. Liberal judges, by contrast, believe the death penalty is unconstitutional and usually seek to avoid imposing it, as well as to prevent its imposition by others.

On many criminal law issues, judges have substantial discretion under the applicable law to rule as they think appropriate. This applies, for example, to many rulings on trial procedure or sentencing. Consequently, Reagan appointees can and have had a big impact in these areas, acting on the basis of a judicial philosophy that favors vigorous and strict enforcement of the criminal law and strong punishment for those who violate such laws. Apparently as a result, criminal convictions and sentences have increased markedly, as discussed further below.[1]

On some criminal procedure issues, however, Reagan judges are constrained by binding Supreme Court precedents. Such precedents, for example, may require evidence establishing guilt to be excluded from the trial because it was improperly obtained. Such precedents may also impose procedural requirements on the gathering of evidence by law enforcement officials, such as issuing Miranda warnings before questioning or obtaining highly specific warrants for searches and seizures.

Reagan judges tend to oppose the required exclusion of evidence from criminal trials and restrictive procedural requirements on law enforcement officials, under the doctrine of judicial restraint, contending such requirements are not mandated by the Constitution or other legal authority, but rather stem from rulings by liberal activist judges who have improperly imposed such requirements based on their own philosophical beliefs. Reagan judges, however, have no choice but to rule in accordance with such requirements until a Supreme Court majority overturns them. Reagan Supreme Court appointees have managed to join with other Justices recently to form majorities ruling to ease these criminal procedure restrictions somewhat.

Another hotly contested area is civil rights. Reagan judges believe that racial and sexual discrimination, and other forms of invidious discrimination, are and should be prohibited by law, so this is not a matter of disagreement. There is disagreement, however, over what evidence is sufficient to prove illegal discrimination. Liberal judges generally favor the view that a statistical disparity between (i) minority participation in an area of employment or other activity and (ii) the proportion of such minority in the local population eligible for the activity, is powerful evidence that discrimination exists, possibly sufficient in itself. Reagan judges tend to believe that clear evidence of actual discrimination is needed. Liberal judges also tend to favor racial quotas and preferences and forced busing as remedies for discrimination while Reagan judges generally do not.

The basis for the position of Reagan judges on these issues is, again, the doctrine of judicial restraint. Reagan judges see racial quotas and preferences, busing and findings of discrimination based on statistical disparities as not authorized by applicable statutes, such as the 1964 Civil Rights Act, or the Constitution, and indeed in some cases directly contrary to these authorities. Rather, Reagan judges see these practices stemming from rulings by activist judges premised on their own liberal policy preferences. Reagan judges, however, are often constrained by binding Supreme Court precedents on these issues. They have some leeway in determining whether actual illegal discrimination has been shown. They also have some opportunity to state the law based on the judicial restraint philosophy on new questions where the Supreme Court has not yet issued a definitive ruling. Certain aspects of the comparable worth doctrine, which would allow a finding of discrimination in some cases based on differential pay for different jobs, may offer such new questions. Another contested area involves religious liberty and establishment of religion issues. Liberal activist judges tend to rule that government benefits to, or involvement with, religion constitutes an unconstitutional violation of the Establishment Clause of the First Amendment. Reagan judges contest such rulings on the basis of judicial restraint, contending that these rulings are not authorized by the Constitution but are based instead on the policy preferences of liberal activist judges and fantasies about the meaning of the Establishment Clause. Reagan judges generally believe that the Constitution authorizes more government accommodation of religion and that the liberal rulings actually restrict the religious liberty favored by the Constitution.

Specific controversial legal issues regarding religion include aid to parochial schools, tuition tax credits and vouchers, formation of student religious clubs in public schools, teaching or textbooks involving either pro- or anti-religious materials, use of public facilities for religious activities, school prayer and other matters. On some of these issues, Reagan judges are, again, constrained by binding Supreme Court precedents. But the doctrines of these precedents are so incoherent and contradictory that on other issues Reagan judges can and have had some impact in restoring a proper understanding of the law.[2]

Abortion presents another key area of disagreement. Liberal judges generally believe almost any restriction on a woman's decision to have an abortion is unconstitutional. Reagan judges largely find this position a prime example of a violation of the doctrine of judicial restraint, contending that there is no basis in the Constitution for this liberal view or for rulings striking down state laws regulating or restricting abortion. Rather, such rulings are, again, based on the policy preferences of liberal activist judges. However, Reagan judges are tightly constrained in this area by binding Supreme Court precedents, and there is little they can do until a new majority on the High Court overturns some of these precedents, or the foundation of all recent abortion rulings itself, *Roe v. Wade* (1973).[3]

A less heavily contested area is economic regulation. Reagan judges generally see liberal activist judges as reading regulatory requirements more severly than the authorizing statutes or regulations suggest, contrary to judicial restraint. They would consequently tend to interpret the authorities as providing for less expansive and onerous regulation. Reagan judges would also, however, be less likely to interfere with the decision of a regulatory agency out of respect for the agency's expertise, based again on the philosophy of judicial restraint. This may often mean, however, upholding an agency decision for less regulation in the face of litigation brought by liberal interests seeking more. There are other subject areas of substantial disagreement as well, such as the scope of the First Amendment's protection for freedom of speech.

What should be most striking is that on the most hotly contested issues the positions taken by Reagan judges are generally supported by strong majorities of public opinion. The public heavily favors stricter attitudes towards crime, more severe punishments for criminals, and the death penalty, and is quite skeptical about excluding evidence based on artificial requirements and technicalities. The public heavily opposes racial quotas and preferences and forced busing. Opinion polls routinely show large majorities in favor of school prayer, while aid to parochial schools has been passed so often by the states as to indicate enduring public support. Tuition tax credits, vouchers, voluntary student religious clubs, and broader religious liberty are popular issues. The public is badly split over abortion, but around half support the position of Reagan and his judges on this issue.

These issues are really what is at stake in the controversy over Reagan's judges. When Reagan critics complain about the qualifications of Reagan's judges or their supposed insensitivity to minority rights, what they are really trying to do is preserve the liberal position on crime, the death penalty, racial quotas and preferences, busing, abortion, school prayer, and government policy toward religion. But given public attitudes towards the liberal positions on these issues, the critics dare not make this the focus of their complaints.

REAGAN JUDGES: THE RECORD

A number of studies confirm that Reagan's judges have generally ruled and decided as described above. In one of the most comprehensive studies of judicial philosophy ever conducted, Craig Stern of the Center for Judicial Studies examined every published opinion during 1981 and 1982 by every Reagan appointee to the district and circuit courts.[4] Stern concluded that of the 62 Reagan appointees included in the study, 31 followed the philosophy of judicial restraint in all their significant cases without exception. Another 16 exercised judicial restraint in nearly all significant cases, and six had not yet published any opinions. Only nine Reagan appointees out of 62 showed any significant departure from judicial restraint.

The raw data shows a trend toward harsher penalties in the federal courts for criminals during the Reagan years. While only 66 percent of those convicted of rape from mid 1980 to mid 1981 received any prison sentence, during mid 1984 to mid 1985 84 percent of those convicted of rape were sent to prison.[5] Only 57 percent of burglary convicts received prison sentences in 1980-81. For 1984-85, however, 75 percent were handed prison terms.[6] Overall, 45 percent of all criminal convicts received prison sentences in 1980-81, compared to 48 percent in 1984-85.[7]

The average prison sentence imposed in the federal courts for murder rose by 70 percent from 1980-81 to 1984-85.[8] The average sentence for first degree murder rose 62 percent during this time, and for second degree murder the average sentence almost doubled.[9] For burglary, the average sentence rose by 44 percent, and for rape the average sentence rose by 45 percent.[10] Overall, average prison sentences in the federal courts for all crimes rose during this period by almost 10 percent.[11]

In a more recent comprehensive study, Jon Gottschall compared the decisions of Reagan circuit court judges with the decisions of circuit court judges appointed by Presidents Carter, Ford, Nixon, Johnson and Kennedy.[12] Gottschall examined decisions in regard to criminal cases, race and sex discrimination cases, First Amendment cases involving freedom of speech, freedom of assembly, right to petition, etc., labor regulation cases involving unions, cases involving welfare or disability claims, and personal injury or wrongful death cases. Gottschall defined as liberal rulings of any type in favor of criminal defendants, unions in labor cases, those working to gain or keep welfare or disability benefits, and plaintiffs alleging claims of race or sex discrimination, First Amendment violations, personal injury or wrongful death. Conservative rulings were defined as the opposite in each instance.

Appellate cases are usually decided by a panel of three or more judges. Gottschall found that in all cases studied combined, covering all of the above issue areas, Reagan judges and Carter judges agreed 74 percent of the time and disagreed 26 percent of the time. This shows the power of precedent and judicial restraint in constraining judges to rule in accordance with the law as established by other authorities. But where Carter and Reagan judges disagreed, Carter judges voted for the activist liberal outcome 95 percent of the time, compared to 5 percent for the Reagan judges.

In race and sex discrimination cases, labor regulation cases and welfare cases, when Carter and Reagan judges disagreed, Carter judges always voted for the liberal position and Reagan judges never did. In criminal cases where disagreement occurred, Carter judges voted 95 percent for the liberal position compared to 5 percent for Reagan judges. Carter and Reagan judges only agreed 60 percent of the time on First Amendment cases, and in disagreements Carter judges voted liberal 87 percent of the time compared to 13 percent for Reagan judges. However, there seemed to be little difference between Carter and Reagan judges on personal injury cases, where Carter and Reagan judges agreed 93 percent of the time. When they disagreed on these cases, Carter judges voted for the liberal position 60 percent of the time and Reagan judges so voted 40 percent of the time

In contrast to the sharp differences between Reagan and Carter appointees, Gotschall found that Nixon and Ford appointees ruled very similarly to Reagan appointees. On all cases combined, covering all of the above issue areas, Nixon and Ford judges agreed with Reagan judges 93 percent of the time and disagreed only 7 percent of the time. Moreover, when they disagreed, Reagan judges voted liberal 51 percent of the time, compared to 49 percent for Nixon and Ford judges. In criminal cases, Nixon and Ford judges agreed with Reagan judges in 94 percent of the rulings. In the few instances of disagreement the Nixon and Ford judges actually voted conservative substantially *more* than the Reagan judges. In race and sex discrimination cases, Nixon and Ford judges agreed with Reagan judges 89 percent of the time, though in the small number of disagreements Reagan judges always voted conservative and Nixon and Ford judges always voted liberal.

Gottschall states:

> That Reagan appointees voted much like those of the Nixon and Ford Administrations tends to contradict the conventional notion that Reagan is appointing radically more conservative judges. Yet direct comparisons between Reagan and Nixon/Ford appointees again suggest that there is little ideological difference between appointees of these three most recent Republican administration.[13]

It should be recalled that while Nixon pursued many liberal policies as President, such as adoption of wage and price controls and support for the ERA, he advocated a tough law and order position on crime and used the appointment of judges as an opportunity to exercise his conservative instincts.

Adding Kennedy and Johnson judges to the picture, Gottschall found that for all criminal cases studied, those with unanimous decisions and those with dissents, Carter judges proved substantially more liberal than Kennedy/Johnson judges, voting liberal 55 percent of the time compared to 44 percent for the earlier appointees. Nixon/Ford and Reagan judges were both much more conservative and quite similar to each other, with Nixon/Ford appointees voting liberal 36 percent of the time and Reagan judges voting liberal in 34 per cent of their rulings.

In race discrimination cases, Kennedy/Johnson judges voted liberal slightly more often, in 51 percent of rulings, compared to 46 percent for Carter Judges. Nixon/Ford judges were much more conservative than these Democratic appointees, voting liberal 36 percent of the time, with Reagan judges again slightly more conservative than this, ruling liberal at only a 31 percent rate. In sex discrimination cases, however, Carter judges were the most liberal by far, voting liberal in 63 percent of rulings, compared to 43 percent for Kennedy/Johnson appointees. Nixon/Ford appointees voted much more conservatively with only 35 percent liberal rulings, while Reagan appointees were slightly more conservative with 30 percent liberal rulings.

In First Amendment cases, Carter appointees were the most liberal with 53 percent liberal rulings compared to 45 percent for Kennedy/Johnson appointees. Nixon/Ford appointees ruled much more conservatively with 34 percent liberal rulings, while Reagan appointees ruled even more conservatively with 31.5 percent liberal rulings. In labor regulation cases, the same pattern again prevailed, with Carter judges voting liberal 69 percent, Kennedy/Johnson judges 67 percent, Nixon/Ford judges 52 percent and Reagan judges 47 percent.

Differences in welfare cases were less pronounced, with Kennedy/Johnson judges voting 67 percent liberal, Carter judges voting 63 percent liberal, Nixon/Ford judges voting 59 percent liberal, and Reagan judges voting 56 percent liberal. There was little disagreement in personal injury cases, with Kennedy/Johnson judges voting 55 percent liberal, Carter judges 48 percent, Nixon/Ford judges 48 percent, and Reagan judges 47 percent.

If we focus only on cases which were not decided unanimously, similar trends appear. But the Nixon/Ford judges have actually voted more conservatively than Reagan judges in non-unanimous criminal cases and First Amendment cases and much more conservatively than Reagan judges in personal injury cases. Reagan judges have voted more conservatively than Nixon/Ford judges in non-unanimous labor and welfare cases, and much more conservatively in race discrimination cases, though both voted about the same in sex discrimination cases.

Carter and Kennedy/Johnson judges all voted liberal about twice as often as Republican judges on all the cases combined. Carter judges were more liberal than Kennedy/Johnson judges in non-unanimous crime, sex discrimination, First Amendment, labor, and personal injury cases, with the Kennedy/Johnson judges more liberal in non-unanimous race discrimination and welfare cases.

Gottschall summarizes these results in part by saying,

When voting on four civil rights and three economic issues which were thought likely to divide judges of different ideological predispositions, Reagan's appointees are not clearly or dramatically more conservative than N on's or Ford's appointees, although they are clearly more conservative n appointees of the Carter, Kennedy and Johnson administration.[14]

Gottschall concludes,

> The impact of the Reagan appointees on case outcomes in the court of appeals is a conservative one, although probably not at this time decisively more conservative than that of appointees of the Nixon and Ford administrations. Thus the Reagan appointees represent not so much the beginnings of a judicial revolution as the continuation of a pattern of Republican conservatism in civil rights and liberties issues which may have begun in 1968 with Nixon's pledge to appoint "strict constructionists" to federal judicial posts ... Viewed in this way, the anticipated transition to a conservative judicial majority on the courts of appeals is an accomplished fact and does not await Reagan's second term appointments, as some commentators have suggested.
> ...this transition appears to have begun not with the Reagan appointees but with the Nixon and Ford appointees who preceded them. Viewed from this perspective, Reagan's appointees represent both the continuation of a judicial revolution and also the continuation of a contemporary Republican tradition.[15]

The decisions of Reagan and Carter judges were also compared in another study, by political scientists C. K. Rowland, Robert A. Carp and Donald Songer.[16] They found that among district court judges Carter appointees were more than twice as likely to rule in favor of a criminal defendant as Reagan appointees. Nixon appointees ruled about the same as Reagan appointees. In women's rights cases, Carter district judges were almost five times as likely to vote liberal as Reagan district judges, and Nixon's judges were three times as likely to vote liberal as Reagan judges. On environmental cases, Carter and Nixon district judges were both about six times more likely to vote liberal than Reagan judges. The authors emphasized, however, that the number of economic rights and environmental cases in the study was too small to justify firm conclusions.

Among circuit court judges, the study found that Carter judges were more than twice as likely as Reagan judges to rule in favor of a criminal defendant. However, Nixon's circuit court judges were found 74 percent more likely to rule for a criminal defendant, contrary to the findings of Gottschall above. In non-unanimous cases, Carter judges were more than four times as likely to vote in favor of a criminal defendant as Reagan judges, while Nixon judges were twice as likely to do so.

A later study by the same three authors focusing only on criminal cases and studying more opinions found similar results, with Carter circuit court judges in non-unanimous cases almost five times as likely to vote in favor of criminal defendants as Reagan circuit court judges.[17] The study also concluded that the differences between Reagan and Carter judges were due not only to a tendency of Reagan judges to be more conservative than their predecessors, but also to a tendency of Carter judges to be more liberal than their predecessors, Democrat and Republican.

In a later study, C. K. Rowland, Robert A. Carp and Bridget Todd examined the decisions of Reagan and Carter district court judges in civil rights and labor cases.[18] They found that Carter judges were more than eight times as likely to rule in favor of parties claiming race discrimination as Reagan judges. Carter judges held in favor of those claiming sex discrimination in 56 percent of rulings, compared to 42 percent for Reagan judges. Carter judges also ruled in favor of those claiming discrimination against the handicapped in 59 percent of such cases, compared to 25 percent for Reagan judges, and ruled in favor of those claiming other forms of discrimination 43 percent of the time, compared to 22 percent for Reagan judges. In labor cases, Carter judges ruled in favor of the union or employee against the company or employer 60 percent of the time, compared to 34 percent for Reagan's judges. The authors conclude by suggesting that these differences are probably due as much to a policy during the Carter Administration of appointing ideologically liberal judges as a policy during the Reagan Administration of appointing ideologically conservative judges.

JUDICIAL INTEGRITY

Though Reagan judges have consistently issued conservative decisions when the law warrants, they have also shown that they have the integrity to rule fairly against conservative policies or Administration positions or allies when the law requires.

In *Synar v. United States* (1986)[19] a three judge D.C. district court judge ruled that the procedure for automatic across the board cuts in federal spending under the Gramm-Rudman-Hollings Act for failure to reach deficit targets was unconstitutional as a violation of the separation of powers. Though conservatives believe in spending cuts and balanced budgets and supported Gramm-Rudman, Reagan appointee Antonin Scalia, later elevated by Reagan to the Supreme Court, is widely believed to have written the unsigned opinion declaring key parts of the law unconstitutional. At the Supreme Court level, Reagan appointee Sandra Day O'Connor, and William Rehnquist, later elevated by Reagan to Chief Justice, voted to affirm Scalia's ruling.

In *United States v. Welden* (1985)[20] Reagan District Court Judge William Acker held that certain provisions of the Victim and Witness Protection Act of 1982, which had been supported by the Reagan Administration, were unconstitutional, because such provisions allowed for deprivation of property without due process of law and for assessment of civil penalties without a trial by jury as required by the Seventh Amendment.

In *Fisher v. City of Berkeley* (1986)[21] the Supreme Court held that rent control did not violate the antitrust laws. Justices Rehnquist and O'Connor concurred in this decision, despite the fact that conservatives strongly oppose rent control as counterproductive and unfair. In *Finzer v. Barry* (1986)[22] Reagan appointee Robert Bork rejected a claim by the Young Conservative Alliance of America that a statute banning all hostile demonstrations within 500 feet of a foreign embassy is unconstitutional.

In *Falwell v. Flynt* (1986)[23] the Fourth Circuit appeals court upheld a damage award to Reverend Jerry Falwell against Larry Flynt, the publisher of *Hustler* magazine, for emotional distress to Falwell caused by Flynt's publication in his magazine of a parody of Falwell. Reagan appointee J. Harvie Wilkenson dissented from the ruling, arguing that Falwell should not be entitled to recover damages for mere emotional distress. In *Lebron v. Washington Metropolitan Area Transit Authority* (1984)[24] a panel of three Reagan appointees held that the D.C. subway authority could not refuse to accept a poster critical of Reagan for display in its subway stations, because the authority had accepted other political advertisements for display.

These are just a few of the many examples of the integrity of Reagan's judges.

CONCLUSION

The record shows that the Reagan Administration has been successful in appointing fair minded judges with integrity who have properly used their judicial authority to issue consistent conservative decisions when the law allows. These conservative decisions, moreover, simply represent an extension of the record of conservative decisions by federal circuit and district court appointees of previous Republican Presidents. (Unfortunately, the Supreme Court appointees of such Presidents have not been nearly as consistently conservative.)

Reagan judges mainly differ from the liberal appointees of President Carter and other recent Democratic Presidents on such issues as crime, the death penalty, racial quotas and preferences, busing, abortion, school prayer, government policy towards religion and economic regulation. The public in fact strongly supports the positions of Reagan judges on most of these issues. These issues are what is really at stake in the Judges War.

But on most of these issues, Reagan's judges are still strongly constrained from issuing conservative decisions by binding Supreme Court precedents. A complete Reagan Revolution in the judicial branch will have to await further Supreme Court appointments.

REFERENCES

Context in the Judges War: Work Product from Reagan's Judges by Peter J. Ferrara

1. *See* discussion, *infra*.
2. For further discussion of the current sad state of the law, particularly concerning establishment of religion issues, see Peter J. Ferrara, *Religion and the Constitution: A Reinterpretation*, (Wash. D.C.: Child and Family Protection Institute, 1983).
3. 410 U.S. 113 (1973).
4. Craig Stern, "Judging the Judges: The First Two Years of the Reagan Bench", *Benchmark*, Vol. 1, Nos. 4 and 5, July-October 1984.
5. Director of the Administrative Office of U.S. Courts, *Annual Report*, 1981, Table D-5. *Annual Report*, 1985, Table D-5.
6. *Id.*
7. *Id.*
8. *Id.*

9. *Id.*

10. *Id.*

11. *Id.*

12. Jon Gottschall, "Reagan's Appointments to the U.S. Court of Appeals: The Continuation of a Judicial Revolution," *Judicature*, Vol. 70, No. 1, June-July 1986.

13. *Id.*, p. 52.

14. *Id.*, p. 54.

15. *Id.*, pp. 53-54.

16. C. K. Rowland, Robert A. Carp and Donald Songer, "The Effect of Presidential Appointment, Group Identification and Fact Law Ambiguity on Lower Federal Judges' Policy Judgements: The Case of Reagan and Carter Appointees," 1985 Annual Meeting of the American Political Science Association, August 29-September 1, 1985.

17. C. K. Rowland, Donald Songer, and Robert A. Carp, "Presidential Effects on Criminal Justice Policy in the lower Federal Courts: the Carter and Reagan Judges," unpublished, Fall 1986.

18. C. K. Rowland, Robert A. Carp and Bridgett Todd, "What if Ron and Jimmy Were Judges? Effects of Presidential Appointment and Legal Context on Judicial Support for Labor and Civil Rights," Southwest Political Science Association, Dallas, Texas, March 20, 1987.

19. 626 F. Supp. 1374 (D.C. Cir. 1986), aff'd, *Bowsher v. Synar* ___ U.S., ___ 106 S. Ct. 3181 (1986)

20. 568 F. Supp. 516 (W.D. Ala. 1983), aff'd in part and re'd in part, 743 F. 2d 827 (11th Cir. 1984), cert. denied, 105 U.S. 2362 (1985)

21. ___ U.S., ___ 106 S. Ct. 1045 (1986)

22. 798 F. 2d 1450 (D.C. Cir. 1986), *cert.* granted, 107 S. Ct. ___ (1987). However, Judge Bork did *not* rule, as some commentators have alleged, on the question of discriminatory enforcement of the embassy law. That subject was not before the circuit court in *Finzer.*

23. 805 F. 2d 484 (4th Cir. 1986)

24. 749 F. 2d 893 (D.C. Cir. 1984)

13

THE STRUGGLE OVER JUDICIAL POWER— THE STRUGGLE FOR REPRESENTATIVE GOVERNMENT

by Jeffrey P. O'Connell

It is seductively easy to view the judicial confrontation of the 1980s as simply a struggle between liberal and conservative opponents. Ideological conflict, however, does not begin to outline the significant dimensions of the confrontation. So long as this struggle is perceived as a political battle, its potentially most enduring product will be missed.

Beyond the political circus of fights over judicial nominations is a far more crucial confrontation—one which, after all the political points have been won and lost, impacts the limits of the democratic process, the jurisdictional limits of the judiciary and contemporary jurisprudence. This struggle is not merely a liberal/conservative confrontation. The underlying concern for a democratic society and an impartial judicial process are uniquely bipartisan. At the turn of the century, a conservative judiciary overextended its constitutional mandate. Today, liberals support the extension of judicial power. The problem is not ideological, but structural. How is the judicial process limited, ensuring that judicial power remains within constitutional proscriptions?

Nothing less is at stake than the proper functioning of the judiciary, in particular, the United States Supreme Court, in a constitutional republic. The fundamental question is the extent to which the judiciary must limit its constitutional adjudication to specific principles embodied in the Constitution. Although the issues have surfaced recently in major daily newspapers as a result of candid speeches by Attorney General Edwin Meese and Associate Justice William Brennan, among others, many individuals (including attorneys) who have not read Court opinions and law review articles are likely to be surprised by the extent and significance of the proposed constitutional role of the judiciary. Essentially two distinctive models of constitutional interpretation—the interpretive and the noninterpretive—exist.

The significance of the judiciary's role in constitutional determinations turns on the decisive effect that a decision has on the operation of government. When a court interprets a statute, federal or state, or determines the common law when no applicable statute exists, a court's declaration of law, if erroneous or poorly decided, can always be overridden by Congress or a state legislature (if state law) by enacting a statute.[1] This includes state law because the federal judiciary has no alternative but to apply state law. But constitutional determinations have quite different consequences. The ease with which a judicial decision can be overridden is foreclosed in constitutional adjudication. The burdensome amendment provisions of Article V of the Constitution must be applied.[2] The alternative means to circumscribe judicial excesses—regulation of jurisdiction as described in Article III, section 2—is a source of controversy, even among critics of judicial activism.

The draconian effect of a judicial declaration of constitutional invalidity, is, by itself, sufficient to suggest that the judiciary has clear limitations in what issues should be considered of a constitutional dimension.[3] Without such limitations, constitutional decisions can weave a broad layer of "higher law" precluding legislative action or a realistic democratic process from emerging. Chief Justice William H. Rehnquist noted the significance of constitutional adjudication:

> An error in mistakenly sustaining the constitutionality of a particular enactment, while wrongfully depriving the individual of a right secured to him by the Constitution, nonetheless does so by simply letting stand a duly enacted law of a democratically chosen legislative body. The error resulting from a mistaken upholding of an individual's constitutional claim against the validity of a legislative enactment is a good deal more serious. For the result in such a case is not to leave standing a law duly enacted by a representative assembly, but to impose upon the Nation the judicial fiat of a majority of a court of judges whose connection with the popular will is remote at best.[4]

One reason the debate has not generated more public notice is that the Supreme Court in its opinions is normally less than candid in expressing the true rationale, and the extra-constitutional basis, for its opinions. Even Paul Brest, one of the boldest advocates for the use of non-constitutional sources in the resolution of constitutional issues, admits:

> It is simply anti-democratic to conceal something as fundamental as the nature of constitutional decisionmaking—especially if concealment is motivated by the fear that the citizenry wouldn't stand for the practice if it knew the truth. If the Court can't admit what it is doing, then it shouldn't be doing it.[5]

Justice Brennan frankly discussed the rationale behind his jurisprudence in a 1986 speech. Rather than seeing the Constitution as a static instrument—one to which he must submit—Brennan visualizes it as an instrument to bring us continually closer to our expectations—as he phrased it, "a lodestar for our aspirations."[6] He continues:

> While the Constitution may be amended, such amendments require an immense effort by the People as a whole.
>
> To remain faithful to the content of the Constitution, therefore, an approach to interpreting the text must account for the existence of these substantive value choices, and accept the ambiguity inherent in the effort to apply them to modern circumstances. The framers discerned fundamental principles ... But our acceptance of the fundamental principles has not and should not bind us to those precise, at times anachronistic, contours. ... Each generation has the choice to overrule or add to the fundamental principles ...; the Constitution can be amended or it can be ignored. ... [T]he ultimate question must be, what do the words of the text mean in our time.[7]

Brennan's honesty in this instance is frequently not found in the opinions of the High Court.[8] Instead, some opinions attempt to instill a false sense of continuity with the traditions of the past. To be sure, some opinions have been blunt in stating that they will not use traditional standards of interpretation to tie the Court to constitutional proscriptions. For example, in *Harper v. Virginia Board of Elections* (1966), the court ruled a Virginia poll tax of $1.50 unconstitutional under an evolving equal protection definition of the Fourteenth Amendment because the tax discriminated on the basis of wealth. The late Justice William O. Douglas wrote:

[T]he Equal Protection Clause is not shackled to the political theory of a particular era. In determining what lines are unconstitutionally discriminatory, we have never been confined to historic notions of equality, any more than we have restricted due process to a fixed catalogue of what was at a given time deemed to be the limits of fundamental rights. Notions of what constitutes equal protection for purposes for the Equal Protection Clause *do* change.[9]

Justice Hugo Black, in dissent, complained:

The Court's justification for consulting its own notions rather than following the original meaning of the Constitution . . . apparently is based on the belief of the majority of the Court that for this Court to be bound by the original meaning of the Constitution is an intolerable and debilitating evil; . . . and that to save the country from the original Constitution the Court must have constant power to renew it and keep it abreast of this Court's more enlightened theories of what is best for our society.[10]

Who Decides? In this discussion, remember that the focus is not whether various judicial decisions are good or bad policy for America. Instead, the issue is whether or not the Court's actions flow from its legitimate role in our constitutional, representative government. As this book's co-editor, Pat McGuigan, phrases it, "The question is, who decides?" In other words, are these determinations more appropriately left for the legislative branch under the democratic process? Archibald Cox, former Watergate special prosecutor, is instructive on this point:

Nearly all the rules of constitutional law written by the Warren Court relative to individual and political liberty, equality, and criminal justice, impress me as wiser and fairer than the rules they replace. I would support nearly all as important reforms if proposed in a legislative chamber or a constitutional convention. In appraising them as judiciary rulings, however, I find it necessary to ask whether an excessive price was paid by enlarging the sphere [of judicial action] and changing the nature of constitutional adjudication.[11]

The common failure of many (including more lawyers than I care to admit) is to focus almost exclusively on the results of given cases. The weakness of this orientation is that results color the role the courts should play, with the result that courts resolve issues based upon what they view as "fair" in each individual case. This a human failing, which, under the proper circumstances, is even a desirable one. The judicial system requires, however, a neutral process blind to favoritism.

COMPETING MODELS OF JUDICIAL INTERPRETATION

Interpretive Model. The interpretive model imposes limits on the extent of judicial review, recognizing that the legitimacy of constitutional determinations arises from the Constitution itself. (Others have phrased their similar concept as judicial restraint, the doctrine of original intention, originalism or strict construction.) Constitutional issues are resolved only by reference to policies or judgments either explicitly or implicitly embodied in the Constitution. This does not mean that the framers necessarily understood or intended a specific result for each factual situation. It is satisfactory if a premise arising from the Constitution exists permitting judges to fashion an answer. Nor does it require that the Constitution explicitly refer to the principle so long as the principles are implicitly embodied in the Constitution. The interpretive model flows from principles inherent in that structure of the government created by the Constitution. Federalism and the separation of powers are just two examples of principles inherent in that structure created under the Constitution.

Judge Robert Bork, an interpretive model advocate, adopted Dean John Hart Ely's understanding of the application of the interpretive model in that:

> [T]he work of the political branches is to be invalidated only in accord with an inference whose starting point, whose underlying premise, is fairly discoverable in the Constitution. That the complete inference will not be found there—because the situation is not likely to have been foreseen—is generally common ground.[12]

When attempting to apply the Constitution, if the Constitution does not reveal any preferred value, the judiciary has no choice other than to leave the value choice to the legislature— the proper forum for departing and choosing among policy alternatives. The ultimate result of the interpretive model is to maintain the judiciary in its original (and limited) role, not because of an attempt to muzzle it from establishing ideological views but because its role, like Congress and the Executive, is limited under our governmental structure.

Some critics of the interpretive model establish a straw man suggesting that the Constitution was written for "another era"— that the framers could not have begun to understand the progress and technology of today. As a result, the argument continues, the interpretive model is completely inadequate to deal with the problems of this generation. But such an attempt to limit the interpretive model fails. Rather than being such a narrow construct, it has the capability of taking the principles drawn from the Constitution and applying them to current problems. An excellent example is the Fourth Amendment's proscription against illegal search and seizures. The Amendment provides that "the right of the people to be secure in their persons, houses, papers, and effects, against unreasonable searches and seizures, shall not be violated" and requires probable cause for the issuance of a warrant. The traditional formulation of the Fourth Amendment's application—originally stated in the days before technology could quietly infiltrate a household—required entry, however slight, into the house before the Amendment applied. Because wiretaps can be connected from outside the house, the rule as originally stated precluded application of the Amendment; and information obtained by a wiretap without an adequate warrant could not violate the Amendment. The Supreme Court, in *Katz v. United States*, acknowledged that the concern of the Fourth Amendment is to protect the individual against unauthorized government searches of the home, however conducted. The historical statement of the principle, while accurate for an earlier era, no longer fit today's technology. To ensure the framers' original concerns are preserved, the old rule had to be restated, not so that a new principle was created but merely to ensure the concept lodged in the Fourth Amendment is adequately applied.

Noninterpretive Model. The noninterpretive model is also known as judicial activism or non-originalism. Unlike the interpretive model, the basis for the formulation of constitutional determinations for the noninterpretive model is dramatically broader. The court looks not merely to constitutional provisions or the governmental structure, but also may found its decision by reference to value judgments formulated outside of the Constitution. Ely's concept of the noninterpretive model stipulates that the "courts should go beyond that set of references [found in the Constitution] and enforce norms that cannot be discovered within the four corners of the document."[13]

Such a formulation has far reaching effects. Brest, for example, is able to subscribe to a noninterpretive model because he gives the Constitution, and its adoption, little significance. Questioning the enduring nature of the Constitution, he writes:

> Even if the adopters freely consented to the Constitution, however, this is not an adequate basis for continuing fidelity to the founding document, for their consent cannot bind succeeding generations. We did not adopt the Constitution, and those who did are dead and gone.
>
> Given the questionable authority of the American Constitution—indeed, of any (quasi) revolutionary constitution at the moment of its inception—it is only through a history of continuing assent or acquiescence that the document could become law.[14]

Ely, like Brest, also questions whether basing substantive value choices on people dead for over a century is "reconcilable with the underlying democratic assumptions of our system."

Brest's role for the judiciary is quite expansive; he argues that the judiciary should constitutionally protect all fundamental rights. The general concept that Brest supports is that constitutional adjudication "should enforce those, but only those, values which are fundamental to our society." The application of this standard would not rule out the interpretive model, Brest insists. But the interpretive model could "no longer be defended *a priori*, but must justify itself in the face of alternative approaches to constitutional decisionmaking."[15] Such a suggestion necessarily emasculates the concept of the interpretive model because it is fundamentally a model to limit the power of the judiciary. By permitting a flexible standard—one determined by the judiciary itself—it defeats the purpose of, and understanding for, the model.

The logic of Brest's theory, which effectively questions the legitimacy of the legal order, is faulty, to put it mildly. If his view is accepted, why should the laws of the nation passed before World War II bind us? Or the laws before the most recent Administration, since one can argue that the people submitted a mandate for the future (or at least the immediate future—until the laws can again be questioned as validly representing the people)? Why should any law passed before the current session of Congress or the state legislature bind them? The truth is the laws do not bind the Congress or state legislatures if they *choose* to revise the law. If they do not, laws remain enforceable as enacted. A stable, sensible government requires changes in law, including the Constitution, through formal assent which ensures that the modification is the will of the people. A fundamental principle that a student of government and civilization learns is that the more important the revision, the more formality and demonstration of assent is required. That is why the amending provisions of the Constitution remain so significant. Judicial modification of a settled and proper understanding of the Constitution would, regardless of the terminology used, amount to little more than a fiction for constitutional revision without the consent of the people.

In a limited sense, Brest follows in the footsteps of Jefferson (in his concern about the laws of a prior age binding a current generation), but a simple answer is that the dead do not bind us. The framers of the original Constitution and its Amendments have no say over us today. *The Constitution, however, does bind us.* If there is a desire for a new Constitution (or a fresh interpretation), it is the people—not an unelected elite—who make that determination. The judiciary, by means of judicial review, has eschewed the significance of that Constitution as an historical document. The fundamental importance of any constitution lies in the stability it provides, and this requires that it possess a settled meaning until the nation, through the proper proceedings, decides to revise or dispose of the Constitution.

The desire of some commentators and even of some justices to make constitutional changes—changes that eliminate the democratic process—without the formal assent of the people is an appalling attempt by a few to change fundamental law without the consent of the people. Justice Brennan referred to the use of the interpretive model as arrogance. To the contrary, a justice who subscribes to the interpretive model is humble enough to accept realistic limitations on his own exercise of power. Those who, in the name of the Constitution, impose their personal interpretations of evolving standards of decency and personal solutions to today's policy problems are possessed of impudence and arrogance when they redefine the constitutional order as *they* deem appropriate.

Invariably present, if rarely articulated, in the noninterpretive model is the desire for the judiciary to assert its judgment in lieu of perceived poor legislative judgment or inaction. Caution must be exercised before thrusting the judiciary into the legislature's role in making the "proper" policy judgments. Even where the legislature simply takes no action, that inaction is action—in the sense that not enacting law, not even having hearings as a prelude to any broader consideration, has the effect of maintaining the status quo. Whether or not that is the most desirable action is ultimately a legislative, not a judicial, branch determination. Having the judiciary make a policy determination is frequently little more than a litigant's or interest group's second bite at the apple. This deliberative function is conferred upon an electorally accountable branch; and no warrant exists for transferring the value determination process to the Supreme Court. If the democratic function fails to produce conscientious legislators, the citizen bears the onus of ensuring those organs of government function properly.

The interpretive model, however, is not favored by the current Court. As some noninterpretive commentators admit, most modern constitutional decisions on humans rights issues are not derived from the interpretive model.[16] Terrance Sandalow somewhat expansively wrote that the "evolving content of constitutional law is not controlled, or even significantly guided, by the Constitution, understood as an historical document."[17] Non-interpretive advocates, such as Michael Perry, have also possessed the honesty to acknowledge that there is no "plausible textual or historical justification for constitutional policymaking by the judiciary—no way to avoid the conclusion that noninterpretive review, whether of state or federal action, cannot be justified by reference either to the text or to the intention of the Framers of the Constitution."[18]

Assuming for the moment that the judiciary should use the noninterpretive model, now does the Court determine the existence of a fundamental value? What characteristics must a fundamental value possess before it can be conclusively said to reach a constitutional threshold—thus leaving limited, if any, control through the democratic process? There are many claimed "fundamental rights." Tribe, for example, would include the sexual preferences of homosexuals as constitutionally protected, believing it is central to the personal identities of individuals.[19] Because homosexuality has traditionally been understood as well within the authority of government to proscribe, this view obviously does not represent any concept of the Constitution understood as an historic document. In fact, attempts to define fundamental rights, even among supporters of the noninterpretive model, only generate disputes. Many of these rights conflict with each other. The balancing approach employed by courts to determine relative constitutional status is, in most situations, too close a call for the decision to be "constitutionalized" and placed beyond the normal democratic process. Leaving it to the Court to place relative priorities on these rights only assists in the institutionalization of a maze of constitutional legislation divorcing any representative voice in the ordering of these rights. This is an approach which, of necessity, must fail. It only manages to leave the discretionary process up to the judiciary. Justice John Harlan recognized the problems associated with the determination of constitutionalizing fundamental values. He wrote that "to pick out particular human activities, characterize them as 'fundamental,' and give them added protection" was tantamount to allowing the justices to legislate over the best interests of the states as their elected representatives understood those interests.[20]

The Growth of the Court's Power. The Supreme Court's understanding of its role in the development of constitutional law has its roots in many occurrences. Theories of expansive judicial power are not unique to the current generation. The understanding of jurisprudence has changed over the years as law schools embraced one theory after another. The nation's Founders, entrenched in the belief that courts discovered, not made law, understood the authority of the judiciary as quite limited. As William Nelson noted:

> [T]he founders did not foresee that the Supreme Court would be an institution that would change the Constitution. The Court was to be an agency of permanence and stability. When opponents of the Constitution argued that "the power of construing the laws according to the

spirit of the constitution [would] enable that court to mold them into whatever shape it may think proper," Hamilton answered in the *Federalist* that such an argument was "made up altogether of false reasoning upon misconceived fact"—a conclusion which could "be inferred with certainty, from the general nature of the judicial power . . ." Contemporary commentators were almost unanimous in assuming that it was "the duty of judges to conserve the law, not to change it . . . They had no power to . . . amend, to alter . . . or to make new laws [for] in that case they would become legislators . . ."[21]

Even in later years when other legal theories arose, the role of the judge was normally seen as passive. People with authority to act, however, invariably find novel ways to expand their power. Law increasingly was transferred from a legislative to a judicial act. At the beginning of this century, John Chipman Gray made perhaps the quintessential argument on the relative power of courts. Statutes, he argued, are not properly viewed as law. At best, they are only sources of law; that is, places to which judges can look for declaring law. Law occurs only after a court actually renders a decision and binds the litigants. According to this argument, a statute has to be interpreted and, therefore, cannot have an ascertainable effect until courts interpret it.

Judge Bork sees today's jurisprudence as a corruption of legal realism. This jurisprudence, which he prefers to call Value Jurisprudence, is the "imposition of the judge's social and political sympathies disguised as conventional legal reasoning."[22] Such a process is a subjective approach to resolving cases, not relying on traditional constraints imposed upon the judiciary in constitutional questions.

NONINTERPRETIVE COMMENTATORS AND THE GROWING DEBATE

Some commentators, wary of the most expansive displays of judicial power under the noninterpretive model, devised special models limiting the "abuse" potential of the noninterpretive model. Ely, in *Democracy and Distrust*, argued that an interpretive model cannot be effectively applied. While advocating a modified noninterpretive model, he objects to the Court's use of substantive due process. As a result, he has concocted a theory permitting considerable judicial latitude in areas affecting representation of the people, such as freedom of expression, reapportionment and equal protection issues. For example, Ely supports the reapportionment decision[23] because legislators cannot be expected to properly define voting, as it affects their ability to stay in office. His argument is interesting. If true, it should have parallel force for the judiciary. If the legislative branch cannot be trusted to perform certain activities because they are vital to their existence, how can the judiciary be trusted with the final authority to determine the limits of its own constitutional authority? The judiciary, if it were voluntarily to curtail its power to determine constitutional issues, would also be limiting its power to affect the nation on many important social and policy issues. Although I would welcome such action by the courts, no convincing case has been made that a judge is any more willing to voluntarily rein in his power (and, therefore, his imprints on the nation) than a legislator.

Although critics of the noninterpretive model have been effective in generating discussion on the validity of the noninterpretive review, much of the debate has been instigated by noninterpretive scholars themselves. They are attempting to justify the Supreme Court's decisions, particularly during the Court's last 30 years. Although noninterpretive commentators are unable to agree on the proper foundations for the Court's actions, of which they generally approve, one area of common agreement is that the Supreme Court has done little to assist the legitimacy of its actions. Even supporters have criticized the Supreme Court's failure adequately to explain decisions and develop new theories consistent with its holdings. Alexander Bickel, late Harvard professor, noted:

> The Warren Court has come under professional criticism for erratic subjectivity of judgment, for analytical laxness, for what amounts to intellectual incoherence in many opinions, and for imagining too much history ... Comparison between the Warren Court and its predecessors really does not matter one way or the other, for intellectual incoherence is not excusable and no more tolerable because it occurred before. The charges against the Warren Court can be made out, irrefutably and amply.[24]

Despite Bickel's comment, the critical reaction would not likely have been so harsh if the years from the beginning of the

Warren Court through at least the 1970s had not witnessed such a massive overhaul in the constitutional landscape. A Court intent on reversing constitutional precedent must be held to a higher standard than if it was merely carrying on tradition. The Court's actions reflected its unprincipled result-orientation. The Supreme Court articulated no common thread justifying its actions because there is none. Its desire to support the "good Cause" has come at a sacrifice to the separation of powers.

The Court's reasoning process has produced *Furman v. Georgia* in which a capital punishment statute was ruled, by a 5-4 decision, unconstitutional as a violation of the cruel and unusual punishment clause.[25] This major case produced a startling *nine separate opinions covering well over 200 pages.* Even Justice Powell noted the majority had five separate opinions with as many different rationales for the decision. The lack of agreement by the majority hampered the Court's credibility, and in the process, left the nation unsure of the status of capital punishment. The decision overturned a statute that gave discretion to the jury in determining the sentence. When the discretionary function was attacked, many states enacted a statute requiring a mandatory sentence. But these statutes were struck down in what Justice Rehnquist called a "pillar to post decision" which now would require discretion be given to the jurors.

Another case more effective in obscuring, rather than clarifying, the Court's rationale is *Griswold v. Connecticut* (1965), which created the constitutional right of privacy.[26] The basis of the decision differs based upon whose opinion you read. In the now infamous opinion of Justice Douglas, one finds that the right of privacy, nowhere remotely suggested in the Constitution, arises from the mist like some warlock's incantation—specific guarantees of the Bill of Rights have penumbras formed by emanations from those guarantees to help give the guarantees life and substance; the guarantees create zones of privacy, and the right of privacy springs from several fundamental, but *unnamed*, constitutional guarantees. Justice Goldberg's opinion is just as imaginative, although not nearly as entertaining. The Ninth Amendment, which provides that the Constitution's enumeration of certain rights is not to be construed as denying or disparaging other rights retained by the people, lends support, according to Goldberg, to the idea that there are other fundamental rights. Goldberg refused, however, to admit that he was suggesting the Ninth Amendment was an independent sources of constitutional rights, notwithstanding that this was the effect that he was giving it. The conservative Justice Harlan merely attempted to use the familiar rational by applying the due process clause of the Fourteenth Amendment.

In *Roe v. Wade*, which created a constitutional right to abortion and effectively declared all abortion statutes unconstitutional, Justice Blackmun justified his rationale with what can only be called an inconclusive conclusion—that the right of privacy which struck down the abortion law was based *either* on "the Fourteenth Amendment's concept of personal liberty and restriction upon state action," *or* "the Ninth amendment's reservation of rights to the people."[27]

The result of these and similar cases has been to shift the burden of providing a satisfactory rationale from the Court to legal commentators. The noninterpretive proponents' problems are compounded by the decades of constitutional growth which now must be justified by noninterpretivists under a coherent theory of the noninterpretive model. But there has been little success or unanimity. It is not easy rationalizing years of decisions, left unencumbered by any attempt by the Court itself to rationalize the process.

THE CONSTITUTION AND JUDICIAL LIMITATIONS

> The concept of the written constitution is that it defines the authority of government and its limits, that government is the creature of the Constitution and cannot do what it does not authorize ... *A priori*, such a constitution could only have a fixed and unchanging meaning, if it were to fulfil its function.[28]

A simple lesson: understand the origins of the Constitution before applying it. The importance placed on the Constitution and its continuing vitality predisposes one to an understanding of the judicial function.

A written, constitutional form of government embodies a distrust of power because it defines, and limits, the government's authority.[29] The Supreme Court, in contemporary decisions, misapprehends the scope of that distrust. A constitution limits not merely *representative* government, that is, the notion that it protects against absolute majoritarianism, it operates to restrain all government, including the unelected judiciary. It would be anomalous to restrict the elected legislative branches, state and federal, without in the process limiting the branch that reviews the constitutionality of government actions. The frustration of the colonists grew, in part, from their lack of representation in Parliament. To have a life-tenured judiciary frustrate the people's ability to rule by removing major decisional areas from the democratic process positions Americans in a situation comparable to that which compelled the nation's founders to spill so much of their own blood.

Abuse of Power. The judiciary's function is not an abstract concept that changes as times change, but one that is tied to the relationship of the other branches of government. The function of the judiciary, and its constraints, are rooted in the Constitution, the document that gives life to the national government and its constituent parts. The Founding Fathers were not as concerned with investing authority in the national government, as they were with limiting it.[30] The whole structure shows a concern for restraint. Their concerns were directed toward dividing power among as many institutions as practicable. *The abuse of power is restrained not by increasing the power of one branch of government but by dividing power.*

The concern for abuse of power predates the American Revolution. As early as the first half of the Seventeenth Century, John Cotton, a minister, was warning Massachusetts "to give mortal men no greater power than they are content [the recipients of the power] will use, for use it they will."[31] Power given is power exercised. Much later, John Adams, a significant framer and second president, sounded the warning against unchecked power: "My opinion is . . . that absolute power intoxicates . . ."[32] Adams' approach, referred to as a "Mixed constitution," was to balance government by pitting power against power. In one sense, then, John Adams advocated that the "generally frailty and depravity of human nature" be used as a stumbling block against itself.[33]

The concept of separation of powers, adapted for the nation from the writings of John Locke and Baron Montesquieu, simply recognizes that unchecked power extends most individuals beyond their reasonable capabilities for self-restraint. The Founders were not idealists viewing utopia and the perfect citizen as just around the corner. They recognized from their collective experiences that the frailty of man requires a measure of control.

These fundamental limitations upon the branches of the federal government illuminate the foundation of the interpretive model. By limiting the scope of judicial authority in constitutional determinations, the interpretive model functions to ensure that the rule of law—not of men and their personal value systems—prevails. The interpretive model grows not only out of a core understanding of the judicial, but also of the constitutional order. Both the Constitution and the interpretive model recognize that the potential for abuse of power by legislators and executives is also reflected in the human condition of judges. The failures of open ended systems of constitutional interpretation are that no realistic limitations on the judiciary exist. Proponents of such systems fail to recognize that the entire basis for the interpretive model is to rein in those who would extend their power extra-constitutionally. Those who complain about the substantive due process in economic issues in the 1890s through the 1930s are nonetheless comfortable giving unrestrained power to the Court in other areas today. The concern for any such abuse—about the very condition of those who, even in good faith, extend power—is precisely why judicial power must be limited.

SOME REFLECTIONS AND A LOOK AT BASIC CONCEPTS

The legislative and executive branches can each be held in check by the judiciary. Congress and the Executive also possess the power to restrain the other. Even the lower courts are constrained because of the Supreme Court's oversight. Who checks the Supreme Court?[34] Currently, the answer is only self-restraint and God. The only way to keep the Court within limits is to ensure that it has a rigid rule to which it must submit. The interpretive model, while not perfect, attempts to establish such a rule. The Constitution is intended to procure stability. It establishes the relationships in the authority structure among the branches. Fundamental to the American experience in its distrust of power is the decision to separate the branches and provide for a set of checks and balances. As fundamental concepts, these are part of the structure of government and of themselves sufficient to ensure that the interpretive model should prevail. But understanding also the need for the people's role in the democratic process, *a fortiori* requires an acceptance of the interpretive model and the rejection of any concept that would permit jurists to look outside the Constitution or to look to evolving concepts of decency for new constitutional proscriptions.

The discussion on constitutional interpretation and the restraints on the role of the judiciary centers on two key issues: the democratic process and the use of neutral principles in the determination of cases.

Democratic Process. If any principle is fundamental to the nation's structure of government, it is the concept of a democratic government and the concomitant understanding of the electoral accountability of our representatives. Alexander Bickel recognized a tension between an unelected judiciary with life tenure and the democratic process:

> [N]othing can finally depreciate the central function that is assigned in democratic theory and practice to the electoral process; nor can it be denied that the policy-making power of representative institutions, born of the electoral process, is the distinguishing characteristic of the system. Judicial review works counters to this characteristic.[35]

John Calhoun saw that suffrage was the "indispensable and primary principle in the foundation of a constitutional government."[36] The Framers structured a representative form of government with frequent elections to assist in the orderly removal of unresponsive representatives. Some express concern that reliance on the democratic process is simplistic because of a lack of effective control over the actions of the elected representatives. Such advocates adopt a variant of Prudhon's pessimistic view of representative government: "It is no use saying that an elected person or representative of the people is only the trustee for the people . . . In despite of principle, the delegate of the sovereign will be the master of the sovereign."[37]

But the electorate is the primary basis for control of government. When the short run goals of the politician conflict with the foundational ideas of a free and responsible civil government, the citizen's actions in maintaining control of the government begin at the polls when he expresses himself through the ballot. But it does not end there. An effective citizen is not an apathetic one. His voice should be heard through active participation in the political process, public interest groups and the continuous assertion of his views. The strange and ill-advised concept of a passive citizen who elects a representative and then hibernates until the next election may be true for many. It should be true for no one. But the paternalistic instinct of the initiators of judicial action to "protect the interests" of the electorate is destructive. This concept of the passive citizenry is wrong not only because, in the long run, it takes significant policy issues away from electoral control, but also because it serves to instill this concept in individual citizens. This judiciary as a constitutional guardian of policy actually serves to undermine the citizen's active participation in government, and that participation is fundamental for the survival of democratic government. Ultimately, the determining factor in a functioning democratic process is the individual's desire to maintain a just civil government. If democratic society fails, only that society's citizens can be faulted.

The Supreme Court's gradual accession of a deliberate policy-making power results in it performing functions intended for politically accountable public offices. This judicial growth to power reduced the effectiveness of the citizen in governance, while frustrating the effectiveness of Congress and state legislatures in enacting society's will. It is sometimes said that the Supreme Court is the conscience of the nation. The conscience of the nation, wherever it properly resides, is effective only when it functions as a persuasive, not a coercive, force. Opinions of the Court might serve to show the deficiencies of the nation's laws, and thus perhaps be a force in the legislature's debate over the wisdom of laws, but it must not serve as a superlegislature, usurping functions that properly reside elsewhere.

The increased reliance on the noninterpretive model produces a willingness to resolve policy questions traditionally within the province of the legislatures. This encroachment into the authority of the other branches and the democratic process betrays the understanding of the relative role of each branch. In determining the role, and limits, of the legislative and executive branches, the crucial choices were made with the original Constitution. Additional choices were made with the passage of each amendment to the Constitution. Those choices were knowledgeably made and limited in scope. Courts or legal commentators possess no privilege to expand those limitations without the necessary consent of the nation—a consent derived only through the amending process.

Neutral Principles. The Court's proclivity for establishing value choices not embodied in the Constitution has produced another problem in securing an acceptable judicial process. These value choices by the Court are a rejection of the Constitution because the source of the new "constitutional" values reside elsewhere, resting largely on the understanding and experiences of the justices themselves. The prose of the justices cannot hide that value choices made are truly personal choices of the justices. At least Douglas was willing to admit that the "'gut' reaction of a judge at the level of constitutional adjudication, dealing with the vagaries of due process . . . and the like, was the main ingredient" of a decision.[38] Gut reaction, even by a distinguished jurist, can never be an adequate basis for constitutional or nonconstitutional adjudication.

The need is for a principled approach to the application of law to the individual case. Using the terminology of Herbert Wechsler, this requires the application of neutral principles:

> [J]udicial action "must be genuinely principled, resting with respect to every step that is involved in reaching judgment on analysis and reason quite transcending the immediate result that is achieved."[39]

Several years later, Professor Bork refined this profound concept of neutral principles. Concerned about a court's capacity for the deliberate avoidance of neutral principles, Bork demanded not only a neutral application of principles, but that the principles also be neutrally defined and derived. Looking solely to the neutral application of a principle may permit some to skirt responsibilities by drawing a principle narrowly enough to be relevant to only a few situations. To adopt neutral principles,

291

the court must demonstrate why one principle was used rather than a narrower or broader one. There must also be a demonstration that the principle was neutrally derived, ensuring that the limitation imposed by the principle is a proper restraint.[40] Under these rules, a constitutional right of privacy and other legacies of substantive due process fail to pass muster. A constitutional right of privacy cannot be shown to be applied consistently to all cases in which privacy would arise. At the some time, there is no derivation of the right from any constitutional issue. Bork makes clear that constitutional adjudication cannot produce fundamental values which are not embodied in the Constitution.

> Where constitutional materials do not clearly specify the value to be preferred, there is no principled way to prefer any claimed human value to any other. The judge must stick close to the text and the history, and their fair implications, and not construct new rights.[41]

RAMIFICATIONS OF JUDICIAL ACTIVISM

The exercise of judicial power under the noninterpretive model has produced several problems with broad effects upon the democratic process and distortion of the judicial process. Some have a major impact upon our understanding of judicial power, and the division of authority among federal branches and among federal and state governments; all play a subtle part in the cumulative understanding of the ability of the judiciary to explore areas considered untouchable in the past. A brief look at some of these issues and their effects shows the problems created.

Levels of Abstraction. One reason that neutral principles have been argued by a core of commentators is that one effect of the noninterpretive model is the judiciary has exercised considerable leeway in the defining of principles. Of course, one method of ensuring the desired result is achieved is to diffuse the factual and legal issues to a level of abstraction that permits whatever result is wished. When this happens, phrases of the Constitution can be redefined so that traditional limitations on the scope of judicial intervention are eliminated. Brest, for example, argues that the use by the framers of the Fourteenth Amendment's equal protection clause "demands an arbitrary choice among levels of abstraction."[42]

The birth of the constitutional right of privacy in *Griswold v. Connecticut* arose with Douglas' labored explanation of the privacy right by basing it on a generalized discussion of privacy. The term privacy is not used in the Constitution, and the use of the term is questionable at best because many of the privacy rights Douglas found in the Constitution are also public rights. Justice Black responded in dissent:

> One of the most effective ways of diluting or expanding a constitutionally guaranteed right is to substitute for the crucial word or words of a constitutional guarantee another word or words, more or less flexible and more or less restricted in meaning . . . "Privacy" is a broad, abstract and ambiguous concept which can easily be shrunken in meaning but which can also, on the other hand easily be interpreted as a constitutional ban against many things . . . For these reasons I get nowhere . . . by talk about a constitutional "right of privacy" as an emanation from one or more constitutional provisions. I like my privacy as well as the next one, but I am nevertheless compelled to admit that government has a right to invade it unless prohibited by some specific constitutional provision.[43]

Legal theorist Ronald Dworkin's advocacy provides a classic example of how such generalization can produce constitutional proscriptions unimaginable to constitutional framers. Dworkin, faced with the realization that the framers of the Fourteenth Amendment had a limited concept of equal protection, tries to avoid a limitation of judicial power by arguing that the framers were not intent on imbuing the Fourteenth Amendment with their narrow *conception* of equal protection, but with the *concept* of equality. A concept of equality expands the limited conception of equal protection understood by the Amendment's framers, thus making the Equal Protection Clause vastly broader in application—certainly broader than the situation that gave rise to the rationale for framing the amendment. Dworkin indicated:

> Suppose I tell my children simply that I expect them not to treat others unfairly. I no doubt have in mind examples of the conduct I mean to

discourage, but I would not expect that my "meaning" was limited to these examples ... I might say that I meant the family to be guided by the *concept* of fairness, not by any specific *conception* of fairness that I might have had in mind.[44]

Dworkin diffuses the constitutional text to such an extent that the Clause's impact is quite different than originally intended. It is different, though, because Dworkin *prefers* a result far broader than the historical meaning. He can only establish a "constitutional basis" for his desired result if the words become so obscure and generalized as to support whatever the interpreter wishes. This is the primary failing of such attempts to raise the constitutional text to higher levels of abstraction. The individual charged with the interpretation of the Constitution wields unrestrained control over the meaning of the Constitution. Such power exceeds acceptable limits for unaccountable offices precisely because the discretion inherent in the exercise of such power has no control.

Judicial discretion, of course, is permissible provided indirect accountability exists. In nonconstitutional adjudication, discretionary functions of the judiciary are subject to control by the legislative branch (state or local, depending on the relevant law) by legislation. Therefore, nonconstitutional determinations by courts enjoy broad discretion. The very nature of constitutional adjudication requires that judicial discretion be limited.

Even indulging the argument for the moment, consider the ramifications if we delegate to the courts the authority to determine a changing meaning to the Constitution, what control—extra-constitutionally—is exerted to maintain a reasoned, limited understanding to those words? In truth, there is no effective constitutional control, nor is there any effective extra-constitutional control. What we have is only faith in justices as individuals. Are they worthy of that faith? On a fundamental level of human nature, one questions unrestrained power. Justices have shown themselves reluctant to relinquish authority—a questionable trait even for enlightened, unelected despots. If such authority is conceded to them, also conceded is a measure of the democratic process and electoral accountability. Acceptance of such authority requires that we, as a people, are willing to submit ourselves to an unelected tribunal. Submission to such authority is submission to each individual until he or God see fit to vacate the chair.

Reapportionment. Until the 1960s, the problems of reapportionment were always considered to be a political question and, therefore, outside the jurisdiction of the judiciary. But with decisions beginning with *Baker v. Carr* (1963)[45] the Supreme Court determined, with occasional ludicrous results, that it was within their competence to examine the realignment of political boundaries. The significance of these reapportionment decisions cannot be overlooked because they signaled a new era in the use of judicial power to effectuate intended solutions to problems of society. The traditional view that reapportionment issues were political questions appropriate for Congress or the state legislatures to address is simply another understanding of the need for the democratic process to address fundamental issues on representation. The ultimate acceptance of a one man, one vote test reflected the Court's decision to accept a single theory of representation as constitutionally obligatory. Egalitarian fervor pushed the High Court to hold that the "State [must] make a good faith effort to achieve precise mathematical equality" in apportioning congressional districts, and that no variance from absolute equality is *de minimis*.[46] One commentator, approving the decisions, noted that they were proof that "ultimate legislative power in the United States has come to rest in the Supreme Court."[47]

Judge, then Professor, Bork indicated that:

> [T]he cases that came after *Baker v. Carr* were not only wrong, but they were wrong in a way that showed that some members of the Court were not really concerned with the constitutional issue of the ultimate power of majorities but were arrogating to themselves a role that does not belong to them. That chosen role was partly philosophical and—partly to be blunt—partisanly political.[48]

There is no historical basis under the Fourteenth Amendment or the history of the nation for a rule which requires that the state and federal governments must have an essentially equal population base. Indeed, the history of the nation suggests it is quite different. One need look only to the electoral college which gives each state a minimum of three votes regardless of size. It is somewhat surprising, therefore, that Chief Justice Earl

Warren indicated the electoral college is an anachronistic feature of another age acceptable only because it was a necessary compromise to join sovereign states into a single nation (and because it is constitutionally mandated!).[49] If it is rational, however, to accept the electoral college under such circumstances, it does not become irrational as a matter of principle for states to follow differing theories of representation. Certainly, the states recognized, from the nation's conception, that the basis for apportionment can differ. The issue is, then, the acceptance of differing conceptions of representation within a democratic framework. A widely accepted principle of representation does not become illegitimate through judicial refinement of a theory of adequate representation.

Frankly, there is no single representation theory which *must* command constitutional allegiance. No such idea is found in the Constitution. The germ of this particular theory of representation ripened in the minds of the justices, not the Constitution. Justice Harlan commented on the egalitarian standards of the Supreme Court:

> Property and poll-tax qualifications, very simply, are not in accord with current egalitarian notions of how a modern democracy should be organized. It is of course entirely fitting that legislatures should modify the law to reflect such changes in popular attitudes. However it is all wrong, in my view, for the Court to adopt the political doctrines popularly accepted at a particular moment of our history and to declare all others to be irrational and invidious, barring them from the range of choice by reasonable minded people acting through the political process. . . . [P]erhaps it is appropriate to observe that neither does the Equal Protection Clause . . . rigidly impose upon America an ideology of unrestrained egalitarianism.[50]

Regardless of the best intentions of the Court, the reapportionment cases imposed unintended consequences. If the reapportionment cases did anything, they simplified gerrymandering on a regular basis. As census data becomes available, district lines were redrawn. Computers were able to provide a facade of neutrality by drawing lines designed to secure or add new seats for the party with control of the legislature. Only recently has the Supreme Court expressed a willingness to review limited gerrymandering cases.[51]

Serious questions arise about the reapportionment cases' impact on federalism. If the federal government could decide that it is permissible to have a system such as the electoral college, it is difficult to justify the states as partners in the federal system being deprived of such rights. The decisions are one of many examples of the speed toward egalitarianism which played such a major part in the machinations of the Warren Court. Reapportionment decisions have been policy decisions, long considered the preserve of the legislature. To etch in granite a one man, one vote system because it may appear popular or appropriate is a disservice to the nation in its ability to seek appropriate responses to the era's problems.

Policy of the Elite—Death Penalty. If the determination of emerging values were a legitimate exercise of judicial authority, how could those values be determined? With what certainty must the value have actually "emerged" or "evolved" before a constitutional label is appended onto it? We must understand that Supreme Court decisions based on emerging or evolving values are unabashed policymaking—but policy made by a minority. This minority may only reflect the interests of a few. The capital punishment cases, beginning with *Furman,* are a prime example. Admitting that the colonies accepted capital punishment,[52] Justice Brennan found that irrelevant. He was convinced that societal values had progressed to such a stage that capital punishment is no longer acceptable to society. As a result, he considered the death penalty cruel and unusual punishment. Brennan drew the contemporary meaning of the cruel and unusual punishment clause "from the evolving standards of decency that mark the progress of a maturing society."[53] Brennan even went so far as to certify the views of the nation by noting that changes in "concepts of justice" resulted in society's "virtually total" rejection of the death penalty.[54] But public opinion polls have consistently shown overwhelming opinion in favor of capital punishment. In an Associated Press poll in November 1986, 85 percent of the respondents favored capital punishment.[55] It became clear that no one bothered to inform society it had rejected the death penalty.

It is interesting to note the two similar, but very different statements that Brennan made. He noted that the standards of society, generally, rejected the death penalty, but he determined that the nation had virtually rejected the death penalty. This points up another failure of any attempt to read "contemporary societal standards" into constitutional proscriptions on governmental behavior. It cannot work. There is no reliable way for justices to possess such clairvoyance—or even an accurate sense—of the standards of the nation. If values change over time, "by what standards are courts to determine whether a particular step in the evolutionary process is or is not permissible?"[56] Ely concludes that what the judge is really discovering are his own values, and judges are by no means "best equipped to make moral judgement."[57] Their isolation in their positions alone hinders a true sense of societal standards. Moreover, the fear is the judges will be swayed by the legal commentators or amicus briefs of interest groups on what societal standards are. The crushing practical result of such erroneous societal determinations is that if the justices are wrong, the only alternative for the American people is a constitutional amendment. But that makes the people mere ombudsmen of the federal judiciary, which turns their relationship on its head.

Elected representatives make policy choices, and these choices do not always reflect the general concerns of the electorate. With admitted faults, at least policymaking invested directly or indirectly in the legislature permits representatives who fail to make the proper decision to be held accountable for their actions. That control is lost when the judiciary wields that authority. At its worst, the judiciary can be an engine run by ego, preserving only the justices' values and *their* personal understandings of propriety. The argument is frequently made that the Court's contemporary actions only follow the command of the Constitution. But values which cannot be rooted in anything other than previously unarticulated views are, conspicuously, stripped of any objective meaning.

If there is a societal change or an evolution of understanding, then it must be reflected in the only legitimate method possible in a free society—through legislation or a more permanent constitutional amendment. An amendment from the people would provide the affirmative change and not be the necessary method for correcting judicial excesses.

Brennan notes:

Because we [the Supreme Court] are the last word on the meaning of the Constitution, our views must be subject to revision over time, or the Constitution falls captive, again, to the anachronistic views of long-gone generations . . . [I]n my judgment, when a Justice perceives an interpretation of the text to have departed from its essential meaning, that Justice is bound, by a larger constitutional duty to the community, to expose the departure and point towards a different path. On this issue, the death penalty, I hope to embody a community striving for human dignity for all, although perhaps not arrived.[58]

A cursory reading of Brennan's words may strike one favorably because it seems to say simply that an incorrect decision of the Court can be corrected. But his is no interpretivist argument. Brennan demonstrates his real meaning through his death penalty example. Under his interpretation, permitting capital punishment today is a deviation from the Constitution's essential meaning. In other words, *his* view of the proper standards of decency, even though never accepted by the Court or the community, is the necessary constitutional standard. His argument, in fact, is not one for returning to the Constitution's essential meaning, but for creating a new meaning.

At least Brennan has been frank enough to admit what other justices have not. He sees that the Constitution is to be adapted along with the "ever-changing conditions of national and international life," and that "those ideals of human dignity—liberty and justice for all individuals—will continue to inspire and guide us because they are entrenched in our Constitution." Willing to interpret the spirit of the Constitution into changed conditions, he necessarily requires a process in which a justice continually gives his view of changed conditions, developing ideals and new meaning. If this is not interpreting or, more accurately, revising the Constitution according to one's personal reflections of what the Constitution should be, it is difficult to comprehend what is. If constitutional standards are not determined according to the individual whim of the justice, as the justices continue to insist they are not, then there should be a coherent, clearly enunciated standard that the court could elaborate to demonstrate adherence to the Constitution. But there is none, and there can be none, except of course for the social conscience of the justice—something unsatisfactory in a frame of government where a constitutional interpretation demands unwavering allegiance.

CONCLUSION

The controversies raging within the Senate Judiciary Committee and, ultimately, on the floor of the Senate cannot properly be evaluated without understanding the tension between the two competing philosophical models for constitutional interpretation. To understand the political struggle over judicial nominations requires a deeper intellectual inquiry into the strengths of our Constitution and the governmental structure it created. The strengths of the Constitution come from the wisdom in limiting power as much as possible and, in the words of John Adams, pitting power against power.

With the Reagan Administration quickly winding down, Americans must recognize that it is impossible to overemphasize the importance of the next President's proper understanding of these basic issues. With two nominations to the current Court, a president—any president—could dramatically change the understanding of the Court's role and substantially redirect America's proud history of republican government.

Even more important than placing justices on the Supreme Court is recreating the persuasive force necessary to ensure both a popular *and* legal consensus in support of the proper, restrained understanding of constitutional interpretation. An informed nation, conscious of both the responsibilities and limitations of each branch of government, is fundamental if the nation is to preserve the value of democratic governance.

REFERENCES

The Struggle Over Judicial Power—The Struggle for Representative Government by Jeffrey P. O'Connell

1. Subsequent legislative action operates prospectively only and will not affect the dispute between the litigants.
2. The severity of the effect of constitutional invalidation is understated with respect to the state statues. Except for particularly sensitive issues, the concern shown for a declaration of unconstitutionality for a federal statute is likely to be attenuated for the state statute. If little interest is generated in other jurisdictions to resolve the matter, the state is left with little recourse.

3. Article V requires that Congress, with two-thirds vote of each house, propose amendments. Alternately, two-thirds of the states can call for a constitutional convention to propose amendments. The Amendments must then be approved by three-fourths of the states or the constitutional convention.

4. *Furman v. Georgia*, 408 U.S. 238, 468 (1972) (dissenting).

5. Paul Brest, "The Misconceived Quest for the Original Understanding," 60 *Boston University Law Review*, 204, 234 (1980) (hereinafter referred to as Brest, "The Misconceived Quest").

6. "The Constitution of the United States: Contemporary Ratification," Text and Teaching Symposium, Georgetown University, October 12, 1985, reprinted in *The Brest Debate: Interpreting our Written Constitution* (Washington: The Federalist Society, 1986), p. 110.

7. *Id.*, p. 16

8. [Editor's note: Whatever jurisprudential disagreements there may have been over the years, we have long admired the intellectual honesty of Justice Brennan.]

9. *Harper v. Virginia Board of Elections*, 383 U.S. 663 (1966). Interestingly enough, the emphasis on the word "do" is that of Justice Douglas. In conjunction with Douglas' concept of equality, see also the argument of Ronald Dworkin under the subsection *Level of Abstraction* below. In addition to questioning the fundamental constitutional framework for the decision, Justices Harlan and Stewart also criticized the failure of the Court to use the less stringent test of whether the state could show a rationale basis for the decision, which they believed was easily met.

10. 383 U.S. at 766 (dissenting).

11. Archibald Cox, *The Role of the Supreme Court in American Government* (New York: Oxford University Press, 1976), p. 102.

12. Robert H. Bork, Speech before the University of San Diego Law School, November 18, 1985, reprinted in *The Great Debate: Interpreting our Written Constitution* (Washington: The Federalist Society, 1986). For another discussion of this same point, *see* Bork's speech reprinted in Patrick B. McGuigan and Claudia A. Keiper, eds., *A Conference on Judicial Reform: The Proceedings* (Washington, D.C.: Free Congress Foundation, 1982), p. 132.

13. John Hart Ely, *Democracy and Distrust*, (Cambridge: Harvard University Press, 1980), p. 1.

14. Brest, "The Misconceived Quest," p. 225. Brest goes so far as to suggest that the "text and original history" should be given "presumptive weight, but" should not be treated as "authoritative and binding. The presumption is defeasible over time in light of changing experiences and perception."

15. Brest, "The Misconceived Quest," p. 227.

16. Michael J. Perry, "Interpretivism, Freedom of Expression, and Equal Protection," 42 *Ohio State Law Journal* 261, 265 (1981) (hereinafter referred to as Perry, "Interpretivism,"); Terrance Sandalow, "Judicial Protection of Minorities," 75 *Michigan Law Review* 1162, 1193 (1977) (hereinafter referred to as Sandalow, "Minorities").

17. Sandalow, "Minorities," p. 1193.

18. Perry, "Interpretivism," p. 275

19. Laurence Tribe, *American Constitutional Law* (1978), p. 943.

20. *Shapiro v. Thompson*, 394 U.S. 618 (1969).

21. William Nelson, "Book Review," 78 *Yale Law Journal* 500, 500-09 (1969).

22. Leonard J. Theberge, *The Judiciary in a Democratic Society*, (Lexington, Mass: Lexington Books, 1979), p. 112 (hereinafter referred to as Theberge, "Judiciary").

23. *Reynolds v. Sims*, 377 U.S. 533 (1964); *WMCA, Inc. v. Lomenzo*, 377 U.S. 633 (New York); *Maryland Comm. For Fair Representation v. Tawes*, 377 U.S. 695 (1964) (Maryland); *Davis v. Mann*, 377 U.S. 678 (1964) (Virginia); *Roman v. Sincock*, 377 U.S. 695 (1964) (Delaware); *Lucas v. Colorado General Assembly*, 377 U.S. 713 (1964) (Colorado). While *Reynolds* is the most cited of these five related cases, all decided on June 15, 1964, they are collectively known as the Reapportionment Cases.

24. See Theberge, "Judiciary," p. 48.
25. 408 U.S. 238 (1972).
26. *Griswold v. Connecticut* 301 U.S. 479 (1965).
27. *Roe v. Wade*, 410 U.S. 113 (1973).
28. Philip B. Kurland, *Watergate and the Constitution* (Chicago: University of Chicago Press, 1978), p. 7.
29. *Cf.* William Hurst, "Discussion," in Edmond Cann, ed., *Supreme Court and Supreme Law* (Bloomington, In.: Indiana University Press, 1954), p. 75.
30. The Framers were concerned about avoiding some of the problems plaguing the states under the Articles of Confederation, and to that extent a stronger national government was desired. But the common thread of the Constitutional Convention was the rejection of a system of government which would permit too much authority vested in one person or one branch.
31. *An Exposition Upon the 13th Chapter of the Revelation* (London: printed for Levelwel Chapman, 1655), quoted in Perry Miller and Thomas H. Johnson, *The Puritans* (New York: American Book Co., 1938), p. 213.
32. C. F. Adams, ed., *The Work of John Adams* (Boston: Little, Brown, 1850-1856), vol. VI, p. 477.
33. Clinton Rossiter, *Conservatism in America* (Cambridge: Harvard University Press, 1982), p. 22
34. There are two arguable checks upon the judiciary. Experience has shown that neither is appreciably effective. This first is the capability of Congress to impeach a judge. The probability of impeachment for the failure to properly apply the Constitution is slight indeed. Only one Supreme Court Justice has been impeached, Chief Justice Salmon Chase, but he was not convicted by the Senate and remained on the bench. The more likely occurence for impeachment is when a criminal act has been committed by the judge. The most recent example is Judge Harry Claiborne, appointed by Jimmy Carter; who was convicted of filing false income tax returns. Congress subsequently impeached and convicted him.
The second check is the use of the Exceptions Clause in Article III, Section 2, which provides that "the supreme Court shall have Appellate jurisdiction . . . with such exceptions and under such regulations, as Congress shall make." Although this has been discussed in recent years on a number of issues including school prayer, there has not been anything close to the majority in each House needed to pass the legislation. The clearest occurrence of a deliberate attempt to prevent the judiciary from hearing certain cases occured during Reconstruction. The statute was upheld in *Ex Parte McCardle*, 7 Wallace 506 (1869). For additional discussion, see Senator John P. East, "The Case for Withdrawal of Jurisdiction," in *A Blueprint for Judicial Reform*, Patrick B. McGuigan and Randall R. Rader, eds., (Washington: Free Congress Research and Education Foundation, 1981), p. 29; Raoul Berger, *Congress v. The Supreme Court* (Cambridge: Harvard University Press 1969).
35. Alexander M. Bickel, *The Least Dangerous Branch* (Indianapolis, in.: Bobbs-Merrill, 1962), p. 19.
36. "A Disquisition in Government," in Richard K. Cralle, ed., *The works of John C. Calhoun* (New York: D. Appleton, 1854-57), vol. 1, p. 2
37. Theory of the Constitutional Movement in the Nineteenth Century.
38. William O. Douglas, *The Court Years, 1939-1975* (New York: Random House, 1981).
39. Herbert Wechsler, *The Courts and the Constitution* (Athens, Ga.: University of Georgia Press, 1966), p. 15.
40. Robert H. Bork, "Neutral Principles and Some First Amendment Problems," 47 *Indiana Law Journal 1* (1971).
41. *Id.*, p. 8
42. Bork's San Diego speech, p. 9.
43. 381 U.S. 479, 509-10 (1965) (dissenting). Black also went on to discuss the other two bases — the Ninth Amendment and the due process clause — for the invalidation of the Connecticut statute by adding that they were merely "different words to claim

302

for this court and the federal judiciary power to invalidate any legislative act when the judges find irrational, unreasonable or offensive."

45. *Baker v. Carr* 369 U.S. 368 (1963).

46. *White v. Weiser*, 412 U.S. 783 (1973); *Kirkpatrick v. Preisler*, 394 U.S. 526 (1969). It appears that this extreme approach will no longer be applied.

47. Theberge, "Judiciary," p. 97, quoting A.A. Berle.

48. Theberge, "Judiciary," p. 111.

49. *Reynolds v. Simms*, 377 U.S. 533, 572-72 (1963).

50. 383 U.S. 684 (dissenting).

51. *Davis v. Bandemer*, 511 U.S.L.W. 4898 (1986).

52. See Raoul Berger, *Death Penalties: The Supreme Court's Obstacle Course* (Cambridge: Harvard University Press, 1982), pp. 44, 48.

53. 408 U.S. 238, 268 (1972) (concurring).

54. 408 U.S. at 295.

55. The survey was conducted from November 7 to November 14, 1986 by Media General and the Associated Press. The accuracy is plus or minus two percent, 95 percent of the time.

56. Sandalow, "Minorities," p. 1181.

57. John Hart Ely, "Foreword: On Discovering Fundamental Values," 92 *Harvard law Review* 5, 16 (1978).

58. William J. Brennan, "The Constitution of the United States: Contemporary Ratification," *supra* n. 6, p. 24.

CONTRIBUTORS

Bruce E. Fein is President of Bruce Fein and Associates, and a Visiting Fellow in Constitutional Studies at the Heritage Foundation. He was a Senior Vice President (Telecommunications and Information Group) at Gray and Company in the nation's capital. He was General Counsel at the Federal Communications Commission and, for two years, Associate Deputy Attorney General at the U.S. Department of Justice. Before that, he served for many years as an attorney in various units of the Department of Justice. The author of many articles in both scholarly and general interest publications, Fein is Supreme Court Editor for *Benchmark*, a publication of the Center for Judicial Studies. He was a contributor to *Crime and Punishment in Modern America*.

Peter J. Ferrara presently practices law in Washington, D.C. He received his A.B. from Harvard College in 1976 and his J.D. from Harvard Law School in 1979. He served as Special Assistant to the Assistant Secretary for Policy Development and Research in the Department of Housing and Urban Development from 1981–82, and was later appointed as a senior staff member in the Office of Policy Development at the White House. He is the author of numerous works dealing with social security and a variety of legal policy issues, including *Religion and the Constitution: A Reinterpretation*.

Paul D. Kamenar is the Executive Legal Director of the Washington Legal Foundation. He is a graduate of Rutgers University and Georgetown University Law Center. He is an adjunct professor at Georgetown University Law Center and a member of the Administrative Conference.

James McClellan is the President and founder of the Center for Judicial Studies, a non-profit educational foundation established in 1983 to promote greater understanding of the Constitution and the role of the judiciary in the American political system. He is the Editor of *Benchmark*, the nation's only conservative journal of legal opinion, and is the author of several books on legal and constitutional topics. McClellan holds both a Ph.D. in political science and a J.D. degree from the University of Virginia, and has taught constitutional law and government at the University of Alabama, Emory University, and Hampden-Sydney College. He has served on the staffs of Senators Jesse Helms, Orrin Hatch, and John East, and was Chief Counsel and Staff Director of the Subcommittee on Separation of Powers of the Senate Judiciary Committee.

Patrick B. McGuigan is Director of the Judicial Reform Project at the Institute for Government and Politics in Washington, D.C. He is the co-editor of six books on legal policy issues, and is the author of *The Politics of Direct Democracy in the 1980s*. McGuigan is a founding father of the Joseph Story Society.

Jeffrey P. O'Connell was Visiting Fellow in Legal Studies at the Free Congress Foundation's Institute for Government and Politics. Formerly an Associate with the firm of Davis, Polk and Wardwell and counsel to Aetna Life and Casualty Company, O'Connell earned his J.D. from the University of Pennsylvania, where he was Editor of the Law Review. In addition, he secured the Master of Arts degree in Public Policy from CBN University.

Dan Peterson is Executive Director of the Center for Judicial Studies, a think tank based in Washington, D.C., that is concerned with the Constitution and the courts. He is also Associate Editor of *Benchmark* magazine, the bi-monthly journal published by the Center. After graduating from the Harvard Law School, Peterson was a judicial law clerk for the Supreme Court of Iowa, and thereafter practiced law with the firm of Fulbright & Jaworski in Houston. He has served as General Counsel for a public interest legal foundation, and has written and spoken widely on legal and constitutional subjects.

Daniel J. Popeo is founder and general counsel of the Washington Legal Foundation, America's largest public interest law and policy center. Popeo received his B.A. from Georgetown University and his law degree from Georgetown Law Center in 1975. Before founding the Washington Legal Foundation, Popeo worked at the White House, Department of Justice and the Department of the Interior. The author of several monographs and many articles, Popeo was a contributor to *Criminal Justice Reform: A Blueprint* (1983), and *Crime and Punishment in Modern America* (1986).

George C. Smith is Chief Minority Counsel, Subcommittee on Technology and Law, Senate Judiciary Committee. Formerly, he served as Director of Litigation at the Washington Legal Foundation. He is author of a major monograph on the death penalty, *Capital Punishment 1986: Last Lines of Defense* (1986). Smith received his B.A. (*magna cum laude*) from Penn State University and his J.D. from Duke University School of Law.

Jeffery D. Troutt is Research Director for the Judicial Reform Project of the Institute for Government and Politics, and Associate Editor of *Judicial Notice*, a newsletter dealing with legal issues. A member of the Virginia bar, he received a B.A. from the University of El Paso, and a J.D. from Northwestern School of Law of Lewis and Clark College, where he was inducted into the law school's Cornelius Honor Society. He is an LL.M. candidate (International and Comparative Law) at Georgetown University Law Center.

OTHER BOOKS ON JUDICIAL REFORM PUBLISHED BY THE INSTITUTE FOR GOVERNMENT AND POLITICS

Blueprint for Judicial Reform – *Edited by Patrick B. McGuigan and Randall R. Rader.* This comprehensive study of judicial reform contains recommendations from numerous leading scholars who advocate major changes in the federal court system. It includes chapters by such well known authors as Dr. Charles E. Rice of Notre Dame University Law School, Dr. Thomas Sowell of Stanford University, U.S. Senators Orrin Hatch, Charles Grassley, Alan Simpson, and the late Senators Sam Ervin and John East. The topics covered include: withdrawal of jurisdiction, constitutional amendments, congressional oversight of the federal judiciary, regulatory reform and the rule-making process. *380 pages - 1981 - $10.95*

A Conference on Judicial Reform: The Proceedings – *Edited by Patrick B. McGuigan and Claudia A. Keiper.* An edited transcript of a conference held on June 14, 1982 at which leading scholars including Professor Raoul Berger, Judge Robert Bork, Attorney General Edwin Meese III, the late Senator John E. East and others presented their views on the proper role of the judiciary in our society. Panel discussions dealt with such topics as regulatory reform, the courts' impact on religious freedom, and constitutional courts and democratic government. Of particular interest is the text of Judge Bork's now historic speech on constitutional interpretation, later reprinted in *National Review.* *139 pages - 1982 - $3.95*

Criminal Justice Reform: A Blueprint – *Edited by Patrick B. McGuigan and Randall R. Rader.* This book focuses on what co-editor McGuigan called "the first half of the criminal justice equation: apprehension of the criminal, trial procedure, and street crime." Contributing authors include: Dr. Steven Schlesinger of Catholic University on the exclusionary rule; Frank Carrington of the Victims Assistance Legal Organization on crime victims compensation; Robert Woodson of the Center for Neighborhood Enterprise on youth crime; Dr. William A. Stanmeyer of the Lincoln Center for Legal Studies on urban crime; Dan Popeo of the Washington Legal Foundation on the "court watch" concept; and Former Attorney General William French Smith on habeas corpus reform. *273 pages - 1983 - $14.00*

A Conference on Criminal Justice Reform: The Proceedings – *Edited by Patrick B. McGuigan and Teresa Donovan.* The edited transcript of a conference held on September 27, 1983 which examined such topics as juvenile justice, the President's anti-crime package, religion and criminal justice, and popular involvement in the criminal justice system. Includes presentations by former Attorney General William French Smith, Attorney General Edwin Meese III, U.S. Senator Paul Laxalt, Al Regnery, Dr. Steven Schlesinger, Russell Kirk and others. *147 pages - 1984 - $4.95*

Crime and Punishment in Modern America – *Edited by Patrick B. McGuigan and Jon S. Pascale.* An historic articulation of "cutting edge" conservative thought on crime, punishment, imprisonment, alternatives to incarceration and privatization of corrections facilities, this book secured rave reviews from across the political and academic spectrum when it was released in the fall of 1986. Now in a second printing, the contributors to this study included Judge J. Clifford Wallace, Dr. Abraham Halpern, Senators Strom Thurmond, Sam Nunn and Bill Armstrong, Prison Fellowship's Daniel W. Van Ness, Professor Herb Titus, Judge Kenneth Starr, former Delaware Governor Pete du Pont, Congressman Jack Kemp and many others. *421 pages - 1986 - $9.95 (paper); $15.95 (hardcover).*

For orders or information, please write or call:

Publications Department
The Institute for Government and Politics
721 Second Street, N.E.
Washington, D.C. 20002
(202) 546-3004